THE COMPLETE HISTORY OF
U.S. Cruise Missiles

From Kettering's *1920s' Bug* & *1950's Snark*
to Today's *Tomahawk*

Bill Yenne

Specialty Press
838 Lake Street South
Forest Lake, MN 55025
Phone: 651-277-1400 or 800-895-4585
Fax: 651-277-1203
www.specialtypress.com

Edit by Mike Machat
Layout by Connie DeFlorin

ISBN 978-1-58007-256-4
Item No. SP256

Library of Congress Cataloging-in-Publication Data

Names: Yenne, Bill, author.
Title: The complete history of U.S. cruise missiles : from Bug to Snark to Tomahawk / Bill Yenne.
Description: Forest Lake, MN : Specialty Press, [2018] | Includes bibliographical references and index.
Identifiers: LCCN 2018008422 | ISBN 9781580072564
Subjects: LCSH: Cruise missiles--United States--History.
Classification: LCC UG1312.C7 Y47 2018 | DDC 623.4/519--dc23
LC record available at https://lccn.loc.gov/2018008422

Written, edited, and designed in the U.S.A.
Printed in China
10 9 8 7 6 5 4 3 2 1

Front Cover: *Chance Vought Regulus II launches on a test flight from the secret North Base complex at Edwards Air Force Base, California. Remnants of Regulus II solid-fuel boosters can still be found there today. (U.S. Navy)*

Front Flap: *North American XSM-64 Navaho Missile being readied for a test launch on the pad at Cape Canaveral, Florida. (Author's collection)*

Front End Paper: *U.S. Air Force Northrop SM-62 Snark blasts off on a test flight from Patrick Air Force Base, Florida. (USAF)*

Title Page: *"Touchdown on the Navaho Trail" depicts a North American X-10 landing on Rogers Dry Lake, California, accompanied by its Lockheed T-33A control ship. (Mike Machat)*

Back Cover:
Top Left: *A Bell GAM-63 Rascal stand-off cruise missile is carried to launch altitude fastened to the fuselage of a modified Boeing YDB-47E Stratojet in 1951. (USAF)*

Top Right: *A Martin TM-67B Mace blasts out of its concrete "zero-length" launch revetment at Patrick Air Force Base, Florida, in 1961. (USAF)*

Center: *A Douglas XGAM-87A Skybolt missile rests on its ground service dolly next to a Boeing B-52 Stratofortress launch aircraft. (USAF)*

Publisher's Note:
In reporting history, the images required to tell the tale will vary greatly in quality, especially by modern photographic standards. While some images in this volume are not up to those digital standards, we have included them, as we feel they are an important element in telling the story.

DISTRIBUTION BY:

UK and Europe
Crécy Publishing Ltd.
1a Ringway Trading Estate
Shadowmoss Road
Manchester M22 5LH England
Tel: 44 161 499 0024
Fax : 44 161 499 0298
www.crecy.co.uk
enquiries@crecy.co.uk

Canada
Login Canada
300 Saulteaux Crescent
Winnipeg, MB R3J 3T2
Canada
Phone 800 665 1148
Fax: 800 665 0103
www.lb.ca

Table of Contents

ABOUT THE AUTHOR

Bill Yenne has written more than three-dozen nonfiction books, mainly on military and historical topics. His work has been selected for the official Chief of Staff of the Air Force Reading List, and he is the recipient of the Air Force Association's Gill Robb Wilson Award for his "most outstanding contribution in the field of arts and letters." He was commended for his "work of over two dozen airpower-themed books and for years of effort shaping how many people understand and appreciate airpower."

His earlier work for Specialty Press has included *Birds of Prey: Predators, Reapers and America's Newest UAVs in Combat*; *Drone Strike: UCAVs and Aerial Warfare in the 21st Century*; and *Convair Deltas*.

Bill Yenne's works have included biographies of men from General Hap Arnold, the father of the U.S. Air Force, to Alexander the Great. His books on military aviation have included profiles of such legendary aircraft as the B-52 Stratofortress and the B-29 Superfortress, the latter coauthored with General Curtis LeMay. His books on aviation and military history have also included his dual biography of Dick Bong and Tommy McGuire, *Aces High: The Heroic Story of the Two Top-Scoring American Aces of World War II*, which was described by pilot and best-selling author Dan Roam as "the greatest flying story of all time."

He has written histories of America's great aircraft manufacturers, including Convair, Lockheed, and McDonnell Douglas, and has been praised for his recently updated *The Story of the Boeing Company*. He has also written histories of the U.S. Air Force and the Strategic Air Command. Mr. Yenne has contributed to encyclopedias of both world wars and has appeared in documentaries airing on the History Channel, the National Geographic Channel, the Smithsonian Channel, ARD German Television, and NHK Japanese Television. His talks and book signings have been covered by C-SPAN.

Surrounded by remarkable children and grandchildren, he and his wife live in San Francisco, California. Visit him on the web at BillYenne.com.

INTRODUCTION

"This new weapon, which has now demonstrated its practicability, marks an epoch in the evolution of artillery for war purposes, of the first magnitude, and comparable, for instance, with the invention of gunpowder in the fourteenth century."
—General George Owen Squier, Chief, Aviation Section, U.S. Army Signal Corps (1918)

The publication of this book marks the centennial of American cruise missiles. In 1918, Colonel Henry Harley "Hap" Arnold, the future father of the independent U.S. Air Force, went overseas to pave the way for the deployment of the new weapon that Squier predicted would mark "an epoch in the evolution of artillery for war purposes, of the first magnitude." However, Arnold reached the front just days before the Armistice, the remarkable new Kettering Bug never saw action, and the cruise missile concept was locked away in a top-secret file not to be revived for decades.

This book tells the story of that revival of the concept on the periphery of the grand scheme of weapons systems during World War II. From there, we turn to the narrative of a postwar generation of cruise missiles directly inspired by the frightening German cruise missile known as V-1. We describe how this postwar generation of missile technology was ambitiously pursued, only to be shelved again and largely forgotten for more than a decade.

This book tells the story of a second rediscovery of the cruise missile concept in the 1970s, when a new generation of guidance systems solved the Achilles' heel of the preceding generation. Because of the revolutionary principles of Terrain Contour Matching (TERCOM), the concept was again reborn, and cruise missiles became a viable modern weapons system.

In the 1980s, "the Cruise," as this genre of missiles was dubbed by the media, grabbed headlines across the world amid great, albeit now-long-faded, controversy. They were of immense concern to the Soviet Union, because with their remarkable capability to fly low and fast, they could evade the then-state-of-the-art defense radar systems of the Eastern Bloc. The Soviets pulled out all the stops in an anti-Cruise propaganda campaign, but when the dust had settled, the Cruise had been proven as a crucial weapons system in checkmating the aggressive posture of the Soviets and bringing an end to the Cold War.

Since the Cold War, cruise missiles have been in the headlines on somewhat less politically contentious missions against terrorist strongholds from North Africa to South Asia. They have been ordered into combat by every American president since George H. W. Bush.

Through the decades since they were first used in combat during the Gulf War in 1991, this new generation of American cruise missiles have proven their value again and again. They have provided National Command authorities the option of precision strikes against specific targets under circumstances wherein an attack by a manned strike aircraft, with the accompanying potential for the loss of a human pilot, is politically unacceptable. From the strikes on suspected al Qaeda facilities in Afghanistan and Sudan that were ordered by President Bill Clinton in August 1998, to the April 2017 attack on Syria's Shayrat Airbase ordered by President Donald Trump, they have afforded the opportunity to project force without endangering the lives of American aircrews.

In celebration of the centennial of American cruise missiles, we return to the days when such legends of American ingenuity as Elmer Sperry and Charles Franklin "Ket" Kettering brought forth the technology to make them possible and when military visionaries such as Colonel Hap Arnold, Admiral Ralph Earle, and General George Owen Squier first created the tactical doctrine that ultimately led to their becoming the weapon of choice for National Command authorities to strike precision targets at arm's length, both tactically and politically.

— Bill Yenne, 4 July 2018

Northrop SM-62 Snark is painted in operational gray SAC markings. It is on display at the National Museum of the U.S. Air Force in Dayton, Ohio. (Author photo)

Sleek lines of the Vought SSM-N-9 Regulus II are evident in this early test version, which is posing on Rogers Dry Lake at the North Base complex of Edwards AFB. (U.S. Navy)

A GAM-77 (later AGM-28) Hound Dog air-launched cruise missile in Strategic Air Command markings on the underwing pylon of a Boeing B-52 Stratofortress. (Author's collection)

Lieutenant Colonel George Owen Squier headed the Aviation Section of the U.S. Army Signal Corps in 1916 when gyroscope genius Elmer Sperry first approached him about his "automatic aircraft." According to U.S. Air Force historian Kenneth Werrell, Squier never returned Sperry's call. A year later, as commander of the entire Signal Corps, he became anxious for the army to have its own cruise missile program. (U.S. Army)

Cruise missiles have been the weapon of choice for National Command authorities to project limited but deadly force to precise locations without risking the lives of American pilots for more than a quarter century. Aside from more than 800 cruise missiles used during the Iraq War in 2003, these presidents made good use of cruise missiles for other missions. Speaking of the use of Tomahawks alone, President George W. Bush (left) ordered more than 50 to be fired, President Barack Obama (center) used more than 170, and President Bill Clinton (right) ordered the use of more than 700. (Official White House photo)

Chapter 1

FROM BUG TO BUZZ BOMB

The Curtiss-Sperry Flying Bomb, which first flew in 1917, was the U.S. Navy's first cruise missile. The airframe was built by aviation pioneer Glenn Curtiss and the guidance system was created by gyroscopic control systems pioneer Elmer Sperry. It was based on the Hewitt-Sperry Automatic Airplane project developed by Elmer Sperry and Peter Cooper Hewitt, which also used a Curtiss airframe. (U.S. Navy)

Barely more than a decade into the era of controlled, manned, powered flight, inventors were turning to powered aircraft that were controlled, not by a *human* pilot, but by robot mechanisms.

The inventors of America's first full-size, unmanned warplane prototypes were among those talented geniuses who populated the technological landscape at the turn of the twentieth century and became folk heroes for many generations of future tinkerers and aspiring inventors. Names of three pioneers in what evolved into cruise missiles loom large in the founding history of controlled, unmanned flight. They included Elmer Ambrose Sperry, Peter Cooper Hewitt, and Charles Franklin Kettering.

Elmer Ambrose Sperry was born in Cincinnatus, New York, in 1860, and he founded the Sperry Electric Company when he was 20. He patented a gyrocompass in 1908, founded the Sperry Gyroscope Company, and began marketing his wares to the U.S. Navy as aids for navigating warships. He patented a gyroscopic autopilot for aircraft in 1912, an invention that earned him a prize from the Aero Club of France and the prestigious Franklin Institute Medal in 1914, the year World War I began.

By 1915, with "the War to End All Wars" having engulfed Europe, there was growing interest in military technology on both sides of the Atlantic. Sperry, who was already toying with the revolutionary idea of unmanned aircraft utilizing his gyroscopic autopilot, presented the idea to the U.S. Navy. Already a customer for Sperry's shipboard gyroscopes, the navy provided a seaplane as a testbed.

In April 1915, Sperry was contacted by Hewitt, who was a fellow electrical engineer and the inventor of both the mercury vapor lamp and a nonmechanical rectifier for converting alternating current to direct current, both widely used in the later twentieth century. Both Sperry and Hewitt had been named to the Naval Consulting Board, created by Secretary of the Navy Josephus Daniels, and both were interested in radio-controlled devices.

Hewitt proposed that they collaborate, Sperry agreed, and development work began for what came to be known as the Hewitt-Sperry Automatic Airplane. The end product was also referred to as a "flying bomb," a term that is clearly synonymous with "cruise missile." It was not the last time this obvious appellation would be applied to a cruise missile.

During the ensuing year, they developed automatic, mechanical, and gyroscopic guidance systems, which Sperry patented in March, April, and August 1916. These were tested in several airframes, including those of a Curtiss C-2

Elmer Ambrose Sperry Sr. was a pioneer inventor and entrepreneur in the field of gyroscopic compasses. He founded the Sperry Gyroscope Company in 1910 and supplied gyroscopic stabilizers for ships to the U.S. Navy. During World War I, he developed a successful gyroscopic autopilot for unmanned aircraft. (Author's collection)

Josephus Daniels, the secretary of the navy during World War I, had an interest in the potential military applications of radio-controlled vehicles, including aircraft. (Library of Congress)

flying boat and a Curtiss N-9, the floatplane variant of the ubiquitous JN-4 "Jenny" biplane.

H. R. Everett, in his extraordinary book *Unmanned Systems of World Wars I and II*, explains the guidance system, writing that "the estimated range to target, corrected for prevailing atmospheric conditions, was measured by [a] wind-driven 'air log,' which was mounted upon an outer wing strut so as to be free of propeller turbulence. The gear-driven clockwork counted down from a preset distance value to close a set of electrical contacts that consequently armed the warhead, shut off the engine fuel supply, and activated a [single-pole, double-throw] relay. This relay in turn switched in an alternate attitude-gyro pick off that allowed the aircraft to descend in a controlled glide. An alternative option activated solenoids to release the wing spars and stabilizing wires, causing the fuselage to plummet to the ground."

To elicit some interest in the project, Sperry contacted Lieutenant Colonel George Owen Squier, who became Chief of the Aviation Section of the U.S. Army Signal Corps in May 1916. According to U.S. Air Force historian Kenneth Werrell, Squier never returned Sperry's call.

The U.S. Navy *did* call back (after all, both Sperry and Hewitt were on the Naval Consulting Board) and a test was arranged that involved installing the robot guidance system

on a manned aircraft. The first flight came on 12 September 1916, with Lawrence Sperry, Elmer's son, at the controls, and a naval observer aboard. The latter was Lieutenant Theodore Stark "Ping" Wilkinson Jr. of the Bureau of Ordnance, who had earned the Medal of Honor two years earlier during the American seizure of the port of Veracruz during the Mexican Revolution. Wilkinson later commanded the battleship

Admiral Ralph Earle, who headed the U.S. Navy's Bureau of Ordnance (BuOrd) during World War I, developed an ambitious plan for massed attacks by hundreds of Curtiss-Sperry Flying Bombs against German shipping in the North Sea. His was a strategic idea many decades ahead of its time. (Library of Congress)

USS *Mississippi* and, during World War II as a Vice Admiral, he was on the Pacific Theater planning staff.

The younger Sperry handled the takeoff, releasing the aircraft to automatic control, during which it climbed to a predetermined altitude, held an appropriate compass course, and flew for about 100 miles. The aircraft had been preprogrammed to dive on a specific target, and it was doing so when Sperry took back control. The test, albeit with a man able to take control, was a success.

"The moral effect of such devices may be great," Wilkinson reported. "They are practically indestructible, unless a well-aimed shot disables [the] engine or control devices, and they cannot be driven off."

Having praised the concept, the naval officer added that the machine was "expensive, required complicated launching facilities," and that its "use in long-range attacks against forts and cities is of doubtful military value on account of [the] difficulty of striking at any desired point rather than at random within the limits of the city or fortress."

His words summarized the guidance problems that would bedevil cruise missile developers for the next half century. However, when the United States entered World War I in April 1917, a five-man panel appointed by Secretary Daniels to study the flying bomb concept endorsed it, and less than a month later, Daniels authorized a budget of $200,000 (nearly $4 million in current dollars). In wartime, funding is far easier to come by.

The Automatic Airplane program, well-funded for its day, got under way at a test site near Amityville on Long Island with six Sperry control systems and five Curtiss N-9 seaplanes. Beginning in June, more than 100 test flights followed the procedure of the one a year earlier, in which the pilot handled the takeoff and landing, relinquishing control in the air.

In the meantime, Sperry was consulting with planemaker Glenn Curtiss on the idea of building an all-new dedicated airframe for the program. He wanted a craft that was faster than the N-9 floatplanes and designed specifically to function as a flying bomb. With the nation at war, time was of the essence and Curtiss was given 30 days to design and build the first of six prototype aircraft. He finished in only 26 days, delivering it on 10 November 1917.

The Curtiss-Sperry Flying Bomb (Hewitt's name was no longer in the title) was 15 feet long with a wingspan of 25 feet. The unmanned aerial vehicle weighed 500 pounds empty and had a projected operational payload capacity of 1,000 pounds and a range of 50 miles. It was powered by a 100-hp Curtiss OX-5 V-8 liquid-cooled engine (also used in variants of the Curtiss Jenny) and had a speed of 90 mph. It was not a seaplane like the N-9, but rather an aerial craft designed to launch from land using a heavy wire as a launch rail. Plans to use a catapult system had been abandoned.

By now the program was deemed so promising that Rear Admiral Ralph Earle, who headed the U.S. Navy's Bureau of Ordnance, conceived of a plan to launch large numbers of Flying Bombs from U.S. Navy warships in the North Sea to attack U-boat bases in northern Germany. His strategy of ship-launched cruise missiles was certainly well ahead of its time. It is recalled that on Earle's watch, the Bureau of Ordnance developed plans for the largest maritime minefield in history, to block the northern entrance of the North Sea against U-boats, and the extensive deployment of 14-inch naval guns as railroad artillery on the Western Front. Each of these projects was carried out.

However, the first attempts to test launch the Flying Bomb, in November and December 1917, ended in failure. In January 1918, the plane was finally able to get airborne after being launched from a 150-foot rail, but it proved tail-heavy and crashed. One of the aircraft was retrofitted with a pilot seat and controls, and Lawrence Sperry undertook a flight test. He barely escaped with his life when the thing went out of control.

Elmer Sperry decided to conduct what amounted to open-air wind tunnel tests, bolting the aircraft to the top of an automobile and accelerating to 80 mph on the Long Island Motor Parkway. This activity, which one wishes had been caught on motion picture film, not only evaluated the aerodynamic properties of the aircraft, but also gave the inventors an idea: to launch it from the top of the car!

The Curtiss-Sperry Flying Bomb became the first unmanned heavier-than-air vehicle to have made a controlled flight, successfully completing its preprogrammed flight regimen on 6 March. Unfortunately, several attempts to follow up on this remarkable milestone flight ended in failure. At last, Sperry decided to revisit the catapult launch concept.

A young Java-born Dutch engineer working for Sperry named Carl Norden (later the inventor of the revolutionary Norden Bombsight) devised a catapult, and tests resumed in

The Kettering Bug was the first cruise missile developed by a predecessor of the U.S. Air Force. Several are seen here in 1918 during flight testing near Dayton, Ohio, by the Aviation Section of the U.S. Army Signal Corps. The program was managed and championed by Colonel Henry Harley "Hap" Arnold, later to command the U.S. Army Air Forces in World War II. He was overseas preparing the way for operational deployment of the Bug when the war ended. (Author's collection)

August 1918. Alas, these too ended in failure with the loss in crashes of the last of the six Curtiss-Sperry Flying Bombs.

The program had a brief reprieve in October 1918, using N-9 floatplanes with a Norden-designed catapult, but World War I ended before the remaining problems could be wrung out of the system. The U.S. Navy's first cruise missile program was suspended.

The Kettering Bug

The U.S. Army, meanwhile, had its own World War I cruise missile program, a system regarded as the harbinger of today's U.S. Air Force cruise missiles and unmanned combat air vehicles. The story of this aircraft began in Dayton, Ohio, just a few miles from the bicycle shop where the seeds of *manned* powered flight were sown, and it took place much closer to the time of those experiments of the Wright brothers than most people realize.

Charles Franklin "Ket" Kettering was born in Loudonville, Ohio, in 1876, the same year that Alexander Graham Bell patented the telephone. A promising engineer, he was hired by National Cash Register immediately after he graduated from Ohio State in 1904. Five years later, he and a colleague named Edward Andrew Deeds struck out on their own to found the Dayton Engineering Laboratories Company (Delco) in a barn on Deeds's property.

Among Kettering's earliest inventions was the electrical starter for automobiles. From there, he developed numerous automobile ignition, lighting, and electrical systems. He developed tetraethyl lead to improve gasoline efficiency and Freon to revolutionize refrigeration and cooling. Though these materials were later to be discredited as environmental

Charles Franklin "Ket" Kettering, an inventor and engineer who held nearly 200 patents, founded the Dayton Engineering Laboratories Company (later Delco Electronics) and created the Kettering Bug. (Author's collection)

villains, Kettering is also celebrated for developing a means of harnessing solar energy. This was not a priority in his own lifetime, but it contributes favorably to a Kettering legacy that includes nearly 200 patents.

In 1917, Ket Kettering created what he called the "aerial torpedo," a term that, like "flying bomb," was clearly synonymous with "cruise missile." Elmer Sperry had also used the term "aerial torpedo" when he patented his flying bomb in December 1916.

Several factors contributed to the Army's decision to catch up to the navy in the field of these cruise missile predecessors. First, George Squier had taken a belated interest in the concept. Now a major general, the former head of the Signal Corps Aviation Section had been promoted to head the entire Signal Corps early in 1917 on the eve of U.S. entry into World War I. Then, in August of that year, Edward Deeds, Kettering's partner, left Delco, divesting himself of all financial interest, to head the joint Army-Navy Aircraft Production Board.

The army embraced the idea enthusiastically after Squier accepted an invitation to join Admiral Earle, along with Curtiss and Sperry, to observe a flight of an autopilot-equipped N-9 Flying Boat on 21 November.

In a memo to Deeds penned five days later, Squier wrote excitedly that "the time has come, in the opinion of the writer, when this fundamental question should be pressed with all possible vigor, with a view to taking to Europe something new in war rather than contenting ourselves as in the past with following the innovations that have been offered from time to time since the beginning of the war by the enemy. Wars are won largely by new instrumentalities, and this Board should be a leader and not follower in the development of aircraft for war."

Squier had been convinced of the concept and he now wanted the army to have its own cruise missile program.

Meanwhile, Orville Wright, who had divested himself of his own interest in his family business after Wilbur died of typhoid in 1912, agreed to come into the project as a consultant. The aircraft, it was suggested, would be mass-produced by the Dayton-Wright Airplane Company, the successor to Wilbur and Orville's Wright Company. Kettering managed to convince Squier that the team he was assembling could produce aerial torpedoes more economically than Curtiss and Sperry could produce their Flying Bombs.

On 8 January 1918, the U.S. Army issued a contract for 25 Dayton-Wright Liberty Eagle aerial torpedoes. (The patriotic name "Liberty" had also been adopted for the famous 400-hp water-cooled aircraft engine, of which American automakers produced more than 20,000 units during World War I.)

The man in the Aviation Section of the U.S. Army Signal Corps who was responsible for the Liberty Eagle aerial torpedo program from the army side was a young officer named Henry Harley "Hap" Arnold. He was the same man who would become the Commanding General of the U.S. Army Air Forces in World War II, and the man regarded as the father of the modern U.S. Air Force. A 1907 grad-

This patent drawing of the Kettering Bug shows, among other details, the pneumatic valve manifold (170) that controlled airflow from opposed-bellows actuators (149 and 150) for rudder and elevator control. (U.S. Patent Office)

These frames from a U.S. Army training film show the modules of the Kettering Bug being reassembled on the launch rail at Carlstrom Field in Florida, circa 1919. The forward fuselage and wing structure was slipped over the fuselage section containing the engine. (U.S. Army)

uate of the U.S. Military Academy at West Point, Arnold was part of the first generation of U.S. Army pilots. Indeed, he was one of those whose flight instructors had been the Wright brothers themselves!

When the United States entered World War I in April 1917, Arnold yearned for a career as a combat pilot, but his organizational skills led to his being sidetracked to a desk job in Washington, DC, serving as assistant to MG William Kenly, the Directory of Military Aeronautics. Promoted to colonel in August 1917, Arnold was, during World War I, what he would be during World War II: the highest ranking army officer in the nation's capital with a pilot's license. In 1917, none of the officers above Colonel Arnold in the hierarchy knew how to fly! In the later war, now-General Arnold commanded tens of thousands of pilots, and wore four, then *five*, stars as the highest-ranking airman ever.

Colonel Arnold's specific job was in acquisitions as the U.S. Army underwent a rapid expansion on a scale unmatched since the Civil War. This was at a time when the "horse cavalry" leadership of the U.S. Army still considered aviation a novelty, if not a folly, an attitude that was a major challenge for Arnold. This mindset prevailed for more than a quarter century. Arnold was part of a generation of airmen who, like those contemporary inventors, embraced technology and looked beyond the horizon.

His work took him to the factories of numerous planemakers and other suppliers. Among these were both Delco and Dayton-Wright, both in Dayton. So, too, was his old friend Orville Wright. Here, Arnold began a collaboration with Ket Kettering that led to the construction and the eventual flight testing of an aircraft he was convinced (by

Kettering and Wright) was superior to the Curtiss-Sperry Flying Bomb. About the latter, Arnold commented in his memoirs that "the necessary precision devices, man-hours to be expended, and so on, made it too expensive to pursue in terms of quantity production."

He went on to say that "under Ket's direction, we then devised a pilotless airplane, or bomb, which we called the 'Bug.'" Indeed, the "Liberty Eagle" name was quickly overshadowed and has largely been forgotten.

The Kettering Bug weighed around 300 pounds and consisted of a wooden structure with the fuselage built of reinforced papier-mâché and wings of doped brown wrapping paper and muslin. It was 12.5 feet long with a wingspan of 15 feet. Designed with the utmost simplicity in mind, the Bug was to be built, packed, and shipped in modules that could be assembled in four to five minutes with a socket wrench and screwdriver.

The Bug carried 180 pounds of explosives, much less than the Curtiss-Sperry Flying Bomb, though Arnold recalled a 300-pound payload in his memoirs. It was launched from a portable track and had a cruising speed of 50 mph with a range of 75 miles. It was powered by a Ford V-4 engine delivering 41 hp that also met, according to Arnold, "the requirements for both pressure and vacuum necessary to operate the automatic controls."

Arnold added that "the actuating force for the controls was secured from bellows removed from player pianos. They rotated cranks, which in turn operated the elevators of the rudder. The direction of the flight was ensured by a small gyro, elevation from a small supersensitive aneroid barometer, so sensitive that moving it from the top of the

A replica of the Kettering Bug on display at the National Museum of the U.S. Air Force. (Bill Yenne Photo)

desk to the floor operated the controls. This kept the Bug at its proper altitude."

In a more detailed description, H. R. Everett explained that "The Bug maintained a prespecified climb attitude during ascent by means of a gyro-based autopilot. Upon reaching cruise altitude, an aneroid barometer overruled the gyro, causing the aircraft to slowly descend until [it was again] below the set point, at which point the gyro took over to resume the climb. Whereas electromechanical flight control actuators had been employed on the Curtiss-Sperry Flying Bomb, Kettering's approach involved pneumatic bellows driven by engine vacuum, inspired by similar mechanisms used in contemporary player pianos and organs. The control system was built by the Dayton Metal Products Company, with components and technical support provided by the Aeolian Organ Company."

Kenneth Werrell pointed out that lateral stability was achieved through a 10-degree wing dihedral suggested by Orville Wright himself. Werrell also reminds us that the control and guidance system depended upon Sperry gyroscopes.

There was a great deal of fine-tuning to the design. Arnold recalled that "at first we relied only on the dihedral of the wings for lateral stability, but later, more positive directional controls had to be installed with orthodox ailerons."

As the Bug program was ongoing during the early months of 1918, the massive buildup of American forces in Europe was taking place, and Arnold certainly imagined that the Bug would play a useful role in World War I. After three manned flights in July, Arnold had grown so excited about the Bug that he was sure that role would be a decisive one. In fact, he went so far as to recommend that the U.S. Army acquire as many as 100,000 Bugs. The original order was increased, but only to 75 aircraft. Around 45 were built.

"By mid-1918, the development of the Bug had proceeded so favorably that we decided to tell General Pershing and the Commanding General of the Air Service in France what we were doing," Arnold wrote. "We were sure we would be ready to send some of the pilotless bombs overseas within a few months. A proposed table of organization was drawn up showing the number of officers and men that would be required in each Bug squadron, and an estimate was prepared showing the number of Bugs each squadron would be able to launch in 24 hours. It was planned to launch thousands every day against German strong points, concentration areas, munitions plants, etc., which would certainly have caused great consternation in the ranks of the German High Command at least."

With this exuberant optimism came the need for security and secrecy. "Our one fear," Arnold fussed, "was that information about it might leak out to the Germans."

Blaming the "complexity of the systems," Arnold noted that the first unmanned flight test was delayed until October 2. The Bug was launched by pointing its portable tracks toward the target. Distance, wind direction, and wind intensity were calculated, as were the number of engine RPM required to reach the objective. A cam was set, and when the engine had turned the precise number of revolutions, the cam fell into position, and the two bolts holding on the wings were withdrawn. As Arnold described it, "the wings folded up like a jack rabbit's ears, and the Bug plunged to earth as a bomb."

Though the target was missed on this try, the team

went back to the drawing board and was ready for another attempt with another Bug two days later.

The 4 October flight was the proof-of-concept mission. As H. R. Everett tells us, the Bug stayed aloft for 45 minutes, reaching an altitude of 12,000 feet, and not coming down until it had run out of fuel. With security of paramount concern, there was a mad dash to get to the crash site, near Xenia on the opposite side of Dayton.

"We had to get to that wrecked Bug before anyone else," Arnold recalled. "In the vicinity where we thought we had seen it come down, we came upon some excited farmers."

"Did you see an airplane crash around here?" the group asked, when it had raced to the crash site in a car.

"Right over there," a farmer replied. "But strange thing, there's no trace of the pilot."

Arnold noted that in the car there happened to be a pilot with his leather jacket and goggles, and as Kenneth Werrell wrote, this "pilot" was Hap Arnold himself. When he stepped out to greet the farmer, the group explained that he had bailed out before the crash. Arnold clarified in his memoirs that army pilots were not yet using parachutes.

In the meantime, General Pershing *had* expressed positive interest in Kettering's cruise missile. Arnold was ordered to pack his bags and travel to France to brief him and prepare the way for the operational deployment of the Bug.

Arriving in New York at the height of the 1918 influenza pandemic, Arnold boarded the SS *Olympic*, only to find himself laid low by pneumonia. When the ship reached Southampton, Arnold was hospitalized for eight days and did not finally reach France until there was already talk of an armistice in the air. In his words, it was "too late to put over the Bug."

The Armistice went into effect on 11 November 1918, with the Bug fleet still in the United States. Though they never saw combat, General Squier remained enthusiastic, writing to the chief of staff, General Peyton March, that "this new weapon, which has now demonstrated its practicability, marks an epoch in the evolution of artillery for war purposes, of the first magnitude, and comparable, for instance, with the invention of gunpowder in the fourteenth century."

In January 1919, a dozen Bugs were shipped to Carlstrom Field in Florida for further testing, during which one flight covered 16 miles. The program was finally closed in March 1920 after only 4 successful flights out of 14 attempts. Though the program ended as less than a roaring success, the Bug was considered sufficiently significant to remain classified until after the start of World War II.

"The Bug was 25 years ahead of its time," Arnold observed in his memoirs, comparing it to the German V-1 of World War II. "It was cheap, easy to manufacture, and its portable launching track would have permitted its use anywhere. Considering the trends in air weapons [in the 1940s], and that the first German V-1 was not launched against Britain until the fifth year of World War II, it is interesting to think how this little Bug might have changed the face of history if it had been allowed to develop without interruption during the years between the two wars. It was not perfect in 1918, of course, and as new gadgets and scientific improvements came out they continued to be incorporated into the Bug until the economy wave of the mid-twenties caused it to be shelved."

As with many aircraft programs throughout history, the Flying Bomb and the Bug were hampered by being at the leading edge of technology. Perhaps the biggest problem was with the newness of autopilot technology, but a close second was the lack of evaluation and diagnostic systems. In the manned flights, a human pilot could "feel" the aircraft and assess what happened when the autopilot misbehaved. In the automatic flights, it was generally guesswork, and often the aircraft were so badly damaged in crashes that it was hard to determine what had gone wrong. In turn, the loss of several aircraft, many, if not most, on their first flights, put an obvious strain on the programs. This was exacerbated by the fact that the aircraft themselves were small and flimsy, a result of making them simple and inexpensive so that they could eventually be mass-produced in huge numbers.

As Kenneth Werrell pointed out, "the developmental method of the day, trial and error, did not work well with unmanned aircraft."

Radio Control

After World War I, both the urgency and the funding for military strength fell off precipitously. The personnel strength of the U.S. Army plunged from 4 million in 1918 to only 202,000 in 1920. By 1923, the U.S. Navy had decommissioned 17 new battleships, the gold standard of

Archibald Montgomery Low was a brilliant but eccentric British engineer and physicist who came to be known as "the father of radio guidance systems" and who was also an early pioneer in what became television. In 1917, he flew the first radio-controlled aircraft, achieving a key milestone in the evolution of cruise missiles. The Royal Flying Corps set up its Experimental Works under Low's supervision. (Author's collection)

naval power, that had been commissioned between 1906 and 1910. In both services, innovative new weapons systems had but a handful of advocates, though some of these few did persevere.

One of these supporters was Secretary of the Navy Josephus Daniels, who continued his interest in pilotless flight. In 1921, he authorized the Bureau of Engineering and the Bureau of Ordnance to continue to study the concept using the N-9 floatplanes that had earlier been assigned to the Flying Bomb program. A key technological advancement in automatic aircraft guidance made in Britain during the war now provided a glimmer of promise.

Archibald Montgomery Low, a British engineer and physicist who came to be known as "the father of radio guidance systems," was also an early pioneer in what became television. On 21 March 1917, he flew the first radio-controlled aircraft, achieving a milestone in the evolution of cruise missiles. In his personal habits, the brilliant Low was easily distracted, the archetype of the "absentminded professor," though he was not a professor and drew the ire of colleagues for calling himself one.

During World War I, Low had joined the Royal Flying Corps (RFC) and, like Sperry and Kettering, pursued the idea of a weapon to ram and destroy the German zeppelins that were attacking London. As with the military hierarchy in the United States, which had a wartime fascination with promising but untried technology, there was official support for Low's idea, and the RFC Experimental Works was established under his direction.

Like Hap Arnold, the RFC was concerned with secrecy and Low's machine was officially designated an "Aerial Target" (AT) to make it seem to be an anti-aircraft artillery target drone. The initial radio-controlled flight featured an airframe built by de Havilland, but other planemakers, including Sopwith and Folland, later built AT aircraft that incorporated Low's radio guidance. As with the early American cruise missiles, the AT never saw combat, and such programs were terminated at war's

The Northrop JB-1A Thunderbug flying wing cruise missile was created and tested in 1943–1944 as part of the USAAF's top-secret MX-543 program, initiated in response to the German V-1. The JB-1A was flown, albeit not entirely successfully, but this was a photograph of one on the ground with the background airbrushed out to simulate an inflight image. (Author's collection)

Russian-born television pioneer Dr. Vladimir Zworykin, seen here demonstrating an early television set to Mildred Birt in 1929, is considered the father of video camera tubes that made modern television possible. He first proposed an "electric eye" for an aerial torpedo in 1934 and consulted on U.S. Navy aerial torpedo projects. (Smithsonian)

with a gyroscopic autopilot designed by Carl Norden, was adapted to perform a function similar to that of Low's in the British AT program. On 15 September 1924, an N-9 made a flight in which all operations from takeoff to landing were completely radio controlled, albeit with a human pilot aboard as a backup to the electronics. Not all flights were successful, however, and by 1925 the program had faded away.

In 1922, the U.S. Army also began testing radio guidance systems for aircraft, with Elmer Sperry again spearheading the effort. The aircraft, known as the Messenger Aerial Torpedo (MAT), was based on the Sperry Messenger, a single-engine sport plane designed to Sperry's specifications by Alfred Verville, designer of the Sperry-Verville R-3 race plane that won the 1924 Pulitzer Trophy. In army tests in 1922, the MAT successfully completed multiple mock air strikes against targets 30 to 90 miles from the takeoff point. After Elmer's son, Lawrence Sperry, was killed in December 1923 while flying over the English Channel in his personal Messenger, the elder Sperry terminated all his aviation activities and army experimentation with radio-controlled aircraft gradually wound to a close. In 1929, Elmer sold the Sperry Gyroscope Company to North American Aviation.

As these navy and army programs were ongoing in the United States, in Britain, both of the corollary services demonstrated a similar interest in unmanned aircraft. The Royal Navy saw value in target drones, ironically, the *cover story* of the RFC AT. Meanwhile, the Royal Air Force (RAF), successor to the RFC, pursued both target drones and the flying bomb concept.

The first major RAF cruise missile project ramped up in 1925, after the parallel American programs had largely come to a close. Developed by the Royal Aircraft Establishment (RAE), the aircraft was known as "Larynx," a clumsy acronym for "Long-Range Gun with Lynx Engine." In size, it lay between the Flying Bomb and Bug, being 14.5 feet long with a wing span of 19.8 feet. Powered by a 200-hp Armstrong-Siddeley Lynx IV radial engine, it had a top speed of 200 mph, making it faster than many contemporary fighters. It carried a 200-pound payload and had a radio guidance system that had evolved from that of Archibald Low's AT.

Larynx testing was initially done over water. The first launch, on 20 July 1927, was by catapult from the destroyer

end. Nevertheless, Low had invented radio control for aircraft.

The U.S. Navy, meanwhile, had its own expert in the field of radio guidance. John Hays Hammond Jr. was an electrical engineering prodigy and a protégé of Thomas Edison, Alexander Graham Bell, and Nikola Tesla. Among other things, Hammond built a radio control system for a 40-foot houseboat and patented photoelectric guidance for torpedoes in 1912. The latter interested the U.S. Navy, and several series of torpedo tests were carried out using various Hammond radio guidance systems through 1921.

In 1922, when the U.S. Navy resumed automatic airplane tests, Hammond's radio guidance system, together

HMS *Stronghold* and ended in a crash. In the second test, a Larynx flew at least 100 miles before disappearing. Three additional tests during the coming year places Larynxes within 1.6 miles of their targets. After one successful test in 1929, the RAF moved the program ashore. The British had seized the oil fields of Iraq as the Ottoman Empire imploded after World War I, so the desert north of Basra was used for the final tests. After the Larynx had completed no better than 60 miles of a 200-mile evaluation course, the program was terminated in 1930.

Target Drones

Through the 1930s, the cruise missile concept that had been so prominent in 1917–1918 lay largely dormant around the world even as radio guidance technology was evolving rapidly. Radio control for aircraft, the stuff of science fiction when Archibald Low pioneered it in 1917, flourished in the 1930s. Indeed, it was so common that the hobby of flying radio-controlled model airplanes became widely popular. Military applications for radio-controlled aircraft centered almost solely on target drones for honing the skills of anti-aircraft gunners. Reginald Denny, a B-movie actor turned model airplane buff, operated a chain of hobby shops in Hollywood before he started building radio-controlled aircraft.

In 1940, the U.S. Army Air Corps (U.S. Army Air Forces/USAAF after June 1941) began ordering large numbers of target drones from Denny's Radioplane Company. The first Radioplane Model RP-4 aerial target was officially designated OQ-1, and the initial production series of Model RP-5s were initially designated OQ-2s, with later RP-5 variants ranging up to OQ-14. The early aircraft were powered by 6.5-hp engines, but the OQ-14 had a 22-hp engine. The speed increased from 85 mph to 140 mph as the models incorporated larger and larger powerplants. The largest Radioplane drones had wingspans of more that 12 feet. Many of the "OQ" aircraft were transferred to the U.S. Navy under the designation "TD" for "Target Drone."

During 1942, so many orders poured in that Radioplane's Van Nuys factory could not handle them, and the USAAF turned to the Frankfort Sailplane Company of Joliet, Illinois, to build thousands of aircraft based on Radioplane RP-5 designs. Radioplane itself built more than 8,550 radio-controlled aircraft during the war, mostly OQ-3s and OQ-14s, while Frankfort built 5,429.

Revival of the Assault Drone

In the interwar period, the lineage of unmanned military aircraft diverged. The fork that included target drones evolved, by the 1960s, into reusable unmanned aerial vehicles for reconnaissance, which in turn evolved into the unmanned combat air vehicles of the twenty-first century. The other fork led to expendable unmanned aerial vehicles to be used as long-range projectiles (i.e., cruise missiles). As the two branches forked, some vehicles originally designed as drones were adapted as precursors of cruise missiles.

The "aerial torpedo" or "flying bomb" concept that had been on the shelf for more than a dozen years was mentioned in various quarters shortly before the United States entered World War II, then quickly revived in 1942. Technological advances in radar altimeters and television guidance now made such systems *seem* more practical than ever.

Just as had been the case at the start of the previous world war, the quest for new and innovative weapons systems awoke with sudden energy and adequate funding. Interestingly, most of the cruise missile types came not from major, established planemakers, those with massive contract commitments for mainstream aircraft types, but from small companies on the fringes of the aviation industry, firms that came and went quickly.

The U.S. Navy acquired its new cruise missiles under the same "TD" designation as its target drones, though that designation was also interpreted as standing for "torpedo drone." The USAAF created several new designations for what it now called "assault drones." Fletcher Aircraft of Pasadena, founded in 1941, developed the FBT-2, a light trainer aircraft of which one was built. Ten were ordered as PQ-11 target drones, but completed under the "BG," or "Bomb Glider," designation. The idea was to attach glider wings to an explosive charge. They were never used as such, and the BG-2 and BG-3 programs were canceled.

Fleetwings of Garden City, New York, a builder of general aviation and light training aircraft, developed its small YPQ-12A assault drone, and manufactured eight of them. In tests, one destroyed a Culver PQ-8 in the air, while another impacted within 30 feet of a ground target.

The principal World War II USAAF cruise missile designation was "BQ," which is said to stand for "Bomb, Guided," though "Q" was the official prefix for unmanned aerial vehicles, including target drones. Fleetwings built single examples of their similar twin-engine, television-guided XBQ-1 and XBQ-2, each of which was designed to carry a 2,000-pound payload. The XBQ-3 designation went to a pair of Fairchild AT-21 trainers that were converted as assault drones, but the first one did not fly until May 1944 and it crashed on its first flight, ending the program.

Another USAAF designation prefix was "JB" for "Jet-Propelled Bomb." It was first used in 1943 within one of an extensive series of USAAF secret development programs that were cryptically designated with the prefix "MX." Meaning "Materiel, Experimental," this nomenclature originated with the Experimental Engineering Section of the Air Materiel Command in 1941.

The JB designation originated specifically within the MX-543 program, which had seen the development of the Northrop Bat, a flying wing cruise missile that was eventually designated as JB-1A. Jack Northrop is famous in the annals of aviation for being a pioneer in the design of aircraft such as the prewar N-1M, also featuring a flying wing configuration.

The Bat evolved from the earlier MX-324 manned, unpowered aircraft and the manned, rocket-powered MX-334 aircraft. MX-543 was a flying wing that began late in 1943 in response to the German V-1 program that is discussed later in this chapter. MX-543 began with a manned glider that evolved into the unmanned, jet-propelled JB-1A, known officially as a "power bomb," and unofficially nicknamed by Northrop personnel as the "Thunderbug." These were 10.5 feet long with a wingspan of 28.3 feet and a launch weight with full ordnance package of 7,000 pounds. Powered by a General Electric turbojet engine, the JB-1A was test launched from a 400-foot rail using solid rocket motors to assist takeoff. Once airborne, the JB-1A was intended to cruise at 427 mph with a range of 670 miles using active radar homing to locate its target. However, the first powered flight on 7 December 1944 ended in a crash after a flight of 1,200 feet because of an engine malfunction. After 2 test vehicles were ordered, the contract was extended for another 11, but these were not produced.

A slightly larger variant, powered by Ford PJ31 pulsejet engines and designated as JB-10, was developed under the MX-554 program and first flown at Eglin Field early in 1945. Northrop listed it with a range of 185 miles, but the best performance it was able to deliver was a flight of 26 miles on 13 April. Ten of a dozen test flights were deemed failures and the JB-10 program ended quietly in March 1946.

America's First Operational Assault Drones

The U.S. Navy, as it had in World War I, was ahead of the U.S. Army with assault drones in World War II, both in their development and in their operational deployment. Lieutenant Commander Delmar Fahrney, a naval aviator with an engineering background, had been assigned in 1937 to develop target drones for the service, and he soon envisioned using the technology to create assault drones.

Developed in-house by the Naval Aircraft Factory, the navy's TDN-1 was later produced under license by Brunswick-Balke-Collender, a company best known for bowling equipment. (U.S. Navy)

Seen here on a blustery day in late 1942 on the Great Lakes aboard the training carrier USS Sable, the Naval Aircraft Factory TDN-1 was the U.S. Navy's first "aerial torpedo" to enter production. It never saw combat. (U.S. Navy)

He worked with Russian-born television pioneer Dr. Vladimir Zworykin at RCA, who had first proposed an "electric eye" for an aerial torpedo in 1934, in the development of television guidance systems for unmanned aerial vehicles. Fahrney is sometimes described as the father of U.S. Navy guided missiles, and Zworykin as the father of video camera tubes that made modern television possible.

In February 1942, Fahrney was assigned to a top-secret effort called Operation Option, which was aimed at assault drone development. Initially, it was planned that existing, but obsolete, manned aircraft should be adapted as assault drones. However, Fahrney created a purpose-built aircraft for the role. The Naval Aircraft Factory TDN-1 was a simple wooden aircraft with a fixed landing gear that could operate from an aircraft carrier. It was 37 feet long with a wingspan of 48 feet and had a cockpit for an optional pilot. Guidance was either by radar or television, and it was powered by a pair of 220-hp Lycoming O-435 piston engines.

The TDN-1 carried 2,000 pounds of ordnance, either a bomb or a torpedo, which were intended to be dropped and the drone recovered. In this sense, the TDN-1 was more of a predecessor to today's unmanned combat air vehicles than to today's cruise missiles.

The XTDN-1 made its first flight on 15 November 1942. Carrier trials were delayed nine months, although an order for the first of 114 production TDN-1 aircraft had already been issued in March 1942. These were built by the Brunswick-Balke-Collender company, better known for bowling equipment. The TDN-1 proved to be a disappointment, so they were used as target drones and Fahrney turned to developing the TDR, one of the best-known American cruise missiles of World War II.

A U.S. Navy Interstate TDR-1 assault drone being prepared for an attack. During September and October 1944, Special Task Air Group One (STAG-1) operated TDR-1s from Banika, Russell Islands, in combat action against enemy targets in the Solomons area. During a two-month period, 50 drones were launched with 31 hits recorded on anti-aircraft sites, bridges, airfields, and grounded ships. (U.S. Navy)

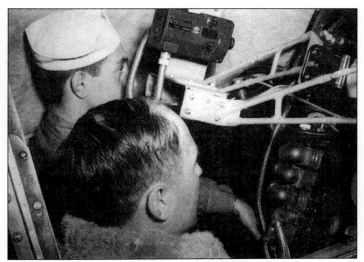

The TDR-1 was controlled from a modified Grumman TBM-1C Avenger torpedo bomber. Seen here is the controller's claustrophobic station with a gun camera focused on the 5-inch television screen that received a feed through the Block I (SCR-550) receiver from the TDR-1's nose-mounted camera. After launch by a ground control crew, control of the TDR-1 passed to the TBM pilot and then to the controller in the aft cockpit, who guided it to the target. (U.S. Navy)

The TDR program originated with the Interstate Aircraft and Engineering Corporation, founded in 1937. This company operated in El Segundo, California, literally in the shadow of giants such as Douglas Aircraft and North American Aviation.

The TDR aircraft, of which 195 were built, was simply constructed of wood over a tubular metal frame. It was 37 feet 11 inches long and had a wingspan of 48 feet. Its two 230-hp Lycoming O-436 piston engines gave it a cruising speed of 140 mph and it had a range of 425 miles. Like the TDN-1, it could carry 2,000 pounds of bombs or a torpedo, and it was intended to drop these rather than crashing into its target.

The SCR-549 television guidance system, code named "Block I," was designed by Zworykin. It could be operated either from the ground or by an operator flying in an accompanying TBM Avenger aircraft using an SCR-550 receiver. Compared to earlier and existing technology, the system was remarkably miniaturized. Zworykin managed to squeeze transmitter, camera, and battery pack into a 97-pound box measuring just 26 inches on its longest dimension.

In addition to Block I television, other components included an RCA radio altimeter control system (code named "Ace"), gyrostabilized hydraulic actuators and controls (code named "Castor"), and an AN/APS-2 radar system and AN/APN-7 radar transponder beacon (code named "Roger"). Input from the TBM mother ship was via a joystick and a rotary telephone dial that had been preprogrammed by the operator with numerically designated commands.

After a first flight in 1942, the TDR flight test program unfolded through 1943 and into 1944, slowed by a

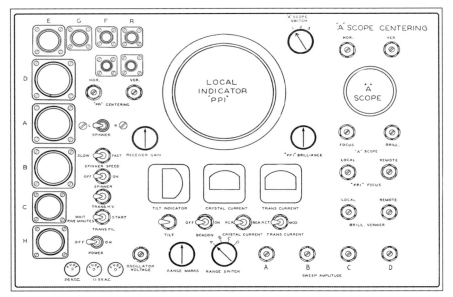

This diagram shows the control panel of the TDR-1's Block I system, incorporating the R-7/APS-2 receiver-indicator of the AN/APS-2 radar system. In the center is the Local Indicator, or Plan Position Indicator (PPI). Designed by the Naval Research Laboratory, it provided 360-degree situational awareness. (U.S. Navy)

The KY-3/APN-7 beacon coder used aboard the TDR-1 converted output from the AN/APN-7 radar transponder beacon (code named "Roger") into one of five predetermined codes to trigger the transmitter. (U.S. Navy, via Maurice Schechter, via H. R. Everett)

diminishing priority for untested technology as the United States achieved the upper hand on world battlefronts with more conventional technology. The TDRs and their TBM mother ships were assigned to a unit called Special Task Air Group One (STAG-1) under Lieutenant Thomas South, which was based at Traverse City, Michigan, and later at Monterey, California, and which conducted training and evaluation flights that included mock bombing runs. A table of organization for a Special Air Task Force (SATFOR) of assault drones drawn up in August 1943 also included STAG-2 under Lieutenant Commander Earl Eastwald, which was intended to be deployed with TDR-1s to the European Theater. STAG-3, under Lieutenant Commander James Smith, was tasked with operating Consolidated PB4Y bombers retrofitted for remote control operations.

In World War I, neither the navy nor army cruise missiles got anywhere near the front, but in May 1944, STAG-1 embarked for the Russell Islands in the Western Pacific. Here, they were based at Sunlight Field on Banika Island, 25 miles northwest of Guadalcanal. On 30 July, the TDR-1 was first tested as a cruise missile when four were sent to deliberately fly into an abandoned Japanese ship that had been beached on an island. Two of them scored direct hits.

On 27 September, four TDR-1s attacked and destroyed two Japanese transport ships off Bougainville and another hit a beached ship that was being used by the Japanese as a fixed anti-aircraft platform.

Through October 26, when STAG-1 was ordered to stand down, the unit flew 46 TDR-1 missions, with 37 reaching their targets and 21 destroying their targets. These included transport ships and gun emplacements ashore. Some of the failures were due to television malfunctions, and others from radio interference, but some TDR-1s were shot down by ground fire.

The lack of success and a lack of enthusiasm from the staff of Admiral Chester Nimitz, commander of the Pacific Fleet, led to the program's termination.

This image shows the location of the KY-3/APN-7 beacon coder situated in an aft fuselage compartment to the left of the R-7/APS-2 receiver-indicator of the AN/APS-2 radar system. (U.S. Navy, via Maurice Schechter, via H. R. Everett)

Meanwhile, the navy had ordered variants with larger engines designated as TD2R-1 and TD3R-1, but only a handful were built and none were deployed. The USAAF assigned the designations XBQ-4, XBQ-5, and XBQ-6 to a possible acquisition of TDR drones. This did not materialize other than the testing of a single TDR-1 under the XBQ-4 designation in April 1943. The U.S. Navy had offered to literally hand the whole program over to the USAAF, but General Hap Arnold, the former champion of the Kettering Bug and now commanding general of the USAAF, declined.

The National Naval Aviation Museum, which owns and displays a TDR-1, calls it "the world's first legitimate cruise missile."

An Interstate TDR-1 assault drone at the National Naval Aviation Museum in Pensacola, Florida. (Greg Goebel, licensed under Wikimedia Commons)

Arnold and Kettering, Together Again

During World War II, Arnold became reacquainted with Ket Kettering on the subject of a new generation of assault drones. Kettering was now president of the General Motors Research Company, with General Motors having acquired his Delco company as an electronics subsidiary after World War I. Kettering proposed an inexpensive aircraft that could be mass-produced, and Arnold had agreed in February 1941 to buy 10 prototype flying bombs. The General Motors A-1 was a high wing monoplane 16.3 feet long with a wingspan of 21.1 feet and weighing 1,400 pounds. It had a range of 400 miles with a 500-pound bomb load and a cruising speed of 200 mph.

The first flight, at Muroc Dry Lake (now Edwards Air Force Base) in California's Mojave Desert, took place on 15 November 1941, just three weeks before the attack on Pearl Harbor brought the United States into World War II. In an inauspicious beginning, the aircraft rolled down the test track on its carriage and immediately crashed. Another A-1, launched on the Friday before Pearl Harbor, flew for 150 seconds. On Sunday, 7 December, as the American fleet was being pummeled by Japanese airpower, an A-1 flew for 10 minutes, and the following day, another made a flight of 95 minutes.

Now using a powered catapult and an altitude control system, the A-1 test program resumed at Eglin Field in Florida in March 1942, but the results from this and from other rounds of flights during the summer of 1942 and May 1943 were disappointing in terms of both duration and directional control. Despite a proposal to try air launching the A-1 from a North American B-25 Mitchell bomber, Hap Arnold canceled the whole program in November 1943.

Project Perilous

By 1944, assault drones with very large warhead capacity had come to the fore through a series of top-secret projects designed around a few specific targets. As necessity is the mother of invention, the necessity in this case was the construction by the Germans of massively reinforced concrete structures in northern France.

In 1942–1943, the USAAF Eighth Air Force committed substantial resources, including countless heavy bomber missions, to attacking heavily reinforced concrete German U-boat pens. The results were negligible, and indeed, these facilities survive to this day. By 1944, the reinforced concrete targets to be attacked also included the launch sites for the German *Vergeltungswaffe*, or Vengeance Weapons, including the jet-propelled V-1 cruise missiles (discussed later in this chapter) and the strange V-3 *Hochdruckpumpe* (HDP, or High Pressure Pump). The V-3 was a massive multi-chambered 150-mm gun, 490 feet long with a range of more than 100 miles from its emplacement at Mimoyecques, near the French port of Calais. The *Vergeltungswaffe* were wreaking havoc against British cities and the Allies were casting about for means of attacking concrete too thick for conventional bombs, which had been so disappointing when used against the U-boat pens.

The proposed solution, developed under Project Perilous, involved turning heavy bombers into 10- to 12-ton bombs. The program, approved by Hap Arnold personally in July 1944, was to be managed by the Third Bombardment Division of the Eighth Air Force.

The first component of Perilous, code named "Aphrodite," called for approximately 25 to 27 "war weary" used Boeing B-17F and B-17G Flying Fortress heavy bombers to be field-modified in England and redesignated as BQ-7. They were stripped of all unnecessary gear and packed with 20,000 pounds of impact-fused Torpex (torpedo explosive), which had about 50 percent more explosive power than TNT.

The idea was for human pilots to handle the takeoff from remote secret bases in southern England, then bail out. The BQ-7s could then be radio-controlled by a ground-based controller "flying" them via a television camera in the nose. Because the range of the television signal was short, however, the operator was shifted from the ground to an accompanying aircraft, like those used in the navy's TDR program.

The Aphrodite program got off to a bad start during the first week of August when the first six missions all failed (with the deaths of several pilots) due to guidance and control malfunctions.

In the meantime, Eighth Air Force Commander General Jimmy Doolittle learned that the U.S. Navy, through its Special Task Air Groups (STAG) in the Pacific, had already developed an operational expertise in assault drone operations in live combat. He requested that they be brought

The last known photograph of Lieutenant Joseph P. Kennedy Jr., taken just before he boarded a Consolidated PB4Y-1 Liberator for his fateful Project Perilous mission against occupied France in August 1944. (Photo by Earl Olsen, licensed under Wikimedia Commons)

into the program, and that they bring their most up-to-date guidance and control technology.

Commander James Smith was asked to reassemble part of his STAG-3 team, including Lieutenant Wilford "Bud" Willy, his former executive officer. In turn, a small number of PB4Y-1 patrol bombers (the navy equivalent of the USAAF B-24 heavy bomber) were added to the Project Perilous fleet under the code name "Anvil." Designated as BQ-8, these aircraft could carry 25,000 pounds of Torpex.

Among the navy personnel brought into the program was a naval aviator with 50 maritime patrol missions in PB4Y-1s, Lieutenant Joseph P. Kennedy Jr. of patrol squadron VP-110. He was the eldest son of former U.S. Ambassador to Britain Joseph P. Kennedy and the brother of future U.S. President John F. Kennedy.

On 12 August, shortly after Kennedy and Willy took off, bound for the V-3 site at Mimoyecques, their BQ-8 exploded. Reportedly, USAAF Colonel Elliot Roosevelt, the son of President Franklin D. Roosevelt, was present that day aboard one of the accompanying aircraft. Because of the size of the explosion, all evidence to the exact cause vaporized along with the plane and pilots, so it will never be known what happened, though it appears to have been a malfunction in the arming system that caused a premature detonation.

Three weeks later, on 3 September, the second and last Anvil BQ-8 mission successfully obliterated a German submarine base on the island of Heligoland.

Meanwhile, Castor, also known under the code name "Abusive," was involved in the development and adaptation of more advanced systems, including SCR-729 "Rebecca" radio beacons and Block III television equipment. This equipment reached England as Anvil was winding down and was installed in BQ-7 aircraft. Despite improvements, the electronics were still problematic. Several missions in mid-September ended in failure, although one of two October BQ-7 missions found its target.

After a BQ-7 belly landed in Germany on 5 December without exploding, it was assumed that the whole project had been compromised, so it was terminated. After the war, it was learned that a German patrol had inadvertently detonated the aircraft while investigating it, destroying themselves and any information the Germans might have learned about Project Perilous.

The concept had a minor postwar footnote in the form of the secret Project MX-767, also known as Project Banshee. This was an effort by the Air Materiel Command to adapt surplus B-29 Superfortresses as flying bombs. The MX-767 program remained alive, albeit only on paper, until finally being terminated in 1949.

The Buzz Bomb

The most widely used cruise missile of World War II, and the only jet-powered cruise missile widely used in combat for

A preserved example of Germany's Fieseler Fi 103, better known as the "Buzz Bomb" or as the V-1, the first in Hitler's series of Vergeltungswaffe (Vengeance Weapons). It was the first widely used cruise missile. More than 8,000 were flown operationally in 1944. (Bill Yenne photo)

nearly half a century, was Germany's Fieseler Fi 103.

Known by many other names, it was designed under the code name "Kirshkern" (Cherry Stone), while the British code named it "Diver." Because of the buzzing sound of its Argus pulsejet engine, people who heard it called it a "Buzz Bomb" or "Doodlebug." However, the Fi 103 is best known by the designation given it by the Reich Propaganda Ministry with Hitler's direct approval, as the first in the Vergeltungswaffe (Vengeance Weapons) series, or "V-1."

Like the Americans, German engineers had been experimenting with gyroscopically stabilized unmanned aerial vehicles guided by radio, and later television, since World War I, and during the late 1930s, the Reich Air Ministry (RLM) encouraged a number of remote-control aircraft projects. In 1937, the RLM opened the Peenemünde Army Research Center on the island of Usedom in the Baltic Sea as an advanced rocket research center for the use of both the German Army and the Luftwaffe. The V-1 cruise missile was developed by the latter, while the "V-2" designation was assigned to the A-4, a vertically launched ballistic missile that was a German Army program.

The first glide test of the Fieseler Fi 103 came in September 1942, with the first flight with the Argus As 014 pulsejet engine three months later. Radio control for precision strikes was initially planned, but the RLM decided to use the missile for barrage attacks against London, so the gyrostabilized autopilot system governed only speed and altitude, not a precise trajectory. As with earlier American cruise missiles, the plan was for simple, inexpensive weapons that could be produced in large numbers, as many at 8,000 a month according to Kenneth Werrell.

In initial tests, the weapon was air-launched, but the RLM decided that operationally it should be catapult launched from "ski jump" launchers on the ground. As noted previously, a large infrastructure of around 150 heavily hardened launch sites had been constructed in northern France, and most of the launches took place from these.

In the summer of 1943, Allied aerial reconnaissance discovered the launch sites under construction, and massive air attacks were undertaken. These, combined with a host of technical issues, delayed the first operational launches from the planned date of December 1943 to 13 June 1944, a week after the Allied invasion of France. By the end of the month, more than 1,000 V-1s had been launched, one of which landed only a quarter mile from Buckingham Palace. Flying at low altitudes and with a top speed of around 400 mph, the V-1s were hard for interceptors and anti-aircraft units to defeat, but tactics emerged to deal with the threat.

After the last launch site was overrun by Allied troops, the Luftwaffe resumed air launches of its V-1s using the

Test operations involving the Republic-Ford JB-2, a reverse-engineered copy of the German Fi 103, involved airdropping the missiles from a B-17G mother ship. The flights began in 1944 and were operated out of Eglin Field in Florida. (USAAF)

He 111 bombers of Kampfgeschwader 3. This unit, known as the "Blitz Wing," outflanked air defenses in southern England to launch its missiles from above the North Sea. An estimated 1,176 V-1s were air-launched, with a success rate of around 60 percent, before these operations were terminated in March 1945.

In the summer of 1944, a manned variant of the V-1, the Fi 103R Reichenberg, was developed and flight tested. Like the American Aphrodite aircraft, it was intended that the pilot should bail out as the vehicle neared the impact point, but such an escape was considered unlikely, making the Fi 103R essentially a suicide plane. Fewer than 200 Fi 103Rs were built and none were used in combat.

The U.S. Strategic Bombing Survey estimated that the Germans produced 30,000 V-1s, of which more than half were used. Basil Collier, writing in the British Air Ministry's 1957 *Defence of Great Britain*, notes that 10,492 V-1s were launched against Britain. Of the total, about 2,000 suffered launch failures and 3,957 were shot down. The V-1 barrage resulted in 6,184 civilian deaths and 17,981 people injured. Around 92 percent of the casualties were in greater London.

As the Allies advanced across northern Europe in the fall of 1944, the Luftwaffe launched as many as 9,000 V-1s against targets on the continent, especially Antwerp, Belgium, which was liberated in September and which became an important disembarkation port for the Allies.

The V-1 was the most widely used cruise missile in history, and one of the most sophisticated, certainly in terms of propulsion, to date. Its legacy would be seen in the subsequent weapons for which it was the technological inspiration.

A Republic-Ford JB-2, a reverse-engineered copy of the German Fi 103, on the underwing mount of a B-17G mother ship, probably at Eglin Field in Florida. (USAAF)

The McDonnell LBD-1 (later KSD-1) Gargoyle, ordered in 1943, was a short-range glide bomb inspired to some degree by similar German weapons such as the Hs.293 and the Bv.143. It was first flown in March 1944 with a small rocket engine attached. Beginning in December, a series of tests demonstrated that when dropped from 27,000 feet, it had a range of 5 miles. It was not technically a cruise missile, but it demonstrated an American interest in winged missiles. (Author's collection)

American Sons of the Buzz Bomb

The V-1 and the technically unrelated V-2 attracted the attention of the Allies in more ways than one. Four years after the most intense part of the Blitz, the deadly power of these "Vengeance Weapons" startled the British populace. Meanwhile, the fact that their technical sophistication was, or at least appeared to be, ahead of Allied capability aroused an eagerness to imitate them.

The emulation of the V-2 led, of course, to postwar ICBMs and ultimately to the launch vehicles that made possible the American and Soviet space programs. Emulation of the V-1 would lead ultimately to the cruise missile systems that came on the scene in the latter half of the twentieth century.

The XAUM-6 Kingfisher, seen here beneath the wing of a Douglas JD-1 (A-26), was an air-launched short-range missile developed late in World War II and test flown after the war. The U.S. Navy considered arming various aircraft with the weapon, from the carrier-based AD-2 Skyraider to the long-range PB4Y-2 Privateer patrol plane and the P5M-1 Mariner flying boat. It was tested by the navy through 1949 but apparently never used in combat. The Kingfisher had a range of 20 miles and a top speed of Mach 0.7. (Author's collection)

Named for the enormous bird of Arabian mythology, the radar-guided Douglas Roc I was acquired by the USAAF under the Vertical Bomb designation VB-9. The VB-10 Roc II, which appeared in 1943, was similar, but was one of the first weapons to successfully exploit the emerging technology of television for guidance systems. Begun in 1940 under secret Project MX-601, the Roc program included four air-launched missiles with a distinctive circular wing that ringed the torpedo-shaped fuselage like a large doughnut. (Author's collection)

In the near term, American military leaders were so impressed with the V-1 that they sought to replicate it through reverse engineering.

In June 1944, Hap Arnold, the USAAF Commanding General, was overseas as part of an inspection tour that would take him to USAAF bases in Britain and to the Normandy beachhead where Allied troops had just landed. While in Britain, he and his staff stayed at a large house near Staines, southwest of London.

Arnold recalled in his memoirs that at 5:30 a.m. on 23 June, he was awakened to the sound of nearby explosions. He stepped outside in time to see that "a pilotless plane was flying through the air, circling right above. . . . It just missed the house. It came down out of the clouds in a dive, leveled off, made a low turn, then crashed into the ground and exploded about a mile and a half away! The force of the explosion lifted most of the staff out of their beds. About seven of these missiles hit within five miles of our house."

He later told Prime Minister Winston Churchill that "if the Germans were as efficient as we were in our fabrication, they could produce these V-1s with about 2,000 man-hours and at a cost of about $600. They could launch them from tracks at the rate of about one every 2 minutes, per track. They could turn them out, headed toward England, at the rate of 14,000 in 24 hours, which would cause great consternation, and finally, might even break down normal life in Britain. . . . If concentrated on central spots, they could even dislocate the war effort. No one could predict where they would hit."

Arnold ordered that wreckage from unexploded V-1s be shipped to the United States, where it could be studied by USAAF engineers with the Experimental Engineering Section of the Air Materiel Command at Wright Field. Designated as Materiel, Experimental Project MX-544, the task of reverse engineering a copy of the V-1 was given the highest of priorities, and the first of an initial batch of 13 was ready in just three weeks.

In August 1944, contracts were issued for the large-scale manufacture of the first 1,000 American Buzz Bombs under the designation JB-2. Republic Aviation Corporation in Farmingdale, New York, received the contract to build the airframes, but they subcontracted the work to Willys-Overland (makers of the famous Jeep). Ford, which had produced jet engines for the Northrop JB-1 cruise missile, received the contract for the JB-2's PJ31 pulsejet engines, while Northrop was to build the launch sleds.

Initially, the USAAF expected to use JB-2s in the European Theater to compensate for air operations that had to be canceled because of weather. However, combat commanders,

A Republic-Ford KGW-1 Loon cruise missile during a test flight at NAS Point Mugu in 1947. The KGW-1 was the U.S. Navy equivalent of the USAAF JB-2. Both were reverse engineered from the German V-1. (U.S. Navy)

including General Carl "Tooey" Spaatz, heading the U.S. Strategic Air Forces in Europe (USSTAF), which incorporated the 8th and 15th Air Forces, was concerned about inaccuracy, the inevitable learning curve, and especially about the diversion of resources away from existing, well-honed operations.

In Washington, an eagerness to get the JB-2 into production and into the field was tempered by a cautiousness that this effort should not interfere with the building of established and proven aircraft. There was an interesting exchange of memoranda in February 1945 between General Barney Giles, Hap Arnold's wartime deputy and the man who served as acting USAAF commander when Arnold was in the field or recovering from one of his several wartime heart attacks, and Dr. Vannevar Bush, the engineering genius and computer pioneer who was the head of the U.S. Office of Scientific Research.

"We believe the JB-2 to be representative of a new family of very long-range weapons whose capabilities will profoundly affect future warfare and especially aerial warfare," Giles observed pragmatically. "We want now to explore the possibilities of very long-range missiles to the utmost extent which will not involve a serious diversion of effort from the essential business of prosecuting this war."

As the war in Europe neared its finish, plans for JB-2 operations against Germany faded. In turn, it was envisioned that the JB-2 would play a key role in Operation Downfall, the invasion of Japan, which was likely to take place in late 1945 and early 1946. With this in mind, the USAAF planned for monthly JB-2 production to reach 1,000 units per month by April 1945, and 5,000 monthly by September 1945. Noting the rapid rate at which the Germans were launching V-1s, General Arnold insisted that the USAAF should have an inventory sufficient to be able to launch 100 JB-2s daily by September 1945 and 500 daily by January 1946. Plans were laid for total orders ranging up to 75,000 JB-2 vehicles.

The U.S. Navy also joined the program, intending to order the vehicle under the designation KGW-1 (later LTV-N-2) and the assigned name "Loon." Its plan was to surface launch them against Japan from LSTs or from escort carriers or to air launch them from PB4Y bombers.

Before these overly ambitious production schemes were ramped up, however, there was the test program. This began with the first JB-2 launch at Eglin Field on 12 October 1944. The first U.S. Navy LTV-N-2 launch did not occur until 7 January 1946. An 80-percent failure rate in early tests demonstrated that there were still bugs to be wrung out of the reverse-engineered system. Even with a radio control guidance system, the aiming accuracy was no better than

A Republic-Ford KGW-1 Loon cruise missile being readied for launch at NAS Point Mugu on the California coast in 1948. (U.S. Navy)

missiles. In 1946, two new Balao-class boats, USS *Cusk* and USS *Carbonero*, were retrofitted with watertight deck hangars that could accommodate Loon cruise missiles. The first submarine launch of a Loon, ushering in an era in naval history that continues to this day, took place from aboard the *Cusk* on 12 February 1947, off Point Mugu, California.

Looking Back on Three Decades

Through the three decades from the height of World War I through the aftermath of World War II, unmanned aerial vehicle technology had evolved almost unimaginably—from rickety wood and paper biplanes to all-metal missiles, from four-cylinder piston engines to turbojet power, and from early gyroscopes to TV guidance. Yet the operational achievements were few and far between. Among American weapons, only the TDR-1 and the Project Perilous weapons saw service, and they could be described as costly near-failures.

It is safe to say that no other aircraft type with a similar, dismal success rate would have had any legacy at all, but a fascination with the *potential* of the cruise missile concept still held the rapt interest of postwar planners.

the preset controls used by the Germans.

When the war ended and Downfall was canceled in September 1945, only 1,391 of the tens of thousands once imagined had been completed.

The USAAF (U.S. Air Force after 1948) continued to test the JB-2 after the war, while the U.S. Navy used its Loons to begin validating the concept of submarine-launched cruise

A Republic-Ford KGW-1 Loon cruise missile being fired from the deck of the submarine USS Cusk *in 1951. This was the beginning of a long series of submarine-launched cruise missiles that would later include the Regulus of the 1950s, as well as the Tomahawk, whose career spans the decades on either side of the turn of the twenty-first century. (U.S. Navy)*

Chapter 2

THE FIRST AIR FORCE CRUISE MISSILES

Given the questionable success and downright failure of the myriad cruise missile programs developed and tried by both the U.S. Army and the U.S. Navy between 1917 and 1947, it is easy to understand why everything else would be abandoned by both services in favor of systems that were essentially V-1 derivatives. After two decades of experimenting with such advanced technology as television guidance, it may seem curious that both services embraced a system in which operators simply pointed in the direction of a distant city and hoped for the best. However, we are reminded that strategic cruise missiles, as they evolved into the 1950s, were intended to deliver nuclear weapons whose blast radii rendered pinpoint accuracy irrelevant.

Captivated by the potential of the V-1/JB-2 program, USAAF planners issued a requirement for a next generation cruise missile in August 1945, before the formal termination of the war. General Hap Arnold, the commanding general of the USAAF, was enthused with leading edge technology. As he had embraced the Kettering Bug during the last year of World War I, he embraced the newly coined concept of "guided missiles" in the last year of World War II, pushing for many thousands of JB-2s.

In October 1945, a month after the war ended, Arnold and his friend Donald Douglas, whose Douglas Aircraft Company had grown into one of the largest planemakers in the world, set up Project RAND (Research and Development). The idea was to use the engineering infrastructure at Douglas to jumpstart

A 1953 launch of a Martin QYB-61 Matador cruise missile using a Zero-Length Launch (ZEL) system. The Matador was operationally designated as TM-61, and later redesignated as MGM-1. (Author's collection)

a permanent research and development institution. Working with them was Arthur Raymond, the chief engineer at Douglas, and his assistant, Franklin Collbohm, as well as Edward Bowles of MIT, who had been a consultant to Secretary of War Henry Stimson. On the USAAF side were General Lauris Norstad, Arnold's assistant chief of staff for plans, and Curtis LeMay. Under a special contract issued to Douglas, RAND began work on 2 March 1946 in an autonomous office located within the Douglas facility in Santa Monica.

So forward thinking was RAND that two months later it completed its first report. Entitled *Preliminary Design of an Experimental World-Circling Spaceship*, it described the design, performance, and deployment of earth-orbiting satellites, more than a decade ahead of the Soviet Sputnik and the American Explorer spacecraft programs. RAND was incorporated in 1948 as a nonprofit "think tank" and was transferred from Douglas to an entity called the RAND Corporation, which still exists.

Meanwhile, Arnold and his friend and chosen successor, General Carl "Tooey" Spaatz, were actively guiding the USAAF toward full independence from the U.S. Army. Recalling how the rug of technology funding had been pulled out from beneath the U.S. Army Air Service after the

Armistice of 1918, Arnold and Spaatz were determined that this should not befall the new U.S. Air Force when it came into being. Guided missiles would have a home, both in the technological vision and in the strategic doctrine of the new U.S. Air Force.

When Arnold and Chief of Staff General George Marshall agreed to the creation of the autonomous USAAF in 1941, its postwar independence was understood. This finally came about through the National Defense Act of 1947, which created the Department of Defense and the U.S. Air Force within it, along with the army and the navy.

There were, naturally, bad feelings at the Pentagon when the former cabinet-level War Department and Navy Department were eliminated and the secretaries of army, navy, and air force were made subordinate to the cabinet-level secretary of defense. Far from creating unity within the new Defense Department, the new arrangement simply added another service into the mix of inter-service rivalry that had existed between the army and navy for decades.

Insofar as missile technology and doctrine was concerned, there would be separate homes for a broad range of missile programs in all three services, at least for the moment.

A Martin Matador cruise missile being rail-launched from a Zero-Length Launch (ZEL) system using rocket assist at Cape Canaveral AFS, near Patrick AFB in Florida. (USAF)

Army Versus Air Force

Military leaders recognized that each postwar service would control separate missiles, but within the pre-1947 army, the ground forces and the airmen found themselves competing for the *same* missile systems. From a ground perspective, surface-launched missiles such as the V-1/JB-2 were *artillery*. However, the USAAF men argued that the same missiles were winged *aircraft* and should therefore remain with them after the two services separated.

This was on Arnold's mind as early as August 1944. In a memo that month to Secretary of War for Air Robert Lovett (a future secretary of defense), Arnold said that a big part of his desire to get the JB-2 into service quickly and in large numbers was to establish cruise missiles as part of *his*, not the army's, arsenal of weapons systems!

As Arnold was aware, negotiations were already ongoing at the newly opened Pentagon with respect to what parts of itself the U.S. Army would relinquish when it divested itself of its air arm in 1947.

A War Department general staff memo dated 14 September 1944 and approved by Lieutenant General Joseph McNarney on 2 October stipulated that any missile, whether launched from the ground or air, that required aerodynamic lift would belong to the airmen. Wingless, ground-launched ballistic missiles not dependent upon aerodynamics would remain under the artillery umbrella. Essentially, the United States had divided the systems in the same way the Germans had. As noted in the previous chapter, the winged V-1 was a Luftwaffe program, while the vertically launched V-2 ballistic missile belonged to the German Army.

At the close of the war in Europe, the USAAF and the U.S. Army operated separate projects related to locating and appropriating German advanced technology, especially missile technology. The USAAF managed its Operation Luftwaffe Secret Technology (LUSTY), directed at aviation and aerodynamic technology, while the army's well-known Operation Paperclip went after German ballistic missile technology, especially that related to the V-2. The latter materiel, along with German rocket scientists such as Wernher von Braun, were brought to facilities such as the Redstone Arsenal and White Sands Proving Ground where they were instrumental in the army's ballistic missile program.

After the war, the 1944 delineation was reopened for

At the beginning of the age of guided missiles, Lieutenant General Joseph McNarney of the USAAF was the man who decided that any missile, whether launched from the ground or air, that required aerodynamic lift would belong to the USAAF, while wingless, ground-launched ballistic missiles not dependent upon aerodynamics would remain under the artillery umbrella. (U.S. Army)

General Carl "Tooey" Spaatz (left) succeeded General Henry "Hap" Arnold (right) as commander of the USAAF. In 1947, he became the first man to command the independent U.S. Air Force. Both men understood the importance of guided missiles in their service and worked hard to integrate them into airpower doctrine. (Author's collection)

negotiation, which was ongoing for some time. When it was formed in September 1947, the new U.S. Air Force tentatively received the lion's share of the army missile arsenal, including winged missiles and strategic ballistic missiles, while the army moved into such systems as air defense missiles.

U.S. Air Force personnel ready a Martin QYB-61 Matador cruise missile for a test launch. (National Archives)

Officially, the army retained vertically launched ballistic trajectory missiles with a range less than 1,000 miles, which included captured German V-2s and their derivatives, while the air force inherited winged, airplane-like missiles and carried forward with the development of longer-range ballistic missiles.

USAAF and U.S. Air Force missile activities were mainly concentrated within a succession of various units at several bases in Florida. The early center of USAAF cruise missile development was at Eglin Field (later Eglin Air Force Base), where the JB-1, JB-2, and JB-10 had been tested. A center of USAAF weapons testing early in World War II, Eglin was home to the USAAF School of Applied Tactics, which became the Tactical Center in 1943, the Air Proving Ground Command in 1946, and the Air Proving Ground Center after 1957.

Also in 1946, the USAAF established its first Experimental Guided Missile Group (incorporating the First and Second Guided Missile Squadrons) at Eglin. This unit became the 550th Guided Missile Wing in 1949 and moved from Eglin to Patrick Air Force Base at Cape Canaveral in 1950, where its activities were absorbed into the 550th Guided Missile Group, and then into the 6555th Guided Missile Wing (later the 6555th Guided Missile Group, and the 6555th Aerospace Test Group between 1971 and 1990). In turn, this organization contained the 6555th and 6556th Guided Missile *Squadrons*, which would handle much of the hands-on work in testing air force cruise missiles for the next quarter century. These organizations were assigned to a series of major commands, including the Joint Long-Range Proving Ground Command and later the Air Research and Development Command, which split off from the Air Materiel Command in 1951.

Patrick AFB itself was part of a complex of missile launch facilities that included Cape Canaveral Air Force Station as well as the facilities that grew into NASA's vast Kennedy Space Center. Patrick AFB originated as the navy's NAS Banana River, became the Air Force Long-Range Proving Ground, and in 1951, the Air Force Missile Test Center (AFMTC). As such, Patrick, like the 6555th, would be an

A 1952 launch, probably at White Sands Missile Range, of a Martin Matador cruise missile from a Zero-Length Launch (ZEL) system. The air force identified this specific missile as an operational B-61. (National Archives)

essential part of early cruise missile development history.

Missile training consolidated around units, such as the 588th Tactical Missile Group at Orlando Air Force Base. In 1956, the 588th and various other units were consolidated into the 4504th Missile Training Wing at Orlando, which operated the U.S. Air Force Tactical Missile School. The wing also operated two detachments, at Cape Canaveral Auxiliary AFS on the Eastern Missile Test Range and at Holloman Air Force Base near the White Sands Missile Range in New Mexico.

Cultural Issues

In concentrating on technical, doctrinal, and strategic issues regarding missiles in the postwar armed forces, we often lose sight of cultural issues. In retrospect, these seem quaint and irrelevant, but in the context of the late 1940s, they were an important dimension to the overall picture.

A Martin Matador cruise missile surrounded by its launch equipment and support vehicles ahead of a 1954 test launch from a Zero-Length Launch (ZEL) system. A year later, Matadors were redesignated from B-61 "bombers" to TM-61 "tactical missiles." (Author's collection)

Missiles, despite their past failures and their past practical insignificance, were there to stay, but many still dismissed them as faddish. An easy comparison is to the perception of airpower itself in the early decades of the twentieth century. In the 1920s, many within the "horse cavalry" establishment of the U.S. Army considered airplanes an expensive novelty at best and a dangerous waste of resources at worst. General Malin Craig, who was the chief of staff until General George Marshall took over in 1939, believed that the army should not waste its money on airplanes because they became obsolete so much faster than other equipment. Of

Even though many air
force officers, as epitomized
by Hap Arnold himself, were
inclined to embrace advances
in technology, many more
saw only the past failures and
could not imagine incorporating these past failures into
future doctrine.

In his 1954 Air War Col-
lege thesis, *The Impact of
Guided Missiles Upon the U.S.
Air Force*, Richard P. Klocko
wrote that "unfortunately,
the actual reaction within the
air force [to the guided mis-
sile] appears to be the exact opposite of that which might
logically be expected. The attitude of air force personnel,
individually throughout the air force and collectively in the
major commands, seems to best be described as a combination of skepticism, indecision, and indifference. This is a
sweeping statement, but it appears to be well supported by
the facts."

A half century later, we saw the same reaction within
the culture of the air force to the advent of unmanned aerial
vehicles, especially unmanned *combat* air vehicles. Many
pilots reacted negatively to an expanding and growing culture of ground-bound drone operators.

Air Force Versus Navy

While the air and ground constituencies of the U.S.
Army were staking out their doctrinal turf with respect
to guided missiles in 1944–1947, the U.S. Navy sought to
define its postwar guided missile future. Like the airmen
of the U.S. Army Air Forces, the U.S. Navy moved quickly
to develop its first generation of surface-to-air missiles for
the defense of its surface forces. When it came to offensive

course, many in the U.S. Navy still believed that battleships
would trump airpower indefinitely.

World War II ended with airpower doctrine fully established, but even many of those in the new U.S. Air Force
establishment who had crusaded upon that issue regarded
guided missiles with great skepticism. Curiously, while the
attitude toward ballistic missiles was one of suspicion, there
seemed to be more tolerance for winged missiles because
there was some similarity to the familiar.

As Robert L. Perry wrote in *Science, Technology, and Warfare: The Proceedings of the Third Military History Symposium*
at the United States Air Force Academy in 1969, "to people who had grown up with the manned bombers before
and during World War II and who had mostly stayed with
them through the early part of the next decade, a cruise missile was a less painful and certainly a less abrupt departure
from what they were familiar with than would be a totally
alien ballistic missile. Those who favored the evolutionary
approach to the creation of a new generation of weapons,
predominantly missiles, were people to whom aircraft had
a meaning as a way of life, a symbol, a preferred means of
performing a military assignment."

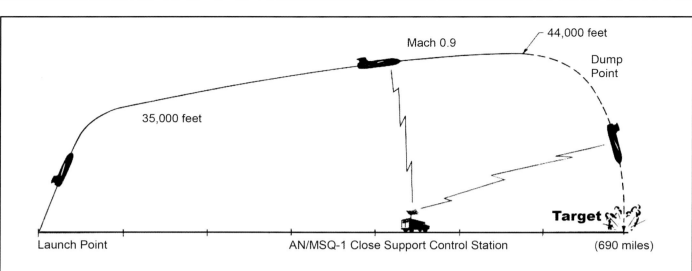

Mach 0.9

44,000 feet

Dump Point

35,000 feet

Launch Point

AN/MSQ-1 Close Support Control Station

Target

(690 miles)

TM-61A Matador Guidance and Control

The TM-61A utilized the Matador Automatic Radar Control (MARC) guidance system consisting of AN/MSQ-1 ground radar and AN/APW-11A airborne radar for midcourse guidance. After launch from the Zero-Length Launch (ZEL) system, longitudinal control of the TM-61A was maintained by a fixed bias pitch controller. When the airspeed reached 210 mph, an airspeed control system phased into operation. The missile climbed under programmed airspeed control to an indicated dynamic pressure of approximately 220 pounds per square foot. The airspeed control period lasted until radar contact with the MARC guidance equipment for midcourse flight. The AN/MSQ-1 ground-based mobile equipment tracked the missile through the use of the airborne AN/APW-11A beacon. In addition, proper commands were developed either automatically or manually in the MSQ-1 equipment and sent over the radar link to the beacon and then to the flight control system to control position. A semi-ballistic transonic dive began at the "dump" point predicted by the MARC midcourse guidance equipment. When dump was signaled, the terminal dive system produced signal voltages that caused the engine to throttle to idle, the warhead to start its fusing operation, and the fuel system to switch to terminal dive condition. Gyro precession with accelerometer corrections ensured that the zero-lift trajectory was maintained until impact. Line-of-sight limitations to microwave propagation restricted the TM-61A with MARC guidance to a 200-mile range ahead of the AN/MSQ-1 equipment. (USAF)

weapons, the navy would throw itself into the notion of a V-1/LTV-N-2 derivative as the initial guidepost to its postwar shipboard cruise missiles.

As for a think tank analogous to Arnold's RAND, the U.S. Navy sponsored the Applied Physics Laboratory (APL) in Howard County, Maryland, which was and is affiliated with Johns Hopkins University, though not part of it. Through the years, APL has been involved in missile and spacecraft design, and in the immediate postwar period, it was involved in the development of the Terrier and Talos surface-to-air-missiles, as well as the Triton cruise missile concept.

In the years immediately after World War II, as the navy sought to define its strategic future, the service was anxious to develop and maintain its own indigenous nuclear weapons delivery capability. At the time, the air force had

a monopoly on long-range bombers capable of lifting and carrying nuclear weapons, which at the time weighed about 5 tons. The navy did not wish to take a back seat to the new service and actively sought a way to establish an offensive strategic nuclear strike force of its own.

The problem was that the navy did not have aircraft capable of carrying a 5-ton payload that could either match an air force bomber, especially the Convair B-36, for range nor did it have a bomber that could take off from an aircraft carrier with such a load. In 1948, the navy ordered a new class of five "supercarriers," beginning with the USS *United States*. These massive ships were to have a displacement half again greater than that of the Midway class carriers and double the displacement of Essex class aircraft carriers. These could accommodate much larger and longer-range aircraft.

At the same time, the navy was moving full speed ahead, to use a nautical term, toward the development of the nuclear-weapons-capable cruise missiles, a process that is discussed in chapter 3.

The Matador

Several guided missile programs began during and immediately after World War II. By the beginning of 1946, carried forward by the momentum that flowed from the

Designation Systems

In 1947, as all three services were developing missiles of all types, from air-to-air to surface-to-air to long-range offensive cruise missiles, they agreed to a common designation system. Under this complicated nomenclature, missiles were designated by two letters that described the launch environment plus the target environment plus an "M" for "Missile."

The choices for the first two were A (air), S (surface), and U (underwater); therefore, a surface-to-surface missile would be an SSM, and an air-launched ground attack missile would an ASM. There would then be a hyphen followed by a letter naming the service—A (air force), G (ground army), or N (navy)—followed by the series number. The U.S. Navy's first *cruise* missile under the system was the SSM-N-8 Regulus, which is discussed in chapter 3. The first air force cruise missile was the SSM-A-1 Matador, discussed in this chapter.

The army continued to use the 1947 system until 1955, and the navy did so until 1963. The air force withdrew from the system in 1951. The air force was so keen to underscore its assertion that missiles were a form of airplane that, until 1955, it designated its offensive missiles with the "B-for-Bomber" designation, and its interceptor missiles, such as the F-98 Falcon and F-99 Bomarc, with the "F for Fighter" nomenclature.

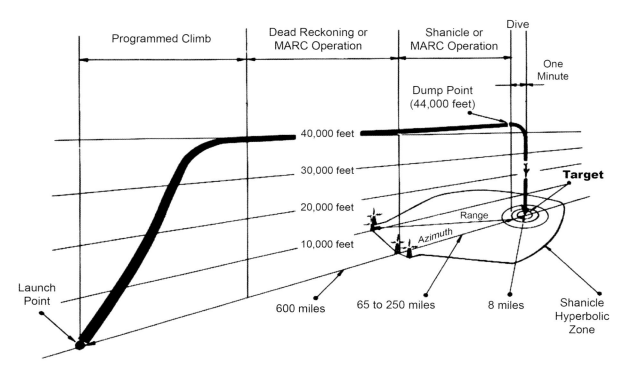

Programmed Climb

Dead Reckoning or MARC Operation

Shanicle or MARC Operation

Dive

One Minute

Dump Point (44,000 feet)

40,000 feet

30,000 feet

20,000 feet

10,000 feet

Target

Range

Azimuth

Launch Point

600 miles

65 to 250 miles

8 miles

Shanicle Hyperbolic Zone

TM-61C Matador Guidance and Control

The TM-61C utilized the Short-Range Navigation Vehicle (SRNV) system, called "Shanicle," which used ground-based microwave emitters to create hyperbolic range and azimuth navigation grids. Shanicle was still limited by its dependence on line-of-sight radio transmissions, but it had a much better reputation for accuracy than the original MSQ-1. The guidance mode for the launching phase was the same as for the TM-61A and lasted until a predetermined point where one of three alternate midcourse guidance systems assumed control. At the discretion of the launching entity, any one of three possible modes of midcourse guidance could be selected. The systems available were Shanicle, the Matador Automatic Radar Control (MARC), or a combination of the two. If the Shanicle hyperbolic system was employed for the midcourse, the missile was programmed into the Shanicle zone. Four base stations (consisting of antenna towers and transmitting equipment) generated two families of LORAN-type constant-time differential hyperbolic signals; one family for azimuth guidance, and one family for range guidance. Airborne equipment measured the time of arrival of these signals and issued corrective commands to the controls in the missile. The missile was guided along the azimuth hyperbola until it crossed the intersecting range hyperbola, at which time the terminal dive was initiated. If the MARC system was selected, the missile was controlled from the ground-based mobile transmitter until arrival at the "dump" point or flown into the Shanicle zone where the Shanicle system assumed control until the terminal dive. While operating under Shanicle guidance, the missile emitted no signal. The terminal dive phase was conducted in the same manner as the TM-61A's. (USAF)

years of wartime urgency, there were 21 distinct missile programs across all the services, and this number more than doubled through the year.

That wartime momentum, however, which had seen American technology and production infrastructure grow on a previously unimaginable scale, foundered on the shoals of dissipating necessity. By December 1946, demobilization had caught up with all the services. For the USAAF, there was no longer an urgency for vast numbers of new aircraft, nor vast numbers of new aircrews. From a wartime peak of 2.4 million, the personnel count had fallen below 400,000. Nor was there an apparent need, by neither army nor navy, for the plethora of research and development programs that had been cropping up.

As the USAAF budget was slashed, new manned aircraft programs withered to minuscule by wartime standards. The missile budget was more than halved from $29 million to $13 million, with the num-

Partially hidden in a West German forest, a Martin TM-61A Matador cruise missile stands cocked and ready on its Zero-Length Launch (ZEL) system trailer. (USAF)

ber of programs reduced to around a half dozen. Among these were two signature cruise missile programs that had begun in August 1945.

In that month, the USAAF had issued requirements for two 600-mph cruise missiles. Project MX-771 was a secret development program that called for a tactical cruise missile with a range of 175 to 500 miles, a weapon similar in size and performance to the JB-2. Project MX-775 was a strategic cruise missile with a range of 5,000 miles with a 1-ton warhead. Both were intended to be capable of delivering nuclear weapons. The former would evolve into the Martin Matador, and the latter became the Northrop Snark program, which is discussed in chapter 4.

The Glenn Martin Company received the nod for the MX-771 tactical missile in April 1946 under the surface-to-surface missile designation XSSM-A-1 and the name "Matador." The USAAF requested proposals for both subsonic and supersonic MX-771 variants, but the latter was canceled.

The Martin Matador, described informally by the air force as being about the size and configuration of a contemporary jet fighter, was 39 feet 7 inches long with swept wings spanning 28 feet 7 inches. By comparison, the famous F-86 Sabre was 37 feet long with a swept wingspan of 37 feet. The Matador weighed 6 tons, roughly the same as the Sabre without fuel, and carried a 3,000-pound payload. The Matador could carry a conventional warhead, but operationally, it was armed with a W5 nuclear warhead. It had a designated operational range of 1,000 kilometers (620 miles) but could be pushed to around 700 miles, a bit less than half that of the Sabre.

Originally, it was planned to use a catapult launch system like that of the V-1/JB-2 to launch the Matador, but Martin discarded this idea in favor of using a Zero-Length Launch (ZEL) system. An Aerojet solid-fuel booster rocket generating 57,000 pounds of thrust for 2.4 seconds got the missile airborne, at 200 mph, after which an Allison J33-A-37 turbojet, delivering 4,600 pounds of thrust, took over.

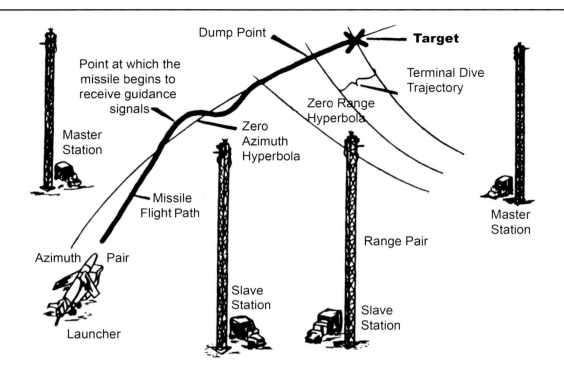

TM-61C Matador Typical Shanicle Flight Pattern

The Shanicle system used to control a TM-61C mission was similar to LORAN. It utilized four ground-based transmitter beacons to create a hyperbolic grid. Two transmitters, master and slave, controlled the range, and two controlled azimuth. A hyperbolic grid system involves the creation of a grid pattern of radio waves by the four radio transmitters, each in a different location. The missile could be programmed in advance to follow a certain sequence of augmented and diminished radio impulses directly to the target without the necessity for manual control by a human operator, as required by the MSQ-1. TM-61C had greater range than TM-61A and was less vulnerable to jamming. Controllers could guide more than one missile at a time. (USAF)

The Matador Automatic Radar Control (MARC) was a radio-link command guidance system that used an airborne AN/APW-11A radar transponder on the missile for ranging, as well as a series of ground-based Reeves Instrument AN/MSQ-1 Close Support Control Stations with direct current analog computers. The MSQ system (nicknamed "mis-cue" by operators), using line-of-sight communications to geolocate the missile, proved problematic because the 250-mile range of the MSQ was less than that of the missile itself.

The tactical doctrine held that guidance for a single missile could be transferred from one ground control site, or Operating Location (OL), to the next, but this also proved problematic and was seldom attempted. The MARC was improved in subsequent Matador variants.

The first Matador flight, occurring at Holloman AFB adjacent to the U.S. Army's White Sands Missile Range on 19 January 1949, ended in a crash. The test program was off to a bad start. In the meantime, the Guided Missile

Committee of the Department of Defense Research and Development Board was considering a consolidation of navy and air force cruise missile programs, and the Matador program faced a complete cancellation after its initial flight test troubles.

The dark clouds of the Cold War were gathering, however, with the Soviet blockade of Berlin and the unexpected first test of a Soviet nuclear weapon in 1949. The fear of having to fight a war, even a nuclear war, was no longer as improbable as it had been just a year or so earlier. After the Korean War began in June 1950, the defense budget pendulum swung rapidly in the opposite direction. Numerous programs throughout the Defense Department were reappraised, and in September, the Matador was elevated in importance.

In 1951, when the U.S. Air Force formally redesignated its offensive missiles using numerals in its "B-for-Bomber" nomenclature, the XSSM-A-1 Matador became the XB-61, and the YSSM-A-1 Matadors, intended to service-test the MARC guidance system, were redesignated as YB-61s. Meanwhile, the First Experimental Guided Missile Squadron at Patrick AFB, which had transitioned from JB-2s to Matadors, became the First Bombardment Squadron Missile.

The first batch of 46 XB-61s and YB-61s was tested through March 1954. However, so great was the newfound urgency to be ready to counter a Soviet attack on Western Europe that a production block of 84 B-61As began appearing in 1952 before testing concluded. The B-61As were first deployed overseas in 1954 by the First Bombardment Squadron Missile, which became the First Pilotless Bomber Squadron, with a new home at Bitburg Air Base in Germany. The Second Pilotless Bomber Squadron was activated and deployed to Hahn Air Base, also in Germany.

In 1955, the air force redesignated its "B-for-Bomber" missiles again, and the B-61 series became TM-61 "Tactical Missiles." The Pilotless Bomber Squadrons in turn became the Tactical Missile Squadrons. During the 1950s, TM-61A Matadors served with the First TMS at Bitburg AB and with the 69th TMS at Hahn AB. TM-61C Matadors were assigned to the 585th TMS at Bitburg and to the 586th TMS at Hahn. In turn, the squadrons were assigned to the 701st Tactical Missile Wing at Hahn, which was superseded in 1958 by the 38th Tactical Missile Wing at Sembach Air Base.

As with the German V-1s that had inspired them, Matadors were kept, ready for immediate launch, in highly reinforced concrete shelters, many of which still exist at various locations in Germany.

Operational testing and training, meanwhile, were conducted overseas out of Wheelus Air Base near Tripoli in Libya, using the Sahara Desert and the Mediterranean Sea as ranges. Built as a military air base by the Italians when they ruled Libya, Wheelus was used by the Luftwaffe early in World War II and taken over by the USAAF in 1943. Named after an airman killed in Iran, the base was used by a broad spectrum of U.S. Air Force units, from the Strategic Air Command to the Military Airlift Command and its predecessors, through 1970, after Muammar al-Qaddafi took power in Libya.

From 1954 through 1958, Wheelus hosted the Annual Missile Launch Operation (AMLO), a training exercise for Matador units stationed in Europe. Run by the 701st TMW and later by the 38th TMW, the AMLOs received code names such as "Suntan," "Sunburst," and "Sunflash." These activities made Wheelus the most active Matador launch location in the world. In a 1957 article, *Aviation Week* Pentagon correspondent Claude Witze noted that 36 TM-61s were launched from Wheelus that year, compared to 25 at Holloman, and only 13 from Patrick and adjacent Florida locations.

Not all the missile tests went according to plan, and, apparently, they routinely did *not*. Famed aviator Chuck Yeager, then commanding the 417th Fighter-Bomber Squadron in Germany, recalled in his memoirs that his unit deployed to Libya with its F-100s, where he "worked out a deal with the gunnery commander [to chase] out-of-control missiles, hammering them with our [AIM-9] Sidewinders." Yeager called this "really good practice."

After the last annual AMLO, Operation Marblehead in 1958, the exercise was discontinued because of problems with Libyan civilians prowling the Matador crash sites looking to salvage scrap metal.

Beyond the TM-61A, there were two further variants of the B-61/TM-61 Matador, the TM-61B and TM-61C. The former, which was significantly different from the TM-61A, became the TM-76 Mace cruise missile (which is discussed later in this chapter), whereas the TM-61C was an operational variant of the TM-61A with an improved guidance system. After 1963, when the U.S. Air Force adopted the

A Matador in Luftwaffe markings photographed at Luftwaffenmuseum Berlin-Gatow in Germany. (Anagoria, licensed under Creative Commons)

A TM-61A Matador preserved at the Warner Robins Museum of Aviation in Georgia. (Alan Wilson, licensed under Creative Commons)

hyperbolic range and azimuth navigation grids.

In a 1992 Air War College research report on U.S. Air Force ground-launched cruise missiles, Lieutenant Colonel Randall Lanning pointed out that the Shanicle system "similar to LORAN, employed four ground-based transmitter beacons to create a hyperbolic grid—two (master and slave) controlling the range, and two for azimuth, along which the missile could fly. . . . A hyperbolic grid system involves the creation of a grid pattern of radio waves by the four radio transmitters, each in a different location. Unlike radar, which is limited to line-of-site, a radio grid may be broadcast for several-hundred miles. The missile could be programmed in advance to follow a certain sequence of augmented and diminished radio impulses directly to the target without the necessity for manual control by a human operator as required by MSQ-1."

Shanicle was still limited by its dependence on radio transmissions, but it had a much better reputation for accuracy than did the original MSQ-1. Its accuracy, measured by a Circular Error Probable (CEP) of around 1,600 feet, was not so good by today's standards, though with nuclear weapons, where this was less than the blast radius, it was probably close enough, and better than the 2,700 feet of the original Matador Automatic Radar Control (MARC).

Matadors joined the U.S. Air Force nuclear arsenal in the Far East in 1958. In South Korea, the 310th Fighter-Bomber Squadron, which had served in the Korean War from Taegu Air Base, moved to Osan Air Base in 1955 and was redesignated as the 310th Tactical Missile Squadron. It was assigned to the 58th Tactical Missile Group in June 1958 and was operational with the Matador until March 1962.

The 17th Tactical Missile Squadron was formed as a

current "M for Missile" designation system, restarting numerals at 1, the Matador was first, becoming MGM-1, while the Mace became MGM-13. The letters indicate a ground-based, ground targeting (MG-) missile (-M).

The TM-61C's Short-Range Navigation Vehicle (SRNV) system, called "Shanicle," first tested in April 1957, in some measure remedied the shortcomings of the MARC system. Shanicle utilized ground-based microwave emitters to create

A Matador, identified by its post-1963 designation as an MGM-1C, on display at Tainan Air Force Base in Taiwan. Tainan was a major Imperial Japanese Navy air base during World War II. (Xuan Nanjo, licensed under Creative Commons)

The U.S. Air Force 6555th Guided Missile Group launches a Martin TM-76A Mace using a Zero-Length Launch (ZEL) system at Cape Canaveral AFS, north of Patrick AFB, in Florida, circa 1960. (USAF)

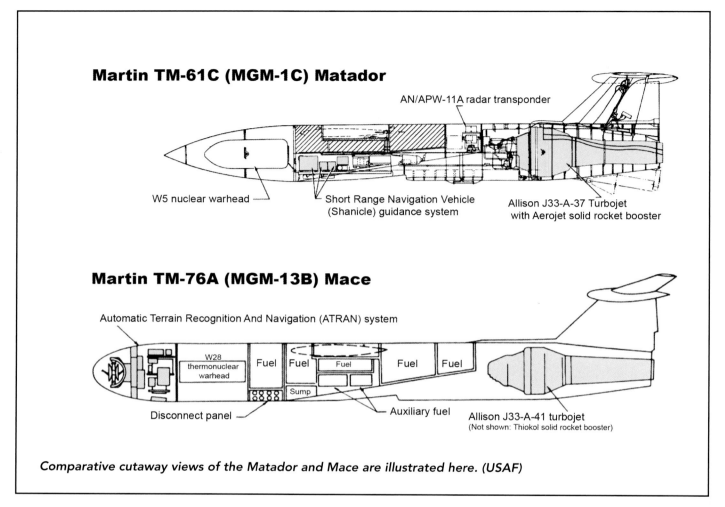

Martin TM-61C (MGM-1C) Matador

AN/APW-11A radar transponder

W5 nuclear warhead

Short Range Navigation Vehicle (Shanicle) guidance system

Allison J33-A-37 Turbojet with Aerojet solid rocket booster

Martin TM-76A (MGM-13B) Mace

Automatic Terrain Recognition And Navigation (ATRAN) system

W28 thermonuclear warhead

Fuel | Fuel | Fuel | Fuel | Fuel

Sump

Disconnect panel

Auxiliary fuel

Allison J33-A-41 turbojet
(Not shown: Thiokol solid rocket booster)

Comparative cutaway views of the Matador and Mace are illustrated here. (USAF)

Matador unit in 1955 at Orlando AFB in Florida as part of the Tactical Air Command (TAC). In 1957, after a period of training, it began the deployment to Tainan AFB in Taiwan in May 1957. Initially, these Matadors were armed with conventional warheads, but they were retrofitted with nuclear warheads by February 1958. Redesignated as the 868th TMS, the unit was formally transferred from TAC to Pacific Air Forces (PACAF) in 1958. By 1962, however, the missiles, similar to Matadors on the frontlines around the world, were being withdrawn.

It is indicative of the Cold War urgency for offensive weapons systems that so many Matadors were forward deployed to so many frontline operational units, and that the deployment took place with a lot of bugs still in the overall system.

The Matador program had been trouble-plagued from the beginning. This was true not only with its guidance component, but with the vehicle itself. In a later program summary, Bernard J. Termena of the Air Materiel Command recalled that in 1953, the air force project officer had written that the "Martin Matador program was delayed excessively because of [Martin's] poor design, inadequate testing, and difficulty in retaining qualified people."

Air force historian Kenneth Werrell observed that "throughout its service, observers criticized the Matador for its low inflight reliability, high CEPs, and questionable con-

A Martin TM-76A (later MGM-13) Mace posed on its FWD MM-1 Teracruzer transport vehicle, circa 1960. (Martin)

trol over long distances."

Meanwhile, an operational analysis dated May 1956 noted that the U.S. Air Force had rushed the whole program, from development to deployment, and that it "did not develop Matador according to procedures and military requirements, but rather devised the missile around existing components and techniques. Further, at the time the air force initially deployed the Martin missile, the weapon had not demonstrated operationally acceptable performance and required major modifications."

Notes on Nukes

Though high explosive warheads were occasionally mentioned in connection with the beginning of the cruise missile story, the primary function of the first generation of American cruise missiles, with both the U.S. Navy and U.S. Air Force, was to perform nuclear strikes. The early missiles, Matador and Mace for the air force and Regulus for the navy, were armed with W5 nuclear fission warheads. These were derived from the Mark 5 nuclear bomb. The Mark 5 was introduced in 1952 and the W5 in 1954. Both remained in operational units until 1963.

Like the Fat Man nuclear weapon of World War II, the W5 was an implosion-type weapon, though while the Fat Man had a plutonium core, the W5 had a composite plutonium-uranium core.

The W5 was 76 inches long and 39 inches in diameter, making it about two-thirds the size of the Fat Man. It weighed around 2,500 pounds, depending on its configuration, which was about one-quarter of the weight of the Fat Man. This reduction in size was made possible by advances in weapon miniaturization. While the Fat Man had a yield of 21 kilotons, variations on the W5 had yields as high as 100 to 120 kilotons.

The successors to the Mark 5/W5 weapons were the Mark 27 bomb and the W27 warhead. These weapons were thermonuclear weapons, meaning that they used a nuclear fission reaction to compress and ignite a secondary nuclear fusion reaction. Because isotopes of hydrogen are used, thermonuclear weapons are called hydrogen bombs, or H-bombs.

Developed at the Lawrence Radiation Laboratory (now Lawrence Livermore National Laboratory) in California, and introduced in 1958, the W27 was 31 inches in diameter, 75 inches long, and it weighed 2,800 pounds. It had a yield of 2 megatons.

Produced at the same time at the Los Alamos National Laboratory in New Mexico were the Mark 28 bomb and W28 (later B28) warhead. Depending upon variant, they were around 22 inches in diameter, up to 170 inches long, and weighed up to 2,320 pounds. The yield, again depending upon variant, ranged from 70 kilotons to 1.45 megatons.

A 1962 launch of a Martin TM-76B Mace from Cape Canaveral AFS, about 10 miles north of Patrick AFB. In the background is the Cape Canaveral Lighthouse. It was built in 1868, but because of erosion it was moved inland in 1894 to its present location about a mile from the beach. (USAF)

A check of known tail numbers confirms that more than 1,000 Matadors were produced, including 388 TM-61Cs ordered in FY 1955–1956. A great many Matadors were expended in testing and training. The first batch of 46 were for sure, and Claude Witze noted that 74, at least, were launched in 1957 alone.

In retrospect, given the numerous technical issues and the high incident rate in testing and training activities, it is a lucky thing that the Cold War never went hot while Matadors were on station. There could well have been a horrific epidemic of friendly fire disasters.

As celebrated in the in-house magazine of the Four Wheel Drive Auto Company, the TM-76A and its FWD MM-1 Teracruzer transport vehicle were featured in President Dwight Eisenhower's second inaugural parade in January 1957. The big vehicle made an impact on spectators, but none on Pennsylvania Avenue as it "gently swayed," borne on its low-pressure "pillow tires." (Author's collection)

FOUR WHEEL DRIVE

News

CLINTONVILLE, WISCONSIN

JAN. - FEB.   1957

TERACRUZER --
New Member of Air Force

Northern Indiana Public Service
Does the Job with FWDs

An FWD Teracruzer with its lethal cargo, the Matador Missile, travels majestically down Washington's Pennsylvania Avenue in Pres. Eisenhower's Second Inaugural Parade Jan. 21. Carrying the huge weapon on its translauncher trailer, FWD's latest addition to the U. S. Air Force might, attracted much attention from spectators as it sways gently on its low-pressure "pillow" tires.

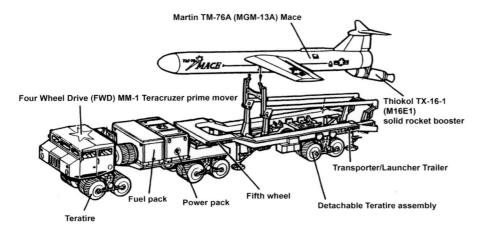

FWD Teracruzer with Martin Mace

Martin TM-76A (MGM-13A) Mace

Four Wheel Drive (FWD) MM-1 Teracruzer prime mover

Thiokol TX-16-1 (M16E1) solid rocket booster

Transporter/Launcher Trailer

Fuel pack

Power pack

Fifth wheel

Detachable Teratire assembly

Teratire

A detailed look at how the TM-76A Mace was integrated with its massive FWD MM-1 Teracruzer transport vehicle. (USAF)

The Mace

The Martin TM-76 Mace cruise missile evolved directly out of the Matador program as an effort to address the latter's shortcomings. The Mace was, in turn, developed and deployed alongside the TM-61 Matador.

As noted previously, the missile that became the Mace originated as the TM-61B variant of the Matador, but the scope of the changes resulted in the system receiving new designations as TM-76A and TM-76B. These variants are often referred to as "Mace A" and "Mace B."

Development of the new missile began in 1954, as the Matador was experiencing its many flight test woes. Flight testing of the first YTM-61Bs began in 1956, with the redesignation to YTM-76A, and the name "Mace," becoming official in early 1958.

Externally, the Mace was longer than the Matador, but with a shorter wingspan. It was 44 feet 9 inches long (about 5 feet longer), with swept wings spanning 22 feet 11 inches, compared to 28 feet 7 inches for the Matador. It weighed 18,750 pounds, compared to 12,000 for the Matador. The Mace was powered by an Allison J33-A-41 turbojet engine and launched

Hobbyists in the 1950s could build their own scale models of the TM-76A mounted on its FWD MM-1 Teracruzer transport vehicle. In contrast to the transporters of the camouflaged U.S. Air Force GLCM of the 1980s, the Teracruzer was painted air force blue. Test missiles were painted orange, but operational missiles went overseas in natural metal finish. Renwal bragged that its kit was "scaled from U.S. Army Ordnance blueprints," but the missile and its transporter actually belonged to the air force. (Author's collection)

This rare view shows a Martin TM-76B Mace being trucked through the town of Gushikawa in Okinawa in the early 1960s. Two Mace B squadrons were located in Okinawa during 1961–1970. (USAF photo by Charles "Chuck" Headlee)

using a Thiokol TX-16-1 (M16E1) solid rocket booster generating 97,000 pounds of thrust.

Like the Matador, the Mace could carry a conventional warhead, but operationally, it was nuclear armed. The warhead was a W28 weapon, weighing 1,700 to 2,320 pounds, depending on variant.

The principal improvement over the Matador was in guidance. The Goodyear Aircraft Corporation developed a system known as Automatic Terrain Recognition and Navigation (ATRAN), an early predecessor of the Terrain Contour Matching (TERCOM) systems that were installed in late twentieth–century cruise missiles. As necessity is the mother of invention, the U.S. Air Force Air Materiel Command had grown frustrated with the early Matador test failures and commissioned Goodyear to develop the all-new system in August 1952. ATRAN was developed in less than two years and entered production in June 1954.

ATRAN was revolutionary because it was the first system to use radar to match terrain to maps carried internally. Unlike line-of-sight radio guidance, ATRAN could not be jammed. However, it was dependent on the preparation of terrain maps that could be matched. This necessitated a lot of low-level reconnaissance missions by manned aircraft. Technically, the reconnaissance aircraft radar was calibrated to a fixed angle that scanned the surfaces ahead and below, with the timing of the radar return signal showing range and landform through an amplitude modulated signal. In turn, this was recorded on photographic film. Later, radar maps were created from topographic maps. This was all, obviously, before the advent of the Global Positioning System (GPS) that we take for granted today.

While ATRAN systems were installed in TM-76A Mace A missiles, the TM-76B Mace B vehicles used inertial guidance systems. The TM-61B also had a longer range. The TM-76A

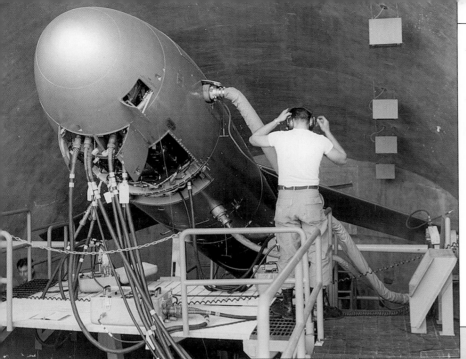

demonstrated that it could reach speeds of up to Mach 0.85 with a range of 540 miles at low level, and 1,285 miles at high altitude. The TM-76B, which was introduced in 1957, had a range of 1,500 miles.

Goodyear also helped to significantly streamline launch procedures, mainly through the development of a mobile launch system. The Matador's launching apparatus weighed 40 tons and required 28 separate land vehicles to support it, but apparatus for the Mace weighed 17.5 tons and required just 2 vehicles.

One of these vehicles was the remarkable MM-1 Teracruzer, a massive diesel truck that made the Mace mobile. It was powered by a 250-hp inline 6-cylinder Series 71 diesel engine made by the Detroit Diesel Engine Division of General Motors. It rode on eight huge, individually self-inflating (or -deflating) 40x42 Goodyear "Teratires" that could be

Technicians at work on a TM-76B Mace cruise missile in a hard-site launcher on Okinawa. The photo was taken in April 1962 and released in July 1964. The original caption explained that "carrying a 1-megaton W28 nuclear warhead, the rocket-boosted, jet-propelled Mace missile could be fired at 6 minutes' notice. Housed in underground concrete and steel 'coffins,' the Mace Bs (TM-76B) had an inertial guidance system and a range which exceeded 1,300 miles. . . . In recent months, a controversy has emerged over whether, during the Cuban Missile Crisis, the Okinawa-based 873d Tactical Missile Squadron received orders to launch missiles against Sino-Soviet targets." (USAF 1353rd Photo Group via National Archives)

A Martin TM-76B Mace screams off its Zero-Length Launch (ZEL) system at Cape Canaveral AFS, north of Patrick AFB, in Florida, circa the 1960s. (USAF)

This Mace B cruise missile displayed at the National Museum of the U.S. Air Force was originally designated as TM-76B, but redesignated as CGM-13B in 1963. (USAF)

adjusted from 3 to 18 psi from the cab. The MM-1 incorporated power steering and a locking differential that powered all wheels when engaged, taking it from four-wheel drive to eight-wheel drive.

The Teracruzer was manufactured by the Four Wheel Drive Auto Company (FWD) in Clintonville, Wisconsin, a firm that originated in 1909 as the Badger Four Wheel Drive Auto Company, founded by Otto Zachow and William Besserdich. One of their early products was known as the "Battleship," which gives an idea of the types of vehicles in which the company specialized. FWD was also known for its fire engines. Incorporated as the FWD Corporation in 1958, the company acquired other fire equipment companies, including Seagrave and Baker Aerialscope, and is today known as FWD Seagrave.

A review of known tail numbers indicates that a total of at least 449 Mace cruise missiles were ordered from FY 1955 through FY 1960. Under the Defense Department renumbering of 1963, the two Mace variants, TM-76A and TM-76B, became MGM-13A and MGM-13B. These letters indicate a ground-based, ground targeting (MG-) missile (-M). For the last 172 Maces, ordered in FY 1959 and 1960, the designa-

tion prefix later changed to CGM, indicating that the missiles were "coffin-based," meaning they were based in nonhardened protective structures.

Overseas deployment of the Mace began in 1959, so it served alongside the Matador for about three years. In Europe, the Mace was controlled by the 38th Tactical Missile Wing, which also owned the Matadors, and was operational in West Germany with the 89th, 405th, and 586th Tactical Missile Squadrons at Hahn AB and with the 71st TMS at Bitburg AB. The 58th Tactical Missile Group in South Korea also received Mace missiles in 1959.

In 1961, the 498th Tactical Missile Group at Kadena Air Base on Okinawa was organized and equipped with TM-76B Maces. Okinawa was under American military administration from 1945 to 1972, but the presence of these nuclear-armed cruise missiles so close to Japan was considered very politically touchy by the Kennedy administration in Washington. Indeed, the Defense Department issued directives insisting that U.S. Air Force missile personnel not talk about what they were doing and not refer to the missiles publicly.

In Europe, Mace operations started to wind down in the 1960s. The 38th TMW was inactivated in September 1966 along with all its squadrons except the 71st TMS, which was transferred to the 36th Tactical Fighter Wing at Bitburg. In turn, the 71st TMS was inactivated on 30 April 1969, marking the end, for the time being, of U.S. Air Force tactical cruise missile activities in Europe. Five months later, the 498th TMG on Okinawa was inactivated.

The CGM-13As and CGM-13Bs were returned to the United States, where the Mace fleet was gradually expended as target drones through 1977.

Today, about a dozen Matadors and at least nine Mace missiles survive as museum pieces, mainly in the United States, though three Matadors are on display in Germany. A handful of MM-1 Teracruzers survive, some owned by heavy equipment buffs, some used for heavy lifting, and one used by a gold mining operation in the remote back country of Alaska.

Chapter 3

U.S. NAVY SEA-LAUNCHED CRUISE MISSILES

The U.S. Navy's Martin KUM-1 (later PTV-2 and PTV-N-2) Gorgon IV was probably the first successful American ramjet missile. This early cruise missile is seen here beneath the wing of a P-61C (navy designation F2T-1N) Black Widow night fighter that was used for air-dropping test vehicles. A dozen test flights were made from the Naval Air Missile Test Center at Point Mugu in California. (Author's collection)

While the air and ground constituencies of the U.S. Army were staking out their doctrinal turf with respect to guided missiles in 1944–1945, the U.S. Navy moved quickly to define its own postwar guided missile future.

As had been the case during World War I with its Curtiss-Sperry Flying Bomb, the U.S. Navy was slightly ahead of the U.S. Army in cruise missiles, or "assault missiles," as they were still known during World War II. Beginning in 1943, even before the Allies were fully cognizant of the V-1 and its capabilities, the Bureau of Aeronautics (BuAer) through the Naval Air Development Center (NADC) and the Naval Aircraft Factory near Philadelphia had developed the ambitious Gorgon family of winged missiles.

Launching a Chance Vought SSM-N-8 (later RGM-6) Regulus Assault Missile (RAM) from the deck of the cruiser USS Helena in the Philippine Sea in June 1957. (National Archives)

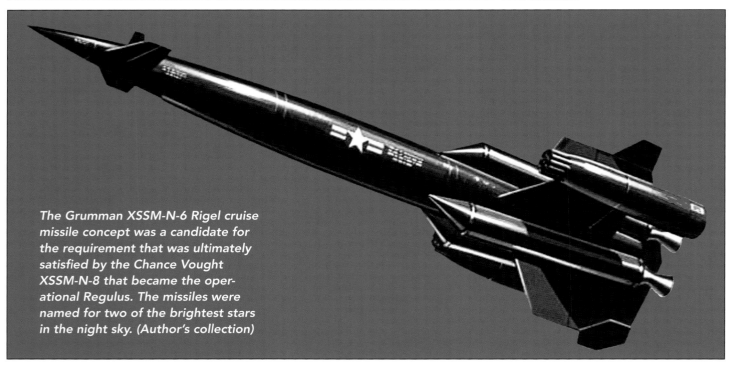

The Grumman XSSM-N-6 Rigel cruise missile concept was a candidate for the requirement that was ultimately satisfied by the Chance Vought XSSM-N-8 that became the operational Regulus. The missiles were named for two of the brightest stars in the night sky. (Author's collection)

A Chance Vought SSM-N-8 Regulus Assault Missile (RAM) being brought aboard the aircraft carrier USS John Hancock *in August 1954. (U.S. Navy)*

The Gorgon series included several dissimilar vehicles, all roughly 18 to 22 feet in length, that were evaluated for a variety of missions from surface-to-surface to air-to-surface to air-to-air. Early Gorgons were rocket or turbojet powered, while the KUM-1 (later PTV-2) Gorgon IV was ramjet powered, and the ASM-N-5 Gorgon V was an unpowered air-launched missile. A variety of guidance systems were tested on the Gorgons, including radar, television, and heat-seeking.

In the history of cruise missiles, the Gorgon program was important because it coincided with the early development of small jet engines. Sam Barlow Williams, who

worked on some of the early navy programs and who later founded Williams International, went on to create the small compact engines that would power the missiles, such as the AGM-86 and BGM-109 Tomahawk that would employ the breakthrough cruise missile technologies of the 1970s and 1980s.

By 1945, the pulsejet-powered KDN-1 Gorgon IIC was being developed to be launched by surface ships against land targets, specifically during the anticipated invasion of Japan. It was for this same mission that the navy would soon be planning to use its first operational KGW-1/LTV-N-2 Loon V-1–derived cruise missiles. The range of Gorgons was

A Chance Vought SSM-N-8 Regulus being launched from the aircraft carrier USS John Hancock *in October 1954. (U.S. Navy)*

Admiral John Harold Sides is the man most closely associated with the development and deployment of the Regulus. Known as the father of the navy's guided missile program, he became involved with navy missiles during World War II. He served as commander in chief of the U.S. Pacific Fleet from 1960 to 1963. (U.S. Navy)

generally less than 20 to 30 miles, while that of the Loon was around 150 miles, so a transition to the V-1 derivative was an obvious step.

Indeed, with the launch of a Loon from aboard the USS *Cusk* on 12 February 1947, the navy was already working toward a future in which missiles could be launched from submarines as well as from surface ships. Submarines could penetrate undetected deeper into enemy waters than a sur-

face ship, allowing a missile launch to occur much closer to the target.

As we have seen, even as the V-1 derivatives were holding the attention of army and navy airmen in 1945–1946, both services were moving ahead with the first postwar generation of cruise missiles. One member of that generation was the air force Matador, while for the U.S. Navy there would be several projects, primarily the Regulus.

Launching a Chance Vought SSM-N-8 Regulus from the submarine USS Halibut. *The missile is painted in its test markings. Operational missiles, like U.S. Navy aircraft of the 1950s, were dark blue. (U.S. Navy)*

Budget Background

Of course, the development of postwar cruise missiles, especially for the U.S. Navy, did not occur in a vacuum. Before turning in detail to the Regulus, it is important to look at the fiscal and doctrinal environment in which it would take form. As noted previously, the Truman administration had pressed hard for postwar demobilization and undertook severe cost-cutting measures. After 1947, this paradigm permeated the newly formed Defense Department.

With the unification represented by the creation of the Defense Department (discussed in the previous chapter) came a concerted effort to eliminate duplication of effort within the services to save money. The Truman administration budget cuts, which aimed to trim expenditures by 90 percent over four years, impacted all the services. With the navy, however, came the graphically unpleasant and disheartening task of scrapping or mothballing numerous new, state-of-the-art warships that had each taken a year or so to build.

Looking ahead to newer programs, the navy was embroiled in the troublesome dispute with the air force over strategic doctrine, and the latter seemed to be winning. Both the Truman administration and Congress had given the highest strategic priority to air force long-range bombers and their nuclear strike capabilities.

The navy, meanwhile, was trying to stake out its strategic position with both a cruise missile program *and* its new class of supercarriers, beginning with the USS *United States*. The budgetary problem with the supercarrier program was that it involved a small number of very large ships, but it was four times as expensive as air force budget requests for bombers. The navy's missile program received the full support of Secretary of Defense James Forrestal, who had previously served as secretary of the navy.

The conflict over the navy's perception of its strategic destiny came to a head in the spring of 1949. Angry with Forrestal for not meeting budget-cutting goals, President Harry Truman asked for his resignation, which came in March. Next, in April, the entire supercarrier program was canceled *only five days* after the keel was laid for the USS *United States*. This became the catalyst for the "Admirals' Revolt," in which numerous retired and active duty naval officers publicly, and before Congress, rancorously disputed the primacy of long-range bombers over supercarriers. A deeper shadow was cast over the whole affair when Forrestal committed suicide at the end of May by jumping out of a hospital window at the Naval Medical Center in Bethesda, Maryland.

In the end, the Truman administration won the debate, both in Congress and in the court of public opinion, although in 1950, the Korean War proved that all conflicts

This photo gives a good indication of the scale of the Chance Vought SSM-N-8 Regulus Assault Missile (RAM) relative to a Grumman F9F-6 Cougar. This jet fighter was used as a Regulus control aircraft aboard the aircraft carrier USS John Hancock *during September 1956 operations. Note the "RAM Detachment" markings on the Cougar. (U.S. Navy)*

could not be won by nuclear weapons and that conventional weapons were still important.

Meanwhile, the navy had continued its ongoing work toward smaller nuclear weapons delivery systems, specifically a cruise missile that could operate from ships other than from aircraft carriers.

Regulus

Even as the Loon cruise missile program was ongoing at the end of World War II, two of the U.S. Navy's leading suppliers of aircraft had been working up proposals for American-born cruise missiles, one of which would result in the first *operational* submarine-launched cruise missile, or "assault missile," in the terminology of

the times.

Grumman Aircraft of Bethpage, Long Island, New York, was responsible for such leading carrier-based warplanes as the F6F Hellcat fighter and the TBF Avenger torpedo bomber.

Unpacking an Aerojet solid rocket booster for an SSM-N-8 Regulus Assault Missile aboard the carrier USS Hancock *ahead of an August 1954 test flight. (U.S. Navy)*

A good view of an SSM-N-8 Regulus Assault Missile on its launch rail aboard the heavy cruiser USS Helena. The launcher took up the space previously occupied by the system that launched observation seaplanes. (U.S. Navy)

Based in Stratford, Connecticut, the Chance Vought component of United Aircraft was the manufacturer of such U.S. Navy aircraft as the OS2U Kingfisher, the SB2U Vindicator, and the F4U Corsair.

In October 1943, BuAer commissioned studies of a cruise missile with a 300-mile range that could carry a 4,000-pound payload. In 1945, revised specs increased the range requirement to 575 miles and stipulated a nuclear payload. Because lighter weight nuclear weapons were coming on line, specifically the same W5 fission warhead that would be used in the air force's Martin Matador, BuAer was able to cut the payload requirement to 3,000 pounds.

In 1946, the U.S. Navy ordered the companies to proceed with design studies, with prototypes ordered in 1947. The Grumman missile would be designated as XSSM-N-6, while Chance Vought was to develop its proposal as the XSSM-N-8. Both were named after two of the brightest stars in the night sky, the Grumman Rigel after the brightest star in the constellation Orion and the Chance Vought

The pilots aboard these FJ-3D Fury drone director aircraft, seen here in 1957, were tasked with guiding the SSM-N-8 Regulus missiles on the final run to their targets. (U.S. Navy)

Regulus after the brightest star in the constellation Leo.

The Rigel was 46 feet 1 inch long with a narrow wingspan of 13 feet 4 inches. It weighed 19,000 pounds with its rocket booster.

While the Rigel was dart-shaped, the Regulus, like the Matador, had the overall appearance of a contemporary jet fighter. The Regulus prototype was 32 feet 2 inches long with a wingspan of 21 feet. These dimensions were 6 and 5 feet smaller, respectively, than those of the air force Matador, though production Regulus missiles were 34 feet 4 inches long. The Regulus, depending upon configuration, weighed around 14,000 pounds with its booster, making it heavier than the Matador and lighter than the Rigel.

The Rigel was to have been a Mach 2 supersonic vehicle powered by a pair of Marquardt ramjet engines and boosted by four solid-fuel rockets each delivering 8,000 pounds of thrust. However, problems with this propulsion system became the undoing of the Rigel, and it never reached flight test status. Starting in 1950, the ramjet was tested repeatedly using subscale flight test vehicles before the whole program was finally canceled in 1953.

The Regulus was, like the Matador, a subsonic vehicle. It was powered by an Allison J33-A-14 turbojet, a variant of the J33-A-37 that was used by the Matador. The Regulus was launched by a pair of Aerojet General solid-fuel booster rockets, each delivering 33,000 pounds of thrust. The Regulus had a range of 600 miles, compared with 700 for the air force missile. Operationally, it would be capable of delivering

SSM-N-8 Regulus Assault Missiles aboard the heavy cruiser USS Los Angeles in the western Pacific in March 1956. The ship was part of the flotilla on patrol in the Taiwan Strait during the Quemoy-Matsu Crisis that year. (U.S. Navy)

A sequence of photos of a 1956 launch of a Chance Vought SSM-N-8 Regulus from the Sturgeon-class attack submarine USS Tunny. Note the Aerojet booster rockets in action. They each delivered 33,000 pounds of thrust, albeit for just a few critical seconds. (U.S. Navy)

the overall cost of the program down significantly.

One of the key people involved in the Regulus development program from the navy side was Captain (later Admiral) John Harold Sides, who has been called the father of U.S. Navy guided missiles. A 1925 Naval Academy graduate, he was chief of ammunition and explosives at the Bureau of Ordnance (BuOrd) during World War II and oversaw development of the High Velocity Aerial Rocket (HVAR) used by all services. In 1948, he became deputy to Admiral Daniel Gallery, the assistant chief of naval operations for guided missiles, beginning his career in his signature field of endeavor. As such, he became the man who kept the Regulus on course during its difficult early years.

In 1949, against the backdrop of the controversy that would boil into the Admirals' Revolt, the Department of Defense noted the similarity between the Matador and Regulus and began to look at the possibility of canceling one

a 3.8 megaton nuclear warhead up to 600 miles at Mach 0.87, making it the first U.S. Navy nuclear system capable of striking targets in the Soviet Union. As with the Matador, the Regulus used radio-control guidance.

Unlike the Matador, though, the Regulus was equipped with landing gear and capable of being recovered. Indeed, Chance Vought print advertising from the era always carried a small line drawing of a Regulus landing with its drogue chute deployed. It was like a logo for the Regulus program, pointing a teasing finger at Martin. Though individual Regulus missiles cost more than Matadors, the fact that they were not routinely expended during testing brought

and adapting the other to serve with both the air force and navy. This review, by the Guided Missile Committee of the joint Defense Research and Development Board, eventually recommended cancellation of the Matador in favor of a joint-service Regulus, but both programs ultimately continued. The navy successfully argued that the Matador was not suited for submarine operations and that its guidance required three communications relay points, versus two for the Regulus. Intended to save money, this committee studied cost development time in both programs.

In the meantime, the U.S. Navy had urged Chance Vought to relocate its manufacturing from Connecticut to

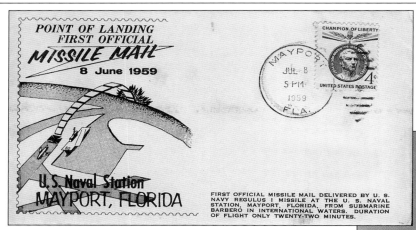

On 8 June 1959, a Regulus missile was used to carry official U.S. Post Office–sanctioned mail from the submarine USS Barbero to a runway at NAS Mayport in Florida. It took 22 minutes and cost just 4 cents for a stamp, but the actual cost was a bit more. There was talk that mail of the future might well be delivered by missile. After more than half a century, we're still waiting for that future. (Author's collection)

This rear view of an SSM-N-9 Regulus II cruise missile shows its retractable landing gear and the exhaust of the General Electric J79-GE-3 turbojet engine that gave it Mach 2 performance. (U.S. Navy)

A high-angle view of a trio of SSM-N-9 (later RGM-15) Regulus II cruise missiles. First flown in 1956, the supersonic Regulus II was larger and faster than the Regulus and promised a significant improvement in capability. However, in 1958, the navy decided to shelve the idea of cruise missiles in favor of submarine-launched ballistic missiles. Two decades later, the cruise missile concept was reborn with the Tomahawk. (U.S. Navy)

Seen here in a 1957 test launch, an SSM-N-9 Regulus II cruise missile screams off its zero-length launcher on a column of fire and the 135,000 pounds of thrust delivered by its Rocketdyne solid fuel booster rocket. (U.S. Navy)

The crew of the guided missile submarine USS Grayback *readies an SSM-N-9 Regulus II for a 1960 launch. Two years earlier, off Port Hueneme, California, the* Grayback *had conducted the first successful submarine launch of a Regulus II. (U.S. Navy)*

Dallas, Texas, where the federal government owned a large state-of-the-art aircraft factory that had been built during World War II to manufacture North American Aviation aircraft, such as the P-51 Mustang. The navy agreed to invest substantially in upgrading this facility, known as Naval Industrial Reserve Aircraft Plant (NIRAP) Dallas, which was located adjacent to NAS Dallas at Helmsley Field.

The move was completed by April 1948, and the company began building F4U Corsairs and F6U Pirates, as well as Regulus prototypes, at NIRAP. With state taxes significantly lower, the company even relocated its headquarters to Texas. NIRAP was greatly expanded during the 1950s to meet demands for aircraft during the Cold War defense buildup.

The U.S. Navy proceeded to order 500 Regulus missiles, with qualification tests on the initial batch of 10 beginning at NIRAP in November 1949. Though they were officially designated as SSM-N-8, the missiles were routinely referred to by the navy under the acronym RAM, meaning Regulus Assault Missile.

These missiles were then shipped to Edwards AFB in California, where flight testing began in February 1950. Most of the ground testing was, however, conducted at the Marine Corps Auxiliary Air Station nearby in Mojave, California. The two-year flight test program eventually moved to NAS Point Mugu on the California coast, which had become the U.S. Navy's center of missile evaluation. Indeed, the adjacent Port Hueneme was to be home to Regulus-armed submarines.

Initial RAM flights were conducted by the contractor, but in October 1952, the U.S. Navy took over and began land-based flight testing with the missiles radio controlled from accompanying aircraft. The first shipboard launch, in November 1952, was made from the deck of the USS *Norton Sound*, a former seaplane tender that had been used for various ongoing tests of other missile types. A month later, the first launch was made from the deck of an aircraft carrier, the USS *Princeton*.

The first submarine launch of a Regulus occurred on 15 July 1953 from aboard the USS *Tunny*, which was a veteran World War II boat with nine war patrols to her credit. The U.S. Navy converted a total of four Balao-class submarines for cruise missile operations, retrofitting them with watertight deck hangars. The first two, USS *Cusk* and USS *Carbonero*, had been earmarked for the Loon program in 1947, but only the *Cusk* joined the USS *Tunny* in the Regulus program.

The fourth, the USS *Barbero*, a veteran boat with two war patrols, joined the *Tunny* and *Cusk*, launching her first Regulus on 14 March 1956. Three years later, on 8 June 1959, the *Barbero* participated in an experiment involving the U.S. Post Office and an inert training Regulus. With a post office officially established aboard the submarine, two sacks of mail were loaded into the Regulus and fired from a point in the Atlantic Ocean to NAS Mayport in Florida, from which it was recovered and individual letters delivered.

"This peacetime employment of a guided missile for the important and practical purpose of carrying mail is the first known official use of missiles by any Post Office Department of any nation," said Postmaster General Arthur Summerfield, who predicted that "before man reaches the moon, mail will be delivered within hours from New York to California, to Britain, to India or Australia by guided missiles. We stand on the threshold of rocket mail." His prediction fell short. "Missile Mail" was never deemed practical.

Meanwhile, Captain John Sides, who had been reassigned away from Washington after testifying before Congress against the air force bomber strategy during the Admirals' Revolt, retired in 1951. He was named to head the technical section in the Defense Department Office of Guided Missiles. A year later, he was promoted to rear admiral and named director of the Guided Missile Division of the Office of Chief of Naval Operations Admiral Robert Carney. As such, he would now direct U.S. Navy missile programs across the board at a critical time in history.

In January 1954, Carney, at Sides's urging, ordered that the Regulus undergo a further operational test program prior to active deployment aboard naval vessels. Lasting from August 1954 through June 1956, this program involved 146 launches that were conducted both ashore and from ships at sea between California and Hawaii, notably with the cruiser USS *Los Angeles* and the aircraft carriers USS *John Hancock* and USS *Randolph*. Most of the radio guidance during the test program was from aboard accompanying manned aircraft, such as Grumman F9F fighters, but one flight in March 1955 involved a carrier-launched Regulus that was controlled from a submarine.

With a success rate officially reported as 82 percent, these ships became the first to deploy with RAM. The first

missiles were deployed aboard surface warships, with the *John Hancock* sailing into the Western Pacific in December 1955. This was at a time when tensions were high between the Republic of China and the Peoples Republic of China over the disputed islands of Quemoy and Matsu.

The *Los Angeles* of the Seventh Fleet became operational with RAM in 1955, followed by three other Baltimore-class heavy cruisers, the USS *Toledo*, USS *Helena*, and USS *Macon*, in 1956. As a Regulus missile ship, the *Macon* served in the Atlantic, while the others joined the *Los Angeles* in the western Pacific. The latter was the longest serving Regulus cruiser, remaining operational with the missile until 1961. The *Toledo*, *Helena*, and *Macon* remained operational with the cruise missile until 1959, 1960, and 1958 respectively.

Among the Regulus-armed carriers, the USS *Randolph* went to the Sixth Fleet in the Mediterranean in 1956, one year after the *John Hancock* had deployed with the Seventh Fleet in the western Pacific. Additional carriers operating with RAM included the USS *Franklin D. Roosevelt* in the Mediterranean and the USS *Lexington* with the Seventh Fleet.

Beginning with the first deployments in 1955, U.S. Navy Regulus operations were organized into two Guided Missile Groups (GMGRU), which functioned in the form of RAM detachments assigned to specific ships. Commanded by Commander R. C. Millard at NAS North Island in San Diego, GMGRU-1 was assigned to the Pacific, while GMGRU-2, commanded by Commander William Coley at NAS Chincoteague in Virginia, covered the Atlantic. When Atlantic RAM operations ended in 1958, GMGRU-2 was redesignated as a Guided Missile Service Squadron (GMSRON-2).

Atlantic and Mediterranean operations routinely included joint exercises with navies of North Atlantic Treaty Organization (NATO) countries, while those in the Pacific involved working with Southeast Asia Treaty Organization (SEATO) navies.

While surface ship Regulus operations were mainly wound down in the 1950s, six submarines were operational with the missile into the next decade. After the Balao-class boats, the U.S. Navy had ordered the two boats of the Growler class, the first class of submarines that would be purpose-built to launch cruise missiles. The Growler was commissioned in March 1958, and the Grayback five months later. Both were fitted with hangars that could accommodate four Regulus vehicles. Converted for RAM operations while under construction, the two boats had originated as sisters to the Tang-class submarines developed from the Greater Underwater Propulsion Power Program (GUPPY) conversion program that incorporated long-endurance technology developed by the Germans for their Type XXI diesel-electric U-boats.

With these boats in service, the U.S. Navy introduced a doctrine under which at least four Regulus missiles should be at sea and forward deployed in the western Pacific and the Mediterranean at all times. This meant either two Balao-class boats or one of the Growlers. Though initially deployed with W5 nuclear warheads, the RAM arsenal was upgraded to the W27 thermonuclear weapon after 1958.

Routine operations included continuing training launches, but these were not always routine. In April 1958, after a booster failure, a Regulus went off course and came within a thousand feet of hitting the *Tunny*. Another time, aboard the *Barbero*, a missile engine went to full power without a booster to launch it and fell onto the deck with tremendous force. Even when the engine was shut down manually, the crew had to contend with a damaged deck and a damaged Regulus with a nearly full fuel tank, two live rocket boosters, and a W5 nuclear warhead. Fortunately, the men were able to secure the missile and contain a potential disaster.

Built at the Mare Island Naval Shipyard on San Francisco Bay and commissioned in January 1960, the USS *Halibut* was the first *nuclear* submarine to be armed with cruise missiles. It was designed to carry five Regulus missiles, or two of the Regulus IIs that are discussed later in this chapter. She was designed with a main deck higher than those of earlier missile submarines so that when she was running on the surface, there was a probability that crews working with the missiles would not have their feet in sea water.

The *Halibut* conducted a number of Regulus test launches beginning on 25 March 1960 during her first cruise into the western Pacific. She made her seventh and final RAM cruise in May–July 1964. Between 1965 and her decommissioning in 1976, the *Halibut* had an interesting career. Its hangar was retrofitted to carry a Deep Submergence Rescue Vehicle (DSVR), and it was used in a series of classified missions. These included Operation Ivy Bells, the wiretapping of Soviet underwater communications cables in the Sea of Okhossk in the 1970s, and Project Astorian (aka "Project Jennifer"), the secret recovery of sunken Soviet submarine K-129 in the Pacific north of Hawaii in 1974 that also involved the infamous Hughes *Glomar Explorer*.

The Regulus missile remained in production until 1959. *Jane's All the World's Aircraft* for various years from 1958 to 1961, as quoted by historian Kenneth Werrell, notes that 514 missiles were delivered. Because of numerous test launches from land in which the missiles were recovered, the same source records more than 1,000 launches, the majority of them successful. After 1963, when all Defense Department missile designation systems were merged into a single nomenclature lineage, the SSM-N-8 Regulus was redesignated as the RGM-6 Regulus. In many accounts that have appeared since the advent of the Regulus II, the Regulus is referred to as the "Regulus I," although during its operational life, it was known without the numeral.

During the later years of Regulus deployment, the U.S. Pacific Fleet was commanded by Admiral John Sides, who had overseen much of its development. By the time he retired in 1963, he had put the U.S. Navy on course toward its transition from the Regulus submarine fleet to George Washington–class nuclear submarines armed with UGM-27 Polaris Submarine-Launched Ballistic Missiles (SLBM), in whose development Sides had also played a key role.

After being withdrawn from the submarines, some of the Regulus missiles had their nuclear warheads removed and they were expended as target drones. Today, nine Regulus survivors remain on display, including one at Pearl Harbor and one at the Intrepid Sea-Air-Space Museum in New York City.

The Regulus is fondly remembered. Admiral Elmo Zumwalt, who served as a naval commander in the western Pacific for many years and as chief of naval operations from 1970 to 1974, wrote in his memoirs that the withdrawal of the Regulus from service was the "single worst decision about weapons made [by the navy] during my years of service."

Regulus II

In the 1950s, against the backdrop of both the Cold War and of rapidly progressing aeronautical technology, it was common for a weapons system to have its withdrawal date written into the program before it was first deployed. So it was with U.S. Navy shipboard missile systems. As early as May 1950, a roadmap existed that marked the milestones of the successors to the Regulus.

However, such roadmaps rarely, if ever, come close to predicting the future. Even Admiral John Sides was overly optimistic. As he explained in a December 1952 lecture to the Air War College, the Regulus was expected to become operational in 1953, though this was three years ahead of when it was actually ready for operations. It was then supposed to have been superseded by the Grumman Rigel in 1955, though this project was to be canceled in 1953. In turn, the Rigel would have been followed in 1960 by the SSM-N-2 Triton, a weapon that had been called, with ebullient overstatement, the "ultimate cruise missile."

Developed by the Advanced Physics Laboratory, the Triton is today remembered as a conceptual missile. Like the Rigel, it was to have been powered by a ramjet engine, and it was to have been capable of supersonic speeds in the Mach 3.5 range. Like the Regulus, it was to have been ship-launched, but it would have had a range more than double that of the Regulus. The first round of design work took place between 1946 and 1950, and it was redesigned several times before the program was canceled in 1957 with no prototype ever built.

Needless to say, the May 1950 roadmap was dead in the water after

This Regulus missile is preserved on its original launcher aboard the USS Growler, a Grayback-class submarine, at Pier 86 in New York City adjacent to the USS Intrepid. The Regulus was redesigned from SSM-N-8 to RGM-6 by the time the last ones left service. (Max Smith, licensed under Wikimedia Commons)

The Regulus missile displayed in Bowfin Park at NAS Pearl Harbor in Hawaii is marked as "Regulus I." The Roman numeral was not used to identify this missile until after the Regulus II had been created. (Avriette, licensed under Wikimedia Commons)

the first milepost. It was, in turn, superseded by a March 1954 roadmap. With Rigel having been canceled in 1953, a new supersonic missile was substituted. This was the Chance Vought Regulus II, which was to become operational in 1957, while the operational capability date for the Triton was pushed back to 1965.

In June 1953, two months before the Rigel program was terminated, the U.S. Navy turned to Chance Vought, which had been working on a supersonic cruise missile concept since April 1952. Now under contract with the navy, this weapon was designated as SSM-N-9. The obvious name, Regulus II, was adopted, though the missile was quite dissimilar to the existing Regulus. While the Regulus had a nose intake, the canard-configured Regulus had a pointed nose with a ventral air scoop near the center of the fuselage.

The Regulus II was 57 feet 6 inches long (24 feet longer than a Regulus) with a wingspan of 20 feet 1 inch, only slightly less than that of a Regulus. Without its 7,000-pound booster, it weighed 23,000 pounds, roughly twice the weight of the Regulus. The range was 650 miles at Mach 2, or around 1,300 miles at subsonic speeds. During the flight test program there were discussions of using wing tanks to extend the range.

First test flown in May 1956, the Regulus II prototypes were designated as XRSSM-N-9. They were each powered by a Wright J65-W-6 turbojet delivering 14,600 pounds of thrust, with an Aerojet General solid-fuel rocket booster delivering 115,000 pounds of thrust to throw it aloft from its zero-length launcher. Like the Regulus, the Regulus II was equipped with landing gear so that test vehicles could be recovered and reused.

The test program for a second batch of prototypes, designated as XRSSM-N-9A, began in 1958 using the powerplants intended for the production series. These were a General Electric J79-GE-3 turbojet delivering 15,600 pounds of thrust and a Rocketdyne solid-fuel rocket booster delivering 135,000 pounds of thrust.

The guidance system also matured. Initially, the Regulus II, like its predecessor, was designed to use a radio control system, but this was switched to inertial guidance, which is less prone to enemy jamming. Later, there was talk of using an automatic terrain recognition and navigation system, a precursor to Terrain Contour Matching (TERCOM),

such as the Automatic Terrain Recognition and Navigation (ATRAN) system that Goodyear was developing for the air force TM-76 Mace cruise missiles.

According to navy records, recoverable Regulus II prototypes made a total of 48 test flights, of which 30 were deemed successful and 14 partially successful. There were four failures. The first submarine launch of a Regulus II came from the back of the USS *Grayback* in September 1958.

In the meantime, the U.S. Navy issued a Regulus II production contract in January 1958 amid ambitious plans to arm four cruisers and 23 submarines with the missile.

In November 1958, having delivered 20 Regulus IIs, Chance Vought had 27 partially completed on the NIRAP assembly line when the "stop work" message arrived from Washington, DC. The Regulus program was suddenly and abruptly over. In December, Secretary of the Navy Thomas Gates, a proponent of the SLBM approach to submarine-based missiles, made it official. Regulus II was canceled and the navy was putting all its eggs in the SLBM basket. It did not help that the unit cost of the Regulus II had spiraled up to a million dollars.

After the cancellation, Chance Vought proposed to keep the assembly line open to produce the Regulus II for other countries, especially within the NATO alliance. The sales pitch was that the missiles could reach the heart of the Soviet Union from bases in Western Europe or Turkey. The proposal was received positively in Europe, but the issue of the United States having to retain control over the American nuclear warheads in the missiles led to the concept being shelved.

Some of the existing Regulus IIs were expended as supersonic target drones, mainly for the U.S. Air Force Bomarc surface-to-air missile program. In 1963, under the Defense Department's merger of designations, the Regulus II was officially redesignated as RGM-15A, though the program had already been done for five years. The target drones, originally designated as KD2U-1, operated under the designations CGM-15A and MGM-15A, with the last of them operational at NAS Point Mugu until 1965.

Three surviving Regulus IIs remain on display, including one at Point Mugu, where it can be seen next to a Regulus.

The termination of the Regulus II program and the phaseout of the operational Regulus would take the U.S. Navy out of the cruise missile business for two decades.

INTERCONTINENTAL CRUISE MISSILES

Before the practical deployment of ICBMs, the first American nuclear-armed missile with an intercontinental range was a cruise missile. Even before the end of World War II, the USAAF had already taken the first steps not only toward cruise missiles in the same class as the V-1, but also toward cruise missiles with an intercontinental range of 3,000 to 5,000 miles. When the USAAF formed its Strategic Air Command (SAC) in 1946, it was with the mandate to deliver a nuclear strike as deep into enemy territory as possible. The idea was that SAC would be able to execute this mission with multiple forms of airpower technology—a manned bomber *or* a cruise missile.

As seen in the previous chapters, both the USAAF and the U.S. Navy were well on the way toward the *tactical* cruise missile systems that became the Matador and Regulus. Meanwhile, the USAAF, which had been extending its reach with manned bombers of increasingly greater range, was ready to develop and deploy unmanned *strategic* missile systems under the same goal.

In August 1945, the Experimental Engineering Section of the USAAF Air Material Command issued a series of highly classified guided missile project summaries designated under the Materiel, Experimental (MX) numbers from 770 through 779. These summaries and the accompanying requests for proposals delivered to major American aircraft manufacturers were handled, of course, with the utmost secrecy.

As noted in chapter 2, Project MX-771 led to the development of the Martin Matador tactical cruise missile. Projects MX-770 and MX-775 both led to intercontinental strategic cruise missiles. These were the North American Aviation Navaho and the Northrop Snark, with the Snark being the first of the two projects to conceptually demonstrate intercontinental potential *and* the only one actually deployed.

Project MX-776, meanwhile, was assigned to the Bell Aircraft Corporation, and it led to two air-launched missiles. MX-776A became the Shrike missile, which was a testbed for the MX-776B, which became the Rascal missile that is discussed in the following chapter.

The Navaho

American postwar cruise missiles were inspired by (if not entirely derived from) the German V-1, and American postwar ballistic missiles had their roots in the German V-2. The Navaho can trace its technical lineage to *both*. The booster stage was a V-2-derived ballistic missile, the upper stage a delta-winged, ramjet-powered pilotless airplane.

At North American Aviation (NAA), as with most American aircraft manufacturers, the experience of observing the V-1 and V-2 in 1944–1945 was convincing evidence that missile technology was a big part of future product lines. NAA President James Howard "Dutch" Kindelberger understood this as well as most, and he had initiated design studies even before the "770-series" requests for proposals came across his desk. The NAA proposal was accepted and the contract for what became the Navaho was signed in April 1946.

In the meantime, specimens of captured V-2 rockets (with their liquid-fuel rocket engines) were delivered to NAA in Inglewood, California, for examination. As NAA developed the missile, the company also developed the liquid-fuel rocket engines to power the Navaho booster rocket; through its Rocketdyne component (formed in 1955), the company went on to become a leading builder of rocket engines.

Because the Rascal missile was preceded by the X-9 experimental vehicle, the first step in the Navaho program included an "X-Plane." This vehicle was originally designated as a Rocket Test Vehicle, the RTV-A-5, but it was soon redesignated as X-10. This vehicle was a winged precursor to

A North American Aviation XSM-64 Navaho on the pad at Cape Canaveral in 1957. The Navaho vehicle was capable of Mach-3 speeds, used an improved V-2 engine, and was boosted into the air by three Rocketdyne liquid-propellant rocket engines of 135,000 pounds of thrust each. Variants of these engines were also developed for the U.S. Army's Redstone and Jupiter vehicles. (USAF)

the winged part of the two-stage Navaho vehicle, which was later designated as XSSM-A-2.

The X-10 was 66 feet 2 inches long with a wingspan of 28 feet 2 inches and had a gross weight of 42,000 pounds. It was to be powered with a pair of Westinghouse XJ40-WE-1 engines rated at 10,100 pounds of thrust.

The NAA team, headed by project engineer H. V. Cooper, also designed the X-10 with retractable landing gear, as Vought had done in its Regulus program so that the test vehicles could be recovered.

The X-10 made its first flight at Edwards AFB on 14 October 1953, achieving an altitude of 20,000 feet while flying 172 miles in 32 minutes and landing at Rogers Dry Lake under radio control. After 14 flights, including 3 failures, the X-10 program was transferred to the Air Force Missile Test Center (AFMTC) at Cape Canaveral, where a dozen test flights were made between August 1955 and November 1956. In 1958–1959, three surviving X-10s were used as target drones in surface-to-air missile tests.

The original contract called for the production Navaho to be a supersonic cruise missile with a specified range of 350 miles, but with the Matador already under way, the air force was more interested in longer range missiles. In 1950, after a long series of design studies, NAA confidently promised an "interim missile" with a

The second North American Aviation X-10, the Navaho precursor, in flight. During the seventh flight of the X-10 program in July 1954, communication with this vehicle was lost, but it continued to maintain level flight until it impacted the ground less than 15 miles from the runway at Edwards AFB. (USAF)

Fueling a North American Aviation XSM-64 Navaho on the pad at Cape Canaveral, circa 1957. (USAF)

The first launch of an XSM-64 Navaho (tail number 52-10989) on 6 November 1956. Unfortunately, the pitch gyro failed 10 seconds after liftoff, and the missile and its booster broke up and exploded 26 seconds into the flight. (USAF)

Navaho Cruise Missile Design Evolution *(USAF)*
(Through three-view drawings of selected variants)

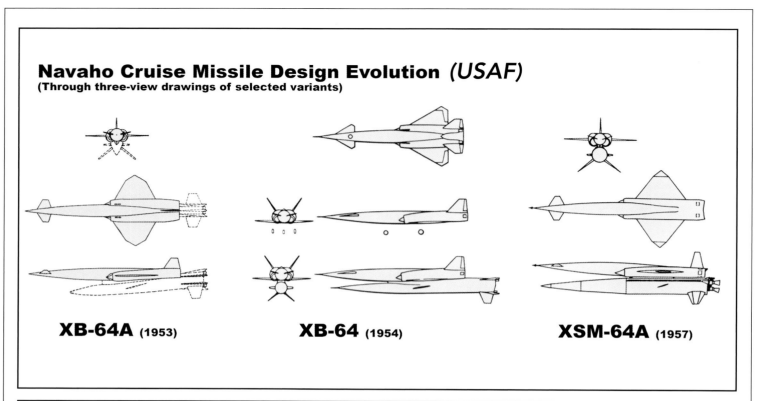

XB-64A (1953)   **XB-64** (1954)   **XSM-64A** (1957)

Selected Navaho Cruise Missile Launch Scenarios *(USAF)*

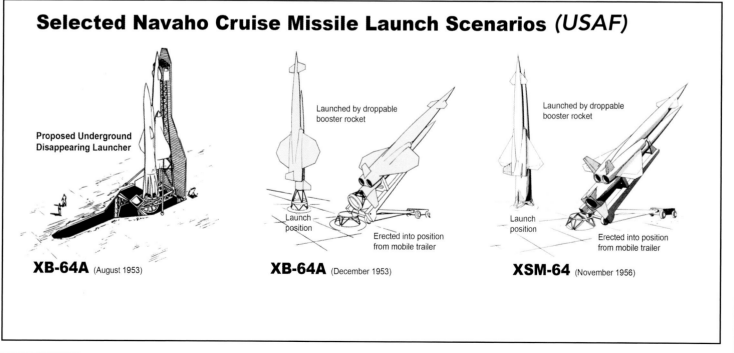

Proposed Underground
Disappearing Launcher

Launched by droppable
booster rocket

Launch
position

Erected into position
from mobile trailer

Launched by droppable
booster rocket

Launch
position

Erected into position
from mobile trailer

XB-64A (August 1953)   **XB-64A** (December 1953)   **XSM-64** (November 1956)

A North American Aviation XSM-64 Navaho on the pad at Cape Canaveral with the gantry withdrawn ahead of launch. After a November 1956 debut, several launches were made during 1957. (USAF)

Looking up at a North American Aviation XSM-64 Navaho on its pad at Cape Canaveral, it was easy to imagine it in flight. (USAF)

range of 4,150 miles and an operational missile with a range of 6,325 miles.

With the range redefined, the Navaho underwent a two-step redesign process, with a long-range interim missile called "Navaho II" designated as XSSM-A-4, and a longer-range "Navaho III" production variant designated as XSSM-A-6. In 1951, when the air force adopted the "B-for-Bomber" nomenclature for missiles, these two became the XB-64 and the XB-64A, respectively, and the Roman numerals were discarded. In 1955, these became XSM-64 and XSM-64A under the new "Strategic Missile" nomenclature.

The XB-64 was 69 feet 9 inches long with a booster that was 76 feet 3 inches long and a wingspan of 28 feet 7 inches.

It weighed 60,000 pounds alone, and 135,000 with its V-2-derived booster. The XB-64A was designed to be 87 feet 7 inches long with a booster measuring 92 feet 1 inch and a wingspan of 42 feet 8 inches. It weighed 120,500 pounds without its booster and 300,500 pounds with.

The XB-64 was powered by a pair of Wright XRJ47-W-5 ramjet engines, each delivering 8,000 pounds of thrust. The XB-64A was to have had two Wright XRJ47-W-7 ramjets with 11,300 pounds of thrust. NAA itself built the liquid-fuel engines for the rocket boosters. The XLR71-NA-1 of the XB-64 was rated at 240,000 pounds, while the thrust of the XB-64A was 405,000 pounds. Guidance was by means of the N-6 celestial navigation system designed in-house by the NAA Autonetics Division.

The U.S. Air Force planned for a first XB-64 flight in 1954 as the X-10 program was still ongoing, but the schedule slipped two years. The first Navaho launch, at Cape Canaveral in November 1956, ended in failure when a pitch gyro faltered and the vehicle broke up just over the pad.

Navaho Cruise Missile Design Evolution *(USAF)*
(Through side view cutaway drawings of selected variants)

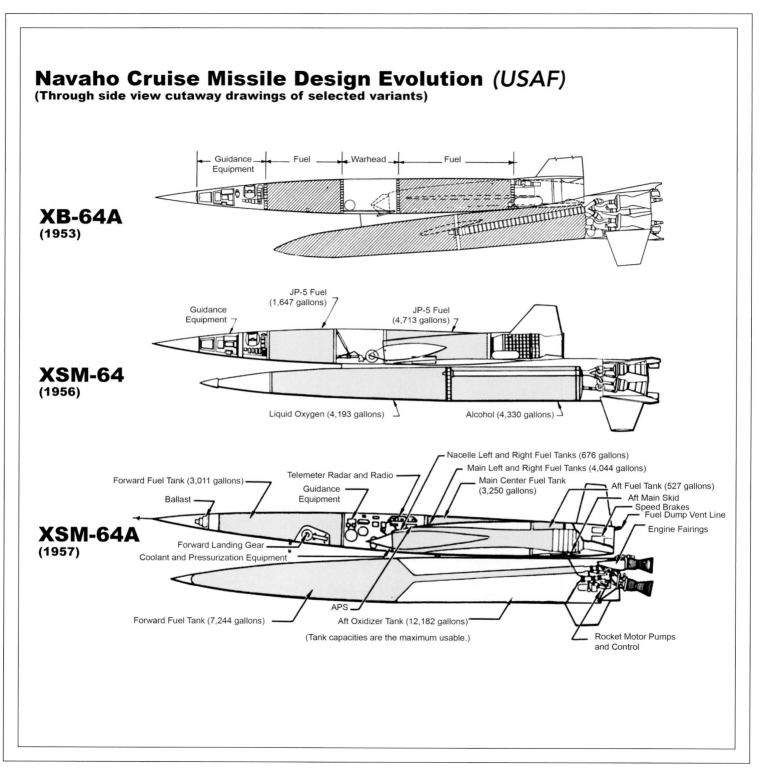

XB-64A
(1953)

Guidance Equipment — Fuel — Warhead — Fuel

XSM-64
(1956)

Guidance Equipment

JP-5 Fuel (1,647 gallons)

JP-5 Fuel (4,713 gallons)

Liquid Oxygen (4,193 gallons)

Alcohol (4,330 gallons)

XSM-64A
(1957)

Forward Fuel Tank (3,011 gallons)

Ballast

Telemeter Radar and Radio

Guidance Equipment

Nacelle Left and Right Fuel Tanks (676 gallons)

Main Left and Right Fuel Tanks (4,044 gallons)

Main Center Fuel Tank (3,250 gallons)

Aft Fuel Tank (527 gallons)

Aft Main Skid

Speed Brakes

Fuel Dump Vent Line

Engine Fairings

Forward Landing Gear

Coolant and Pressurization Equipment

Forward Fuel Tank (7,244 gallons)

APS

Aft Oxidizer Tank (12,182 gallons)

(Tank capacities are the maximum usable.)

Rocket Motor Pumps and Control

Preparing a North American Aviation XSM-64 Navaho for launch at Cape Canaveral in 1957. Though it never reached operational status before cancellation in 1957, Navaho development contributed to the advancement of aeronautical research. (USAF)

Three more missions through June 1957 also suffered malfunctions, though the last one saw the missile fly 42 miles before its ramjets failed to function and it crashed. The missile was soon referred to among the personnel involved as "Never go Navaho."

Two subsequent flights to test the NAA N-6 celestial navigation system also failed, although one in September saw the Navaho make it 1,075 miles downrange before it suffered a ramjet failure. With its test flights measured in minutes, or even seconds, the Navaho program was officially terminated in 1957, but the seven missiles, now designated as XSM-64, were expended in various research projects. One of these achieved a speed of Mach 3 and an altitude of 77,000 feet in November 1958 before it disintegrated.

Today, the only surviving X-10 resides at the National Museum of the U.S. Air Force, and the sole remaining XSM-64 is on display at the entrance to Cape Canaveral AFS.

On 25 April 1957, this North American Aviation XSM-64 Navaho fell back on the launch pad after climbing just 4 feet. The explosion and fire did substantial damage to the pad. (USAF)

An artist's conception of the North American Aviation XSM-64 Navaho climbing into the sky over a mountainous landscape, definitely not south Florida, while strapped to its booster. (USAF)

The only surviving X-10 vehicle resides at the National Museum of the U.S. Air Force at Wright Patterson Air Force Base in Dayton, Ohio. It is painted in the markings of the first X-10. There are no surviving Navahos today, the last one having been a gate guard at Cape Canaveral that was destroyed in a hurricane. (USAF)

Two Imaginary Creatures

As the highly classified requests for proposals for the "770-series" MX projects arrived over the transoms of America's major aircraft companies, one of them landed in the Hawthorne, California, office of Jack Northrop, the imaginative genius who was sufficiently forward-thinking to have developed large aircraft with flying wing configurations at a time when most such airplanes inhabited only the covers of science fiction literature. His Northrop Corporation was no stranger to cruise missiles, or assault missiles, as they were then known, having developed the flying wing configured JB-1 and JB-10 during World War II.

In January 1946, Northrop submitted a pair of cruise missile proposals, a subsonic MX-775A and a supersonic MX-775B, which carried the respective internal Northrop model numbers N-25A and N-25B. Northrop himself supplied the given names, calling the MX-775A the "Snark" and the MX-775B the "Boojum."

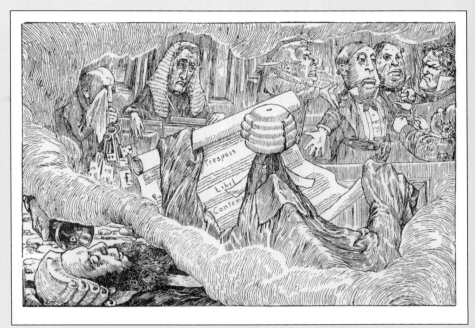

In January 1874, Lewis Carroll commissioned Henry Holiday to illustrate "The Hunting of the Snark." This illustration is the only one that shows the Snark himself. He is in the foreground, in a barrister's robe and wig, defending his client. (Author's collection)

As might have been expected from the imagination of a man like Jack Northrop, the two names were originally the creation of Lewis Carroll, the creator of *Alice's Adventures in Wonderland* and its sequel *Through the Looking-Glass*. The names appear in Carroll's fantasy poem "The Hunting of the Snark (An Agony in 8 Fits)," published in 1876. The fanciful story tells of a group of 10 people in search of an imaginary creature called a Snark, which was part snake and part shark, while being wary of a dangerous anti-creature called a Boojum. Only 1 of the 10, a baker, found the Snark, but when the others rushed to see it, the baker vanished. With this, the narrator concludes that "the Snark was a Boojum, you see."

Carroll's Snark and Boojum may or may not have been one and the same, but Jack Northrop's creatures were two parts of the same proposal. The air force accepted his proposal in March 1946 and contracted with Northrop to develop both N-25A and N-25B.

The N-25A/MX-775A Snark concept was the smaller of the two, weighing 28,000 pounds, while the N-25B/MX-775B Boojum weighed 112,000 pounds. The N-25A/MX-775A was 52 feet long with swept wings spanning 42 feet. The N-25B/MX-775B, delta-winged in the final configuration proposed, was 85 feet 4 inches long with a wingspan of 14 feet 9 inches. The Snark was powered by a single Allison J33 turbojet engine within the fuselage, while the Boojum was designed for two wingtip-mounted General Electric J47 turbojets. Operationally, the N-25B/MX-775B Boojum was designed to climb to 70,000 feet at subsonic speed, then accelerate to Mach 2 for a supersonic dash to the target.

Both missiles were designed to deliver a new generation W39 nuclear warhead with a yield of 3.8 megatons that was a cousin to the Mark 39 bomb that would arm Boeing B-52 Stratofortress bombers. Weighing around 6,400 pounds depending on configuration, the W39 was twice as heavy as the W5 warhead carried by tactical cruise missiles. It was 106 inches long and measured 35 inches in diameter.

During the round of severe budget cuts imposed by the Truman administration at the end of 1946, the USAAF looked at the MX-775 program and decided to cancel the smaller Snark and push forward with an operational Boojum. However, during 1947, as the USAAF became the independent U.S. Air Force, Jack Northrop was successful in lobbying Chief of Staff General Carl Spaatz to reinstate the SSM-A-3 Snark to the

A Northrop N-25A Snark on the ramp at Holloman AFB on 15 April 1950. Developed under Project MX-775A, it bore the air force designation XSSM-A-3. (USAF)

program. At this time, the air force officially designated the N-25A/MX-775A Snark as the SSM-A-3 and the N-25B/MX-775B Boojum as the SSM-A-5.

Yet, two years after Jack Northrop opened the MX-775 envelope, his Snark and Boojum were, like Carroll's, still merely on paper, imaginary creatures ambiguous as to form, and indeed ambiguous as to whether they would ever exist at all. At one moment, the Snark, like Carroll's, was gone and the Boojum was front and center on track to become a real creature.

Before 1947 was over, though, the Boojum was back on the shelf, postponed and eventually canceled, and the Air Materiel Command ordered 10 XSM-A-3s for testing. Northrop engineers now embarked upon their hunt for a Snark configuration that would satisfy the needs of the U.S. Air Force.

The Snark

Leading the N-25/MX-775 team was veteran Northrop engineer S. E. "El" Weaver. There had been just 22 employees at Northrop when Weaver joined the firm in 1939, and in less than a decade, he had seen both his company and aviation technology itself evolve well beyond anything a layperson could have imagined in the 1930s. Still, the development of an intercontinental cruise missile using 1940s

technology presented further immense challenges.

Among these challenges had been developing airframes capable of intercontinental range at a time when only a few aircraft types and no jets were capable of such a thing. The initial work with the N-25A and N-25B concepts had begun to address this.

It was originally anticipated that the Snark would be ready for flight testing in 1949, but the program was delayed by a combination of technical issues and wavering air force enthusiasm for the program. As we have seen, the late 1940s were a time of budget pinching in which untried systems were low-hanging fruit for those keen on pruning budgets. Early in 1950, before the Korean War changed everything, the as-yet-unflown Snark project was briefly trimmed to just a guidance system development program.

This guidance system had already broken new ground, after confronting early technological challenges. The line-of-sight radio guidance used for the Matador and Regulus programs could not be used for intercontinental flights deep into enemy airspace, so something new had to be invented.

As the company's program summary notes, "it soon became apparent to Weaver that the guidance system was beset with almost overwhelming problems, while the airframe and ground support areas fell within the range of reasonability. In 1946, the art of long-range automatic

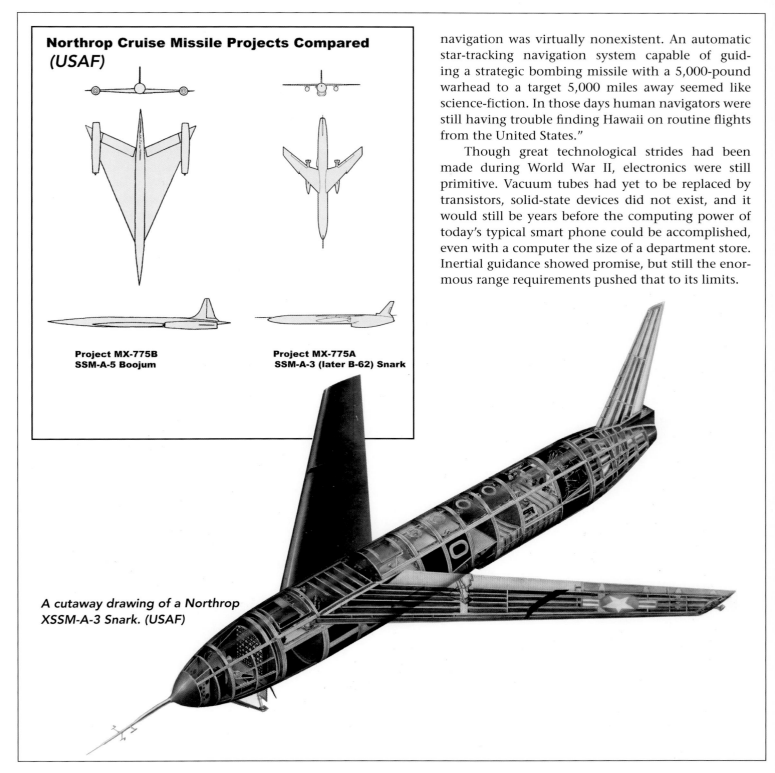

Northrop Cruise Missile Projects Compared
(USAF)

Project MX-775B
SSM-A-5 Boojum

Project MX-775A
SSM-A-3 (later B-62) Snark

A cutaway drawing of a Northrop XSSM-A-3 Snark. (USAF)

navigation was virtually nonexistent. An automatic star-tracking navigation system capable of guiding a strategic bombing missile with a 5,000-pound warhead to a target 5,000 miles away seemed like science-fiction. In those days human navigators were still having trouble finding Hawaii on routine flights from the United States."

Though great technological strides had been made during World War II, electronics were still primitive. Vacuum tubes had yet to be replaced by transistors, solid-state devices did not exist, and it would still be years before the computing power of today's typical smart phone could be accomplished, even with a computer the size of a department store. Inertial guidance showed promise, but still the enormous range requirements pushed that to its limits.

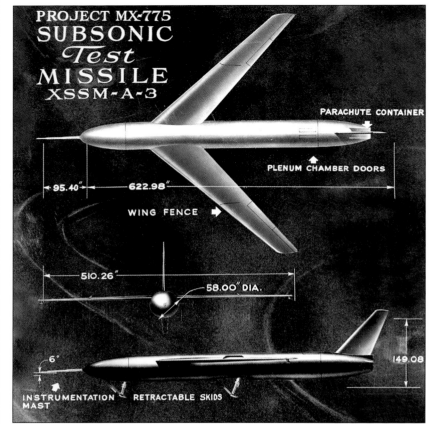

PROJECT MX-775
SUBSONIC
Test
MISSILE
XSSM-A-3

PARACHUTE CONTAINER

PLENUM CHAMBER DOORS

95.40"   622.98"

WING FENCE

510.26"

58.00" DIA.

6°

149.08

INSTRUMENTATION MAST   RETRACTABLE SKIDS

A three-view illustration, very much in the early 1950s industrial style, of a Northrop XSSM-A-3. (USAF)

38 minutes and was deemed a complete success. The test program continued through March 1952, with the Snarks using a modified Sperry A-12 autopilot and radio control from a North American B-45 Tornado director aircraft as well as ground control stations.

Air force historian Kenneth Werrell has stated that 21 N-25A flights were made, but Fred Anderson, in Northrop's program summary, recalls 25. In any case, some of the flights ended with the N-25A/XSSM-A-3 successfully recovered, and 5 of the original 16 vehicles ultimately survived. During the test program, the Snark demonstrated a top speed of Mach .9 and a maximum duration of 2 hours and 46 minutes.

In June 1950, as the test program was getting under way, the air force requested that Northrop add supplementary capabilities to the package, including greater payload, the same supersonic "dash to the target" capability that had been planned for the Boojum, and greater range. Indeed, the potential range capability of the N-25A/XSSM-A-3 was still significantly less than the 5,000 miles imagined in the original XM-775 specifications.

This necessitated going back to the drawing board to come up with the larger Northrop Model N-69 in which wings were moved back and an external engine air intake replaced the N-25A's flush duct. Early N-69 models were powered by an Allison J71 turbojet, but later variants were equipped with more fuel-efficient Allison J75 engines.

Kenneth Werrell mentioned that the N-69 was initially called a "Super Snark," but the adjective was soon dropped. Whereas the N-25A was 52 feet long with a wingspan of 42 feet, the N-69 Snark was 67 feet 2 inches long with a wingspan of 42 feet 3 inches. The N-69 weighed 49,600 pounds without its boosters, nearly double that of the first-generation N-25A Snark.

Solid rocket boosters made zero-length launches possible for the N-69 Snark. They were developed at the Allegheny Ballistics Laboratory in Rocket City, West Virginia, a facility

Ground-based, daytime star tracking was still in its infancy in 1948 when Northrop developed and tested the "time-specified trajectory" concept, in which a predetermined flight plan was computed in advance using a ground-based computer. By 1951, the system was being tested aboard B-29s on flights of 2,500 miles.

With the Snark program back on track in mid-1950, Northrop was ordered to deliver 16 N-25A/XSSM-A-3 test airframes powered by Allison J33-A-31 turbojet engines. The experimental flights were launched using a rocket sled on the famous 3,550-foot test track at Holloman AFB, adjacent to the White Sands Missile Range in New Mexico. The vehicles were supposed to be recovered after flight using landing skids and a drogue parachute. Sometimes this system actually worked.

The Snark's first test flight, on 21 December 1950, was a dismal failure, and to add insult to injury, a second crash soon followed. However, in April 1951, the third flight lasted

A mysteriously shrouded Northrop B-62 Snark is off-loaded from a U.S. Air Force Douglas C-124 Globemaster. (USAF)

that was started by the U.S. Army in 1944 but soon transferred to the Naval Air Systems Command (NavAir), which still owns it today. The early rocket boosters, which were tested with existing N-25As between November 1952 and March 1953, had thrust ratings of 47,000 pounds, but production N-69s would each have a pair of boosters that delivered 130,000 pounds of thrust for 4 seconds.

With a Lockheed T-33 chase plane in hot pursuit, a Northrop XSSM-A-3 Snark impacts the ground on landing on the White Sands Missile Range in New Mexico after a 26 June 1951 test flight. (USAF)

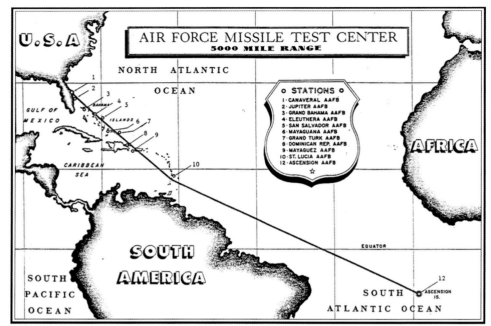

AIR FORCE MISSILE TEST CENTER
5000 MILE RANGE

The Eastern Test Range managed by the U.S. Air Force Air Research and Development Command. It was established for the Navaho and Snark programs. When it was decided in 1952 to extend the range to a length of 5,000 miles, agreements were negotiated with the governments of Britain, St. Lucia, Brazil, and Ascension to authorize construction. The St. Lucia site was activated in December 1956, and Antigua and Ascension were ready for operations in October 1957. The Fernando de Noronha station was activated off the coast of Brazil in September 1958. Twelve small telemetry ships were positioned downrange to fill in the gaps between Antigua and Ascension in 1957 and 1958. The Eastern Range supported its first 5,000-mile mission, a Snark flight, on 31 October 1957. (USAF)

Northrop field test crew, a cadre of air force personnel from the 6555th (later called the B-62 Operations Section) was trained at Northrop in California and placed under the command of Major Richard Eliason in June 1952.

The program began with 13 Snark aerodynamic performance test articles that were designated by Northrop as N-69A and N-69B. They were radio controlled and recoverable.

Booster tests by the 6555th, using the surviving N-25As, began in November 1952, with the first N-69 launch in August 1953. However, the N-69 portion of the test program got off to a rocky start. Mark C. Cleary, the historian for the 45th Space Wing at Cape Canaveral, has noted, "The Snark suffered almost continuous set-backs after the N-69 made its debut at the Cape in the summer of 1953. Part of the trouble centered on the new missile's engine: though the N-25s had been powered by reliable J33A-31 or J35-A-23 Allison engines, the N-69's YJ71 powerplant malfunctioned repeatedly. Quality control became a problem at the Hawthorne plant, as evidenced by the incidence of missing parts and damaged components. In the last half of 1953, rework orders were posted against almost every Snark sent to AFMTC for testing."

Having adopted the "B-for-Bomber" nomenclature in 1951, the air force designated the N-69 series as B-64, with the test articles being designated as XB-64. Whereas the N-25A program had been centered at Holloman, the N-69/B-64 program relocated to the Air Force Missile Test Center (AFMTC) at Patrick AFB on Cape Canaveral, Florida. Here, the program had the use of the Eastern Missile Test Range that extended for 5,000 miles into the South Atlantic.

Though the Snark was destined for operational service with the Strategic Air Command (SAC), it was assigned for testing and evaluation to the 6555th Guided Missile Wing of the Air Research and Development Command (ARDC) at AFMTC. To conduct launches in cooperation with the

The first round of N-69A and N-69B flight tests lasted through May 1955. In addition to zero-length and short-length launch methods, tests looked into booster rocket performance. As had been the case with the early N-25A tests, efforts were consistently made to recover test missiles, but none of the attempts with early N-69A or N-69B missiles succeeded. So many of the missiles were lost that a joke circulated in which the ocean southeast of Cape Canaveral was referred to as having "Snark-infested waters."

A confusing variety of designation systems followed the Snark through this period. Northrop instituted a series

A Northrop SM-62 Snark on the skid strip at Cape Canaveral Auxiliary Air Force Base after a landing mishap on 16 April 1957. Note the drogue chute on the ground. (USAF)

of designations, such as N-69A, N-69B, and N-69C, to describe various configuration changes, and these did not correspond to air force designations, where the XB-62 designation applied to the first three N-69 variants, and "B-62A" came later. The air force also planned a reconnaissance drone variant that would have been designated as XRB-62. To complicate matters, in 1955 the air force abandoned the "B-for-Bomber" nomenclature and the Snark became the SM-62 strategic missile.

As the flight test program unfolded, significant problems emerged. It had been assumed that the Snark, like other cruise missiles, would impact its target in a terminal dive. However, by May 1955, both wind tunnel tests and the flight test program confirmed that stability problems in such a dive could cause the missile to go out of control.

Since 1953, a Northrop team headed by Roy Jackson had been studying a "ballistic nose" option in which a nose-mounted warhead would be released to impact the target independent of the rest of the missile. In 1955, this team, with Art Nitikman heading aerodynamics and Ralph Hakes leading mechanical design, incorporated a ballistic nose into a series of 15 modified N-69C (XB-62) Warhead

Delivery Test Missiles. These were first flown in 1955.

As Northrop's Fred Anderson writes, "Five of these missiles were flight-tested to evaluate terminal-dive warhead delivery, warhead arming and fusing systems, and aerodynamic performance. One of the terminal dive missiles was also flown to evaluate the entry maneuver for the ballistic nose method of warhead delivery and to obtain aerodynamic and system performance data at high dynamic pressures."

The next iteration of the Snark development series was the N-69D Guidance System Test Missiles, which incorporated the Mark I day/night celestial/inertial guidance system. The N-69D was also the first variant to be powered by the J57 turbojet engine. The N-69D first flew in November 1955, but guidance flight tests were suspended in February 1956 for reliability issues. These resumed with the third N-69D launch in September 1956. The N-69D finally accomplished its first celestially guided flight in October 1956, and

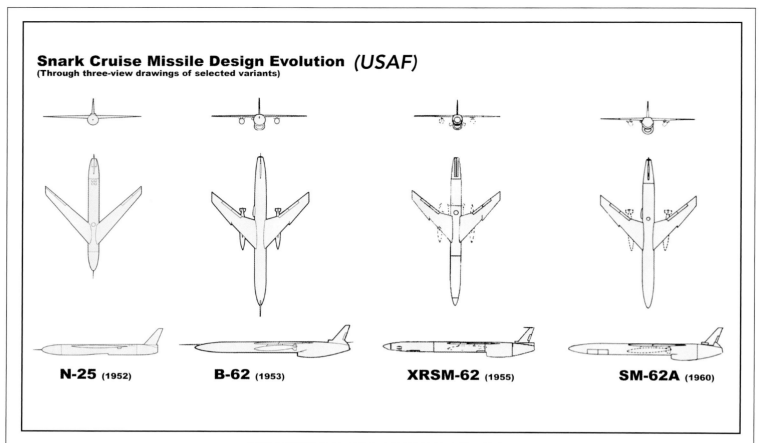

Snark Cruise Missile Design Evolution *(USAF)*
(Through three-view drawings of selected variants)

N-25 (1952)   **B-62** (1953)   **XRSM-62** (1955)   **SM-62A** (1960)

most of the additional guidance test flights that ensued through September 1957 were deemed successful.

The N-69D was a further success insofar as 20 airframes were assigned for flight tests, but the project objectives were met by November 1957 with just 15, and 8 were successfully recovered, 3 of which were subsequently re-flown.

The final Snark test variant was the N-69E Operational Concept Test Missile, which made its first successful flight on 16 August 1957. In this series, which continued through September 1958, N-69Es were used to study aerodynamic performance and system performance at high

A Northrop SM-62 Snark in Strategic Air Command markings shares the ramp with a stylishly finned 1958 Nash Rambler station wagon. The national insignia was at an angle so that it would appear straight when the missile was elevated to 45 degrees. (USAF)

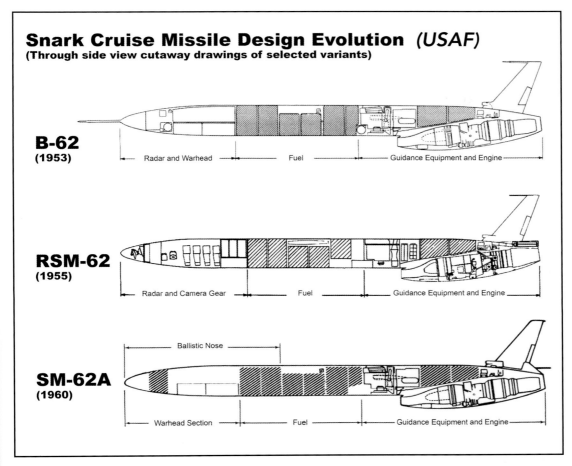

Snark Cruise Missile Design Evolution *(USAF)*
(Through side view cutaway drawings of selected variants)

B-62
(1953)

Radar and Warhead — Fuel — Guidance Equipment and Engine

RSM-62
(1955)

Radar and Camera Gear — Fuel — Guidance Equipment and Engine

SM-62A
(1960)

Ballistic Nose

Warhead Section — Fuel — Guidance Equipment and Engine

dynamic pressures in both terminal dives and ballistic nose drops. It was also during this phase that Snarks began to make flights to the full extent of the Eastern Missile Test Range, traveling 5,350 miles to Ascension Island. The first two were on 31 October and 5 December 1957.

The N-69E proved the desired range of 5,000 miles for the Snark, but the news was not so good when it came to accuracy. Prior to 1954, the air force had demanded that the Snark be capable of striking a target within a Circular Error Probable (CEP) of 1,500 feet. However, with

A Northrop SM-62 Snark painted in operational Strategic Air Command markings at Cape Canaveral in December 1960. (USAF)

the advent of thermonuclear weapons with a greater blast radius than uranium atomic bombs, the accuracy requirements were relaxed to a CEP of 8,000 feet. Even this was overly optimistic for the Snark reality. Most actual flights of more than 2,100 miles could not hit a target within a CEP of 20 miles. The best accuracy is said to have been a CEP of 4.7 miles that was achieved in 1958.

It was in this test that a Snark was flown to Ascension Island, where it was supposed to be recovered. However, it crashed into the South Atlantic within sight of its destination. As it turned out, the predetermined flight path had been calculated based on British navigation charts that had been produced with a slight inaccuracy irrelevant to maritime navigation but representing a serious flaw for a robot control system. There was no second attempt to get it right.

The most famous story in the folklore of Snark flight testing began in December 1956 when a missile headed down the Eastern Missile Test Range veered to the southwest and vanished into the Amazon jungle 3,000 miles from Cape Canaveral. By this time, flights were routinely publicized and the air force announced the loss. It was reported that a remote-destruct system failed as operators attempted to turn the Snark around. The media had a field day, poking fun at the air force for having allowed their million-dollar missile to slip its leash. A reference to an American missile launched from Cape Canaveral that landed in Brazil is made in the 1962 James Bond film *Dr. No*, although the Snark is not mentioned by name.

Efforts by both American and Brazilian teams to locate the missing Snark came up empty handed. It was finally discovered in January 1983 by a Brazilian farmer. The serial numbers that he reported from the crash site were confirmed.

The final Northrop-managed launch took place on 28 May 1958, and the flight test program formally concluded in September 1958 after six years. It had been comprised of four N-25A launches and 62 test launches of the various N-69 variants from the AFMTC. The weapon was now ready for deployment.

However, the U.S. Air Force Strategic Air Command (SAC), the intended user, had been troubled by the Snark's inaccuracy, its cost, and a test program that had dragged on for the better part of a decade.

"Although some may suspect the motives of a unit dominated by bomber pilots regarding a pilotless bomber that would take the man out of the machine, valid questions concerning the weapon's reliability and vulnerability emerged at this point," observed Kenneth Werrell. "As early as 1951, SAC decried Snark's vulnerability both on the ground and in the air. On the ground, the missile would be based at unhardened fixed sites. In the air, the subsonic (Mach 0.9) Snark lacked both defensive armament and the ability for evasive maneuver."

In an official SAC history, E. Michael del Pappa wrote that, in 1954, the SAC command position was "conservative concerning the integration of pilotless aircraft into the active inventory in order to ensure that reliance is not placed on a capability which does not in fact exist." Meanwhile, the Defense Department's Strategic Missile Evaluation Committee found the Snark to be an "overly complex" missile that would not become operational until "substantially later" than scheduled. By the time it was ready for operational deployment, SAC was already deploying the Douglas SM-75 Thor intermediate-range ballistic missile (IRBM), and the Convair SM-65 Atlas intercontinental ballistic missile (ICBM) was close behind.

General Tom Power, who assumed command of SAC in 1957, asserted that the Snark "added little" to the command's strength. Nevertheless, air force headquarters overruled Power, and he accepted it into the SAC inventory, albeit assigning it to only a single operational squadron: the 556th Strategic Missile Squadron, which had been a bomber squadron during World War II and was now reactivated under the command of Lieutenant Colonel Richard Beck at Patrick AFB in December 1957.

In January 1958, as the Snark test program was winding down, crews from the 556th were receiving technical training from the experienced 6555th Guided Missiles Wing, whose personnel had been flying Snarks for six years. The 556th's first launch, and the first by a SAC crew, came on 27 June 1958, and it was followed by additional launches later in the year.

In March 1959, SAC officially assigned the 556th to the 702nd Strategic Missile Wing, which received its first SM-62 Snarks in May at its new home at Presque Isle Air Force Base in northern Maine. Having served during World War II as a waypoint for aircraft traveling to the European Theater, the base was used during the Cold War by various interceptor units of the Air Defense Command.

At Presque Isle, the Snark Missile Launch Complex consisted of six hangars, each with two circular concrete launch pads with a diameter of 160 feet. The idea was that five Snarks would be lined up inside the 420-foot hangers, with the first in each being ready for launch in 15 minutes, and the second ready in 30. The others were to be ready in four hours, three days, and five days, respectively.

The first Snark achieved 15-minute alert status on 18 March 1960. By December, though, only 4 were on alert despite 30 operational missiles having been delivered. The 702nd finally achieved full alert status on 28 February 1961, one month into the new Kennedy administration.

Kennedy and his secretary of defense, Robert McNamara, viewed cruise missiles, and manned bombers, too, for that matter, as relics of past strategic doctrine, and embraced ICBMs as the future of strategic offensive weaponry. In his message to Congress on the defense budget on 28 March, President Kennedy announced "a very substantial increase in second-generation solid-fuel missiles of increased invulnerability (Polaris and Minuteman) . . . [and] the immediate phase-out of the subsonic Snark airbreathing long-range missile, which is now considered obsolete and of marginal military value in view of ICBM developments, the Snark's low reliability and penetrability, the lack of positive control over its launchings, and the location of the entire wing at an unprotected site."

On 25 June, the 702nd was inactivated and the Snarks were withdrawn. The Snark Missile Launch Complex base was sold to the City of Presque Isle in 1962. The concrete launch pads, which never saw a launch, still exist. So, too, do the huge hangars, which have been used intermittently through the years for various small-scale industrial activities.

The SM-62 Snark, which had been in preflight development for six years and in flight testing for another six, served on alert duty for 15 months, and on alert at full strength for only 4 months. Today, four Snarks are on public display, and one remains in storage in mint condition, out of public view at Cape Canaveral.

Project Pluto

Numerous unusual, cutting-edge, and downright improbable weapons systems were proposed and developed during the 1950s and 1960s when defense research funding was in its heyday. One such area of experimentation was that of nuclear propulsion systems, a source of power that provided potentially unlimited range for any vehicle.

The U.S. Navy developed nuclear propulsion for ships, commissioning the USS *Nautilus*, the world's first nuclear submarine, in 1954 and the USS *Enterprise*, the world's first nuclear-powered aircraft carrier, in 1961. The U.S. Air Force looked to nuclear propulsion for intercontinental manned bombers and undertook the X-6 program to develop a nuclear-powered aircraft. This idea got as far as a Convair NB-36H aircraft making multiple flights in 1956–1957 with a functioning nuclear reactor aboard. The reactor did not actually power the aircraft. That would have come later had the program not been canceled.

Meanwhile, plans were afoot for a nuclear-powered cruise missile to address the ongoing quest for intercontinental range. In 1957, the air force and the Lawrence Radiation Laboratory (now Lawrence Livermore National Laboratory) initiated Project Pluto, an effort to develop a nuclear ramjet powerplant small enough to be used for cruise missiles. Because the range of such a missile would be unlimited, it could remain aloft indefinitely, ready to strike at a moment's notice.

Lawrence built the prototype engine, and Marquardt Corporation, a firm specializing in ramjet engines, was selected to build the production variants. In 1963, the air force chose an airframe contractor for the cruise missile itself, which was to be called the Supersonic Low-Altitude Missile (SLAM). This company was Ling-Temco-Vought (LTV), which had been formed through a 1960 merger of Ling Electric and Temco Aircraft, with the 1961 hostile takeover of Chance Vought, maker of the Regulus cruise missiles.

The SLAM was to have been 88 feet long and to have weighed 61,000 pounds, but it was not built. The nuclear ramjet engine *was* completed, and it was tested at the Nevada Test Site (NTS) north of Las Vegas. Short-duration live firings took place in 1961 and 1964 before the project was canceled.

The true legacy of Project Pluto is that during its work toward the SLAM airframe, LTV developed the Terrain Contour Matching (TERCOM) guidance system. Though it would not be used in Project Pluto, TERCOM (discussed in more detail in chapter 6) would revolutionize the entire future of cruise missile operations.

Chapter 5

NOTHING BUT A HOUND DOG

An artist's conception of an AGM-28 Hound Dog, marked with the Strategic Air Command shield, headed for its target. A B-52 Stratofortress can be seen banking away in the distance. The concept of the air-launched cruise missile is to extend the range of the bombers and keep the crews out of harm's way. (Author's collection)

The Hound Dog stands at the crossroads of cruise missile history as the first successful operational American air-launched cruise missile. It is a bridge between past failures (going back to the ambitious attempts of the World War I era, through Aphrodite and Project Perilous) and the successes that were still a quarter century in the future.

When we use the phrase "nothing but a Hound Dog," we are clearly referencing lyrics of the 12-bar blues song,

"Hound Dog," by Jerry Leiber and Mike Stoller that was recorded by Big Mama Thornton and made iconic by Elvis Presley. We do so because the song was a hit for Elvis in 1956 and 1957 at the same time the missile was in development, and it is widely believed to have been the catalyst for the naming. Indeed, air force historian Kenneth Werrell stated categorically that his service "lifted the name from the title of an Elvis Presley hit song."

We also use the phrase because no American offensive

The Bell Aircraft Company's XGAM-63 Rascal was developed under the heading of Project MX-776. The name was an acronym for the missile's "RAdar SCAnning Link" guidance system. (USAF)

A Bell XGAM-63 Rascal carried aboard a Boeing YDB-47E bomber. The first successful Rascal launch from a YDB-47E came in July 1955. By December 1957, the Strategic Air Command's 445th Bomb Squadron was training with the missile. (USAF)

cruise missile before it had come close to the Hound Dog's level of deployment. It was fielded for more than a decade and served with more than four dozen Strategic Air Command (SAC) squadrons. Through the years of that deployment, there certainly was nothing quite like the Hound Dog.

While the Navaho and Snark programs sought to create a cruise missile with intercontinental range, the Hound Dog was a shorter-range missile that was conceived as a means of extending the intercontinental reach of SAC bombers.

Though the Hound Dog was technologically a bird of a new generation, it did have its conceptual roots in the V-1 program, but with a difference. The Matador, Regulus, and Mace were all ground launched from protected bunkers, as were the majority of V-1s. However, the V-1s that were air-launched by the Luftwaffe's Kampfgeschwader 3 had been, if not an inspiration, the precedent for this later generation of air-launched cruise missiles.

Very short-range, line-of-sight, air-launched guided missiles and unguided aerial rockets were becoming commonplace late in World War II, but the concept of using cruise missiles to extend the range of bombers was also considered. Clearly that was the mandate of Kampfgeschwader 3. After the war, both the USAAF and the U.S. Navy experimented with air-launching V-1-derived JB-2 and LTV-N-2 missiles, but these were only part of the story. McDonnell produced weapons such as the XAUM-6 Kingfisher tactical missile, which the U.S. Navy imagined could be used to arm long-range PB4Y-2 Privateers in missions against Soviet shipping. The Naval Air Development Center's Gorgon series of cruise missiles included some that might have been adapted for this purpose.

The origin of the first air-launched cruise missile developed specifically to extend the range of SAC bombers dates back to Project MX-776, one of the classified Materiel, Experimental (MX) guided missile project summaries issued by the Experimental Engineering Section of the USAAF Air Materiel Command in August 1945.

The Rascal

Taken up by Bell Aircraft Corporation, the MX-776 program led to two air-launched missiles. MX-776A became the Shrike missile, which was a testbed for the MX-776B that became the Rascal missile.

Some sources list the Rascal as a cruise missile, though it was designed with stabilizing fins rather than wings and had a range of only around 100 miles. Because it is seen as having common roots with the Matador in the German V-1, and because it was being developed for the Strategic Air Command, a discussion of it is a worthwhile preface to later air-launched missiles.

Conceptual work on the project began in March 1946 under Project Mastiff, which called for a pilotless bomber with a 300-mile range. In January 1948, the Air Materiel Command (AMC) divided this program, with MX-776A seen as an airframe test vehicle and the MX-776B for guidance system testing and a step closer to an operational configuration.

The MX-776A vehicle was originally designated as a Rocket Test Vehicle (RTV-A-4), but it was soon redesignated with an "X-for-experimental" research aircraft designation as the X-9. Officially named "Shrike," it is not to be confused with the unrelated AGM-45 Shrike anti-radar missile that entered service in 1965. Between 1949 and 1953, 31 X-9 Shrikes were delivered and approximately 28 were test fired.

The M-776B project resulted in the Rascal vehicle, its name was derived from the term "RAdar SCAninning Link," which describes the Bell-developed inertial guidance system. Though that phrase yields the acronym RASCAL, the name is usually seen written as "Rascal." The missile was originally designated as ASM-A-2, but in 1961 it received the "B-for-Bomber" designation B-63. In 1955, it was given the Ground Attack Missile designation GAM-63.

The Rascal was 32 feet long, just under 10 feet longer than a Shrike, and had a wingspan of 16 feet 8 inches, compared to 7.8 feet for the X-9. It weighed 13,500 pounds, four times the weight of the X-9, and was powered by a Bell XLR-67-BA-1 liquid-fuel rocket, with which it was able to achieve speeds greater than Mach 2.

The Rascal was designed to carry the W5 nuclear warhead, which equipped other early missiles such as the Matador and Regulus, though it was later earmarked to be retrofitted with the thermonuclear W27 warhead.

The flight test program began when an XB-63 Rascal was first test launched from a DB-50 "Director-Bomber" mother ship in September 1952. SAC planned to air-launch operational B-63s from its huge Convair B-36 bombers, in which a single Rascal would be partially retracted into the bomb bay to minimize aerodynamic drag. In 1953, a dozen specially designed YDB-36H aircraft were ordered. When the first YDB-36H was in hand, at least two launches over the White Sands Missile Range were made through 1955.

Meanwhile, U.S. Air Force headquarters insisted that the faster and newer Boeing B-47 Stratojet should be used as a Rascal carrier. However, SAC objected because the Rascal could not be carried internally and carrying it externally would increase aerodynamic drag and thereby degrade performance. The Pentagon prevailed and a Stratojet was converted, designated as YDB-47E, and delivered in January 1954. Plans for 30 YDB-47Es and for a whole squadron of Rascal-armed Stratojets never materialized, and only two of the Boeing bombers were converted. The first launch from a Stratojet came in July 1955.

Even after seven years of tests, the Rascal's performance left much to be desired. A later program review cited by Marcelle Size Knaack in *The Encyclopedia of U.S. Air Force Aircraft and Missile Systems* stated that more than half of the program's 65 test launches scheduled for 1958 had to be canceled for technical reasons, and only one of those that took place was a success.

The first operational GAM-63 was delivered to Pinecastle Air Force Base in Florida in 1957. This was two years ahead of the target date for construction of ground facilities, which was a good thing insofar as a program ahead of schedule is always desirable, but obviously it could not be deployed. Ultimately, this did not matter. The whole Rascal program was terminated in September 1958 in anticipation of the North American Aviation GAM-77 Hound Dog, a much more capable, and less trouble-plagued, air-launched cruise missile with five times the range.

Four Rascals are currently on public display, and one remains in storage in mint condition, out of public view at Cape Canaveral.

The Hound Dog

By the mid-1950s, the Soviet Union had cloaked its cities within the most extensive and comprehensive air defense system that the world had ever seen, and this system continued to be improved. American bomber crews had experienced tenacious air defenses over Germany in World War II and the air force understood the potential for catastrophic human losses in any mission against Moscow.

The necessity for a weapon to extend the *reach* of SAC's B-52 Stratofortress bombers had nothing to do with the *range* of those bombers. It had everything to do with keeping them out of the furnace of air defenses into which they might be tasked with penetrating. The idea was to allow bomber crews to send their weapons hurtling into the furnace, while they turned toward home without feeling the heat.

In March 1956, the air force sent out its General Operations Requirement GOR-148, which called for a thing

GAM-77 (later AGM-28) Hound Dog air-launched cruise missiles on the assembly line at the North American Aviation Missile Division facility in Downey, California. (Author's collection)

referred to as Weapon System WS-131B, which included a Mach 2 supersonic cruise missile and ancillary equipment. The missile itself was required to have a range of at least 350 miles (triple that of a Rascal), a ceiling of at least 55,000 feet, and a weight of no more than 12,500 pounds. These weapons would be carried in pairs on underwing pylons installed inboard of the engine nacelles of a B-52.

Both Chance Vought and North American Aviation (NAA) submitted proposals in July 1977, and the latter got the production contract in October 1958 for the missile that would be known as Hound Dog.

A grainy color image, possibly a still from a 16mm film, showing the first launch of the North American Aviation GAM-77 Hound Dog missile in April 1959. (Author's collection)

These would be delivered under the designations XGAM-77 for the 25 initial test articles, and GAM-77 for the operational missiles. The numeral, if not the prefix, was in the B-for-Bomber lineage.

The Hound Dog weighed 10,000 pounds, was 42 feet 6 inches long with a 12-foot wingspan, and had an overall configuration similar to NAA's Navaho missile with small canards and a delta wing. It was powered by a single Pratt & Whitney J52-P-3 turbojet engine delivering 7,500 pounds of thrust. The missile was armed with a W28 Class D thermonuclear warhead weighing 1,742 pounds that could be programmed for ground impact or for an air burst at a specific altitude.

The missile's range, which was more than 700 miles, was more than double that of the original requirement and far greater than any previous American air-launched missile.

The navigation system was based on the N-6 celestial navigation system originally designed for the Navaho by NAA's Autonetics Division. It included a KS-120 star tracker developed by the Kollsman Instruments Company, orig-inally founded by the eccentric German-born American inventor Paul Kollsman, whose instruments were later used in the Apollo program. The Kollsman system was used to continuously update and correct the missile's inertial navigation system through celestial observations. The Hound Dog could be programmed so that the missile could fly mission profiles at various altitudes and combinations thereof.

The KS-120 system was designed so that while the missile was mated to the B-52, the bomber crew also could use it for navigation. The overall guidance package gave the Hound Dog a Circular Error Probable (CEP) of 2.2 miles, which was deemed satisfactory for the W28 thermonuclear weapon.

The first dummy air drop of a Hound Dog came in November 1958, with the first test flight of a powered XGAM-77 on 23 April 1959. Flight testing of 25 XGAM-77 preproduction Hound Dogs took place over the White Sands Missile Range in New Mexico and out of both Eglin AFB and over the Eastern Missile Test Range out of Cape Canaveral AFS in Florida.

A GAM-77 (later AGM-28) Hound Dog air-launched cruise missile in Strategic Air Command markings on the underwing pylon of a Boeing B-52 Stratofortress. (Author's collection)

General Thomas Dresser White served as the fourth chief of staff of the U.S. Air Force from 1957 to 1961. He oversaw the deployment of the Hound Dog cruise missile and planned for the Skybolt as its potential successor. (USAF)

A North American Aviation GAM-77 (later AGM-28) Hound Dog air-launched cruise missile in flight over the high desert of California. (USAF)

In contrast with other missiles described in previous chapters, which were under development for 5 to 10 years, the Hound Dog program took just 30 months, with only 14 months elapsing between the issuing of the production contract and December 1959, when the first production GAM-77 missile was formally accepted into the U.S. Air Force by SAC Commander in Chief General Tom Power.

In his annual budget message to Congress in January 1960, President Dwight Eisenhower declared, "I am recommending additional acquisitions of the improved version of the B-52 [the turbofan-powered B-52H, and] funds are also included in this budget to continue the equipping of the B-52 wings with the Hound Dog air-to-surface missile."

The first Hound Dog to be test flown by a SAC crew was launched from a B-52G of the 4135th Strategic Wing on 29 February 1960.

As the development of the Hound Dog occurred in record time, NAA maintained a brisk pace on the assembly

Operational Strategic Air Command Hound Dog Units

2nd Bombardment Wing: Barksdale AFB, Louisiana
20th Bombardment Squadron
62nd Bombardment Squadron
596th Bombardment Squadron

5th Bombardment Wing (Heavy): Travis AFB, California/Minot AFB, North Dakota
23rd Bombardment Squadron

6th Bombardment Wing (Heavy): Walker AFB, New Mexico
24th Bombardment Squadron
40th Bombardment Squadron

11th Bombardment Wing (Heavy): Altus AFB, Oklahoma
26th Bombardment Squadron

17th Bombardment Wing (Heavy): Wright-Patterson AFB, Ohio
34th Bombardment Squadron

19th Bombardment Wing (Heavy): Homestead AFB, Florida/Robins AFB, Georgia
28th Bombardment Squadron

28th Bombardment Wing (Heavy): Ellsworth AFB, South Dakota
77th Bombardment Squadron

39th Bombardment Wing: Eglin AFB, Florida
62nd Bombardment Squadron

42nd Bombardment Wing (Heavy): Loring AFB, Maine
69th Bombardment Squadron
70th Bombardment Squadron

68th Bombardment Wing: Seymour Johnson AFB, North Carolina
51st Bombardment Squadron

70th Bombardment Wing: Clinton-Sherman AFB, Oklahoma
6th Bombardment Squadron

72nd Bombardment Wing (Heavy): Ramey AFB, Puerto Rico
60th Bombardment Squadron

92nd Bombardment Wing (Heavy): Fairchild AFB, Washington
325th Bombardment Squadron

97th Bombardment Wing (Heavy): Blytheville AFB, Arkansas
340th Bombardment Squadron

306th Bombardment Wing: McCoy AFB, Florida
367th Bombardment Squadron

319th Bombardment Wing (Heavy): Grand Forks AFB, North Dakota
46th Bombardment Squadron

320th Bombardment Wing: Mather AFB, California
441st Bombardment Squadron

340th Bombardment Wing: Bergstrom AFB, Texas
486th Bombardment Squadron

379th Bombardment Wing (Heavy): Wurtsmith AFB, Michigan
524th Bombardment Squadron

397th Bombardment Wing: Dow AFB, Maine
341st Bombardment Squadron

410th Bombardment Wing: K. I. Sawyer AFB, Michigan
644th Bombardment Squadron

416th Bombardment Wing: Griffiss AFB, New York
668th Bombardment Squadron

449th Bombardment Wing: Kincheloe AFB, Michigan
716th Bombardment Squadron

450th Bombardment Wing: Minot AFB, North Dakota
721st Bombardment Squadron

454th Bombardment Wing: Columbus AFB, Mississippi
736th Bombardment Squadron

456th Bombardment Wing: Beale AFB, California
744th Bombardment Squadron

465th Bombardment Wing: Robins AFB, Georgia
781st Bombardment Squadron

484th Bombardment Wing: Turner AFB, Georgia
864th Bombardment Squadron

4038th Strategic Wing: Dow AFB, Maine
341st Bombardment Squadron

4039th Strategic Wing: Griffiss AFB, New York
75th Bombardment Squadron

4042nd Strategic Wing: K. I. Sawyer AFB, Michigan
526th Bombardment Squadron

4043rd Strategic Wing: Wright-Patterson AFB, Ohio
42nd Bombardment Squadron

4047th Strategic Wing: McCoy AFB, Florida
347th Bombardment Squadron

4123rd Strategic Wing: Clinton-Sherman AFB, Oklahoma
98th Bombardment Squadron

4126th Strategic Wing: Beale AFB, California
31st Bombardment Squadron: Beale AFB, California

4130th Strategic Wing: Bergstrom AFB, Texas
335th Bombardment Squadron

4133rd Strategic Wing: Grand Forks AFB, North Dakota
30th Bombardment Squadron

4134th Strategic Wing: Mather AFB, California
72nd Bombardment Squadron

4135th Strategic Wing: Eglin AFB, Florida
301st Bombardment Squadron

4136th Strategic Wing: Minot AFB, North Dakota
525th Bombardment Squadron

4137th Strategic Wing: Robins AFB, Georgia
342nd Bombardment Squadron

4138th Strategic Wing: Turner AFB, Georgia
336th Bombardment Squadron

4228th Strategic Wing: Columbus AFB, Mississippi
492nd Bombardment Squadron

4238th Strategic Wing: Barksdale AFB, Louisiana
436th Bombardment Squadron

4239th Strategic Wing: Kincheloe AFB, Michigan
93rd Bombardment Squadron

4241st Strategic Wing: Seymour Johnson AFB, North Carolina
73rd Bombardment Squadron

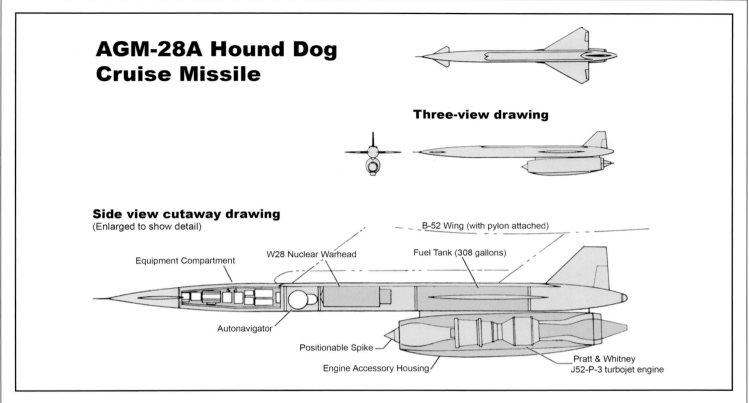

AGM-28A Hound Dog Cruise Missile

Three-view drawing

Side view cutaway drawing
(Enlarged to show detail)

B-52 Wing (with pylon attached)

Equipment Compartment

W28 Nuclear Warhead

Fuel Tank (308 gallons)

Autonavigator

Positionable Spike

Engine Accessory Housing

Pratt & Whitney
J52-P-3 turbojet engine

line, producing a total of 697 GAM-77s by March 1963, when manufacturing ended. There were 547 Hound Dogs in the SAC inventory by the end of 1962, and the number reached a peak of 593 a year later. More than 500 remained in service through 1966.

In 1961, meanwhile, NAA began a Hound Dog upgrade that included an improved KS-140 star tracker and a radar altimeter for low-level terrain-following operations. A total of 452 missiles, or 65 percent of total production, received the upgrade and were redesignated as GAM-77A. In 1963, under the Defense Department nomenclature merger, the GAM-77s were redesignated as AGM-28A, and the GAM-77As were redesignated as AGM-28B.

An Unexpectedly Long Phaseout

Even while it was being widely deployed, the Hound Dog was on track for withdrawal from the SAC inventory. Under the prevailing standard of the 1950s and early 1960s, weapons systems were mapped for replacement even as they

were entering service. SAC's B-36 fleet was gone by 1959 after 11 years, and the B-47s were phased out in 1967 after 14 years.

Meanwhile, a look at SAC records shows a vigorous phaseout program for early model B-52 Stratofortresses within a couple of years of the B-52H entering service. The ongoing search for a B-52 replacement was supposed to have been resolved by the end of the decade. Of course, the Stratofortress would famously still be in service after more than *five decades*.

As the Hound Dog was being deployed, its designated successor was the Douglas GAM-87 (AGM-48 after 1963) Skybolt, an air-launched ballistic missile (ALBM) with a two-stage solid-fuel rocket engine. It weighed about the same as a Hound Dog and was 4 feet shorter. It was designed to have a range of 1,150 miles, half again greater than the Hound Dog's.

Douglas had received the contract in May 1959, and full-scale development received the green light in February 1960. Three months later, Air Force Chief of Staff Thomas

A B-52F Stratofortress takes off with North American Aviation GAM-77 (later AGM-28) Hound Dog air-launched cruise missiles on its underwing pylons. (USAF)

Dresser White said that the Skybolt would be operational in 1968, but the Defense Department announced that this was "an accidental mistake," and it would instead be ready in 1964 or 1965.

In the meantime, the United States had convinced the United Kingdom to join the program and acquire the Skybolt for deployment aboard Royal Air Force (RAF) strategic bombers. The British went all in, abandoning a plan to improve their own Avro Blue Steel standoff missile. The RAF even sent a Vulcan bomber to call on Douglas Aircraft in Southern California for compatibility tests.

The range offered by the Skybolt was promising, but the political and budgetary value of bringing the British aboard the program clinched the deal. In his message to Congress on 28 March 1961, the same one in which he canceled the Snark, President Kennedy brought up the Skybolt, stating that "its successful development and production may extend the useful life of our bombers into the missile age, and its range is far superior to the present Hound Dog missiles."

However, the test program was anything but positive. Beginning in April 1962, the first five test flights of XGAM-87 were all failures. Operational capability within two years was impossible, so Kennedy decided to pull the plug.

Unfortunately, the British were already fully committed. Kennedy waited to drop the bad news until a face-to-face meeting with British Prime Minister Harold Macmillan in the Bahamas in December 1962. According to the official White

House statement, Kennedy "explained that it was no longer expected that this very complex weapons system would be completed within the cost estimate or the time scale which were projected when the program was begun [and] informed the prime minister that for this reason and because of the availability to the United States of alternative weapons systems, he had decided to cancel plans for the production of Skybolt for use by the United States. . . . As a possible alternative

A Strategic Air Command alert crew rushes to board its B-52 bomber with an AGM-28 Hound Dog air-launched cruise missile in the foreground. This famous image released by the air force was widely published in the 1960s. (USAF)

A long lineup of Strategic Air Command B-52 bombers, each armed with a pair of AGM-28 Hound Dog air-launched cruise missiles. (USAF)

A close-up view of a brace of North American Aviation AGM-28 Hound Dog air-launched cruise missiles. (USAF)

This excellent photo of a Strategic Air Command B-52G armed with AGM-28 Hound Dog air-launched cruise missiles was taken from a KC-135 aerial refueling aircraft. (USAF)

A B-52G armed with four XGAM-87A (later AGM-48) Skybolts. This missile represented a state-of-the-art in long-range stand-off weaponry that was not to be matched again for two decades with the AGM-86. (USAF)

He added that he also had offered both the Hound Dog and the U.S. Navy's Lockheed Polaris submarine-launched ballistic missile as alternatives. Ultimately, the British chose the latter and only SAC operated the Hound Dog. At the time, SAC's inventory was still increasing and would not reach its peak until later in 1963.

The phaseout of the Hound Dog, baked into its overall operational scheme for 1964, did not happen. Under its new AGM-28 designation, it remained on alert in significant numbers through the decade and into the 1970s. More than 300 were still in service at the end of 1975.

During the 1970s, the Hound Dog was tested with a TERCOM guidance system, and consideration also was given to adapting Hound Dogs with anti-radar seekers. However, no AGM-28s thus equipped are known to have been deployed operationally.

Hound Dogs remained on alert deployment until 1975, with the last one retired

the president suggested that the RAF might use the Hound Dog missile. The prime minister responded that in light of the technical difficulties he was unable to accept this suggestion."

Naturally, there was a firestorm in the media, especially in Britain, where it appeared Macmillan had been blindsided.

"Well, I think it would seem to me that if anybody bothered to read the pact in detail," Kennedy defensively explained to reporters on New Year's Eve, "that we made several offers to the British. First, the British position on it has been, I know, somewhat critical. In the first place, we did offer the Skybolt. We offered a 50-50 split in finishing the Skybolt, even though we, ourselves, weren't going to buy any, and the British could have bought them. So I don't think it can be charged that the United States was in any way attempting to make a political decision rather than a technical one. The fact is this administration put a lot of money into Skybolt. We increased the funds substantially after 1961 in an effort to finish it successfully. We speeded up the program."

from the 42nd Bomb Wing at Loring Air Force Base in Maine. Subsequently, they remained in storage until 1978, after which time they were formally deleted from the SAC roster.

In the mid-1960s, several studies for a Hound Dog replacement were conducted that centered on significantly smaller missiles. Tactically, the idea was no longer for a single missile flying a single strike mission against a single target, but rather a "swarm" of smaller missiles attacking multiple targets simultaneously.

The Hound Dog's eventual replacement was the Boeing AGM-69 Short-Range Attack Missile (SRAM), which was first deployed in 1972. Like the Skybolt, it was a ballistic-type standoff missile. Its 100-mile range was a throwback to the days of the Rascal, but the idea of swarming a target with larger numbers was seen as offsetting that shortcoming.

The SRAM was also much smaller and lighter than a Hound Dog or Skybolt. It was just under 16 feet in length and weighed 2,230 pounds, which meant that a bomber could carry many more than just two. Even an FB-111 could carry six of them, and a rotary launcher was designed for the

B-52 bomb bay that allowed eight SRAMs internally. In addition, the B-52 could carry a dozen more SRAMs externally.

One of the lasting legacies of the Hound Dog is that the external underwing pylon designed for the Hound Dog, and on which a B-52 would carry SRAMs, gravity bombs, guided bombs, and future cruise missiles, continued to be known as the "AGM-28 pylon" long after the Hound Dog itself was just a memory.

Also keeping that memory alive are the more than two dozen retired Hound Dogs displayed in varying levels of preservation at locations across the United States.

Decoy Missiles

An important footnote to the story of the first generation of Strategic Air Command cruise missiles involves the decoy missiles. These are important because the technology that evolved during their development played a role in future cruise missiles.

The decoys were small winged missiles without warheads that were designed to have a large radar signature. They were intended to be carried by SAC bombers and released near a target area to confuse enemy interceptors and surface-to-air missile systems. To do so, they were armed with radar reflectors and electronic countermeasures simulators.

Some of the earliest official interest in decoy programs can be traced to the early 1950s and the Air Force Materiel, Experimental projects designated as MX-2223 and MX-2224. However, the contractors who would later receive contracts under these programs had apparently been working on similar projects previously.

The MX-2223 study incorporated a project designated as Weapons System WS-123A that called for a missile with a range of 5,750 miles, while MX-2224 envisioned a much shorter-range missile with a half-hour flight duration. Contracts were issued in the summer of 1954 to Fairchild and Convair, respectively.

Fairchild's MX-2223 proposal was a subsonic, delta-winged, ground-launched vehicle that was 33 feet 6 inches long with a wingspan of 24 feet 5 inches. It weighed 7,700 pounds without its booster and was powered by a Fairchild YJ83-R-3 turbojet engine.

The Convair proposal was for a straight-winged, air-launched vehicle resembling a glide bomb that was

When General Thomas White (right) retired as Chief of Staff of the Air Force in June 1961 and handed the baton to former Strategic Air Command leader General Curtis LeMay, the AGM-28 Hound Dog was deployed and the AGM-48 Skybolt was in the pipeline. Secretary of the Air Force Eugene M. Zuckert is on the left at the retirement ceremony. (USAF)

13 feet long with wings spanning 14 feet that could be folded so that several could fit into the bomb bay of a Convair B-36. It weighed 1,550 pounds and was to have been powered by an Aerojet XLR85-AJ-1 liquid-fuel rocket engine.

Both missiles were given names of waterfowl modified by incongruous adjectives. Being considered a strategic weapon, the Fairchild missile received a B-for-Bomber designation as XB-73 (later XSM-73), and it was named "Bull Goose." The Convair vehicle was designated as XGAM-71 and called "Buck Duck."

The Buck Duck was canceled in 1956 without ever having made a powered flight, but the Bull Goose flew more than a dozen times between March 1957 and the end of 1958. The air force made plans for 2,328 operational Bull Geese to be deployed between 1961 and 1963 to equip 10 squadrons. Construction of launch sites was under way in Minnesota and Vermont when the program was canceled in 1958. It had been demonstrated in radar testing that the Bull Goose could not convincingly simulate a B-52 bomber.

A third SAC decoy did make it into production. In 1955,

An August 1961 view of a Douglas XGAM-87A (later AGM-48) Skybolt on its hydraulic loading trailer, parked next to a Stratofortress. (Author's collection)

A Douglas XGAM-87A (later AGM-48) Skybolt air-launched ballistic missile on the ramp in August 1962, three months before the program was terminated. (Author's collection)

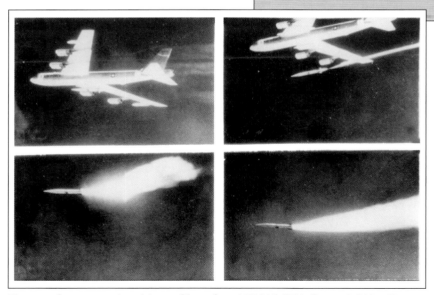

Frames from a grainy 16mm film of an XGAM-87A (later AGM-48) Skybolt being test fired from a Stratofortress. This may be of the first successful launch on 19 December 1962. Ironically, this was the same day as the program termination. (USAF)

the air force undertook the WS-122A program aimed at a short-range, air-launched B-52 simulator. In February 1956, McDonnell Aircraft was awarded a contract to build the GAM-72 Quail (originally Green Quail). It had the size and shape of a refrigerator with stubby wings, but it successfully emulated the big bomber.

The Quail was 12 feet 11 inches long with a wingspan of just 5 feet 5 inches. It weighed 1,200 pounds and was powered by a General Electric J85-GE-7 turbojet delivering 2,450 pounds of thrust. It had a range of 400 miles and a service ceiling of 50,000 feet.

Air-drop glide tests of the Quail began in 1957 at Holloman AFB, with a first powered flight happening over the nearby White Sands Missile Range in August 1958. A production contract was issued that year, and the first test of a production series Quail came in March 1960. McDonnell delivered 616 Quails, 585 of them operational

A B-52G with a GAM-72 (later ADM-20) Quail in the foreground, as seen in June 1960. The Quail was operational with Stratofortress units early the following year. (USAF)

series birds, through May 1962. In 1963, under the Defense Department's nomenclature merger, the designation was changed from GAM-72 to ADM-20.

By the 1970s, advances in radar technology made the Quails obsolete and they were gradually withdrawn from service. Nevertheless, more than 350 were still deployed as late as 1977, and they remained on alert status with B-52 Stratofortress squadrons until June 1978. Today, 15 Quails remain on display at locations throughout the United States.

During the last decade of the Quail's service, various Defense Department research programs studied technology for possible successors. Though none of these ever became operational, the thinking behind them remained part of the knowledge base that could, and would, be drawn upon when the next generation of strategic planners began to once again think about cruise missiles.

The Fairchild XSM-73 Bull Goose ground-launched decoy cruise missile was developed under Project MX-2223. Test and evaluation began in February 1957 with rocket sled tests at Holloman AFB in New Mexico. In June 1957, the test program moved to Patrick AFB at Cape Canaveral, where this photo was taken. Between March 1957 and December 1958, 15 flights were made. (USAF)

Chapter 6

THE AIR-LAUNCHED CRUISE MISSILE

A Boeing AGM-86A, the first but never operational variant of the Air-Launched Cruise Missile (ALCM) series, on display at the Smithsonian's Steven F. Udvar-Hazy Center near Washington, DC. It was similar in size and configuration to its predecessor, the notional vehicle at the heart of the Subsonic Cruise Armed Decoy (SCAD) program. (Cliff, licensed under the Creative Commons)

After technical development of the Hound Dog as a weapons system concluded in the 1950s, it would be two decades before the U.S. Air Force and the U.S. Navy again returned to the idea of deploying a subsequent generation of cruise missiles. In those years, both the air force and the navy had shifted precepts and embraced a strategic doctrine that leaned heavily on ballistic missiles. Intercontinental Ballistic Missiles (ICBMs) and Submarine-Launched Ballistic Missiles (SLBM) ruled the doctrine inside the Pentagon and filled the headlines in the media and popular culture.

In the 1950s, air force ICBMs had included the liquid-fuel Convair B-65/SM-65 (later HGM-16) Atlas and the Martin B-68/SM-68 (later HGM/LGM-25) Titan, but these had been withdrawn in the 1960s in favor of the solid-fuel Boeing LGM-30 Minuteman ICBM, which could be placed on alert indefinitely. The Minuteman, which is still in service in the twenty-first century, has an intercontinental range of more than 8,000 miles and a Circular Error Probable (CEP) accuracy of about 600 feet.

The navy, meanwhile, turned to Lockheed, which developed a series of solid-fuel SLBMs that included the UGM-27 Polaris, the UGM-73 Poseidon, the UGM-96 Trident, and the UGM-133 Trident II. The UGM-133, like the Minuteman, has an intercontinental range of more than 8,000 miles and a CEP accuracy of about 300 feet. However, at the same

A heavily retouched image showing an AGM-86B Air-Launched Cruise Missile (ALCM) in flight. (USAF)

time, on several completely different tracks, more obscure and esoteric research was examining technology that would come to figure in future cruise missiles.

During the 1960s, advances had been made in the field of small, high-performance unmanned jet aircraft. Perhaps none is more emblematic of these developments than the Firebee, a 22-foot, 2,000-pound vehicle that was originally created and manufactured in the late 1950s by Ryan Aeronautical as a high-speed target drone. During the Vietnam War, the Ryan Firebee family of vehicles proved itself as a high-speed *reconnaissance* drone, operating with the armed forces under the AQM-34 and BQM-34 series of designations, and with the CIA under the Ryan company designation Model 147 and with code names such as "Firefly" and "Lightning Bug." This aircraft was never used as a cruise missile, but it did demonstrate the performance and reliability that was possible in a small unmanned package. It also served as a practical test bed for small jet engines.

Meanwhile, the track that would ultimately lead to the Air-Launched Cruise Missile (ALCM) had inauspicious beginnings in an effort to build an air-launched decoy that many people in the air force did not really want.

SCAD and SCAM

By 1967, as noted in the previous chapter, the air force was investigating configurations for possible successors to the ADM-20 Quail decoy, all of which were roughly the same size as the Quail or Firebee. Among them was the Subsonic

Cruise Unarmed Decoy, whose acronym (SCUD) is not to be confused with the NATO code name for the Soviet R-11 and R-17 tactical ballistic missiles that have been widely proliferated around the world.

The SCUD as a decoy concept faded into obscurity, but on its way out, it was noticed by General Glenn Kent of the Air Force Systems Command (AFSC), who suggested arming it and making it into a cruise missile. In his idea, the SCUD would become the SCAD, the Subsonic Cruise Armed Decoy, with an emphasis on *Armed*. Kent was a brilliant research and development man and strategic thinker who became the air force's deputy chief of staff for studies and analysis in 1968. He was later deeply involved in numerous programs from the Airborne Warning and Control Systems (AWACS) to the Joint Surveillance Target Attack Radar System (JSTARS).

The SCAD apparently evolved into the idea of the Subsonic Cruise Attack Missile (SCAM), taking the emphasis off the decoy mission. It might be added that this was one of the first uses of the capitalized term "Cruise" in the name of a missile system.

Pentagon Director of Defense Research and Engineering (DDRE) Dr. John S. Foster concurred with Kent, but surprisingly, there was opposition from SAC, which wanted a decoy to *aid a bomber* in penetrating enemy air space and *not* another standoff weapon. The Short-Range Attack Missile (SRAM) was already being deployed.

As air force historian Kenneth Werrell recalls, "The issue of arming or not arming the new missile remained unresolved for the next number of years and proved critical to the SCAD's ultimate fate. On 12 January 1968, Headquarters Air Force issued a Requirements Action Directive to Air Force Systems Command for a subsonic, armed cruise missile, superseding a document issued only three weeks earlier that called for a pure decoy. Strategic Air Command issued a Required Operational Capability (SAC ROC 68-1) for an improved unarmed decoy on 19 January."

In turn, as the air force was reviewing SCAD internally, contractor study contracts were awarded to Beech, Boeing,

General John Dale Ryan became the seventh chief of staff of the U.S. Air Force in August 1969 and authorized development of the Subsonic Cruise Armed Decoy (SCAD) program, the first step toward the ALCM, in June 1970. (USAF)

and Lockheed to develop a SCAD system that would be compatible with the existing SRAM launchers then being installed in B-52 Stratofortresses. These launchers, intended to be installed in B-52 bomb bays, were also being designed into the North American Rockwell B-1 bomber, which was now under development. Use of this launcher was a key part of SAC's manned bomber program for the 1970s and beyond.

By July 1970, both U.S. Air Force Chief of Staff General John Dale Ryan and Deputy Secretary of Defense David Packard had signed off on the development of the SCAD, but primarily as a decoy. They were cool on the idea of a cruise missile when the SRAM was already in development.

Ironically, it seems that members of Congress saw greater potential in SCAD than did the air force. It was New Hampshire Senator Thomas McIntyre on the Committee on Armed Services who insisted that it should be armed as a standoff weapon and be used to replace the AGM-28 Hound Dog instead of replacing the ADM-20 Quail. Nevertheless, Congress proceeded to cut the budget for the project by half.

The formal request for SCAD proposals was finally issued in February 1972, with airframe, engine, and guidance requests going out to a total of 64 companies. Congress and the comptroller general complained that the program should involve competitive prototypes, but the air force successfully argued against this. Only in the case of engines would there be two systems to compare.

By August 1972, the contractors had been chosen, with the two competing engines to be built by Williams Inter-national and Teledyne Turbine Engines. Litton Industries got the contract to develop the LN-35 inertial navigation system, while the lion's share of the budget went to Boeing to both build the SCAD airframe and to integrate it into the rotary launcher system. Boeing was already the contractor for SRAM, so this made sense.

Still, the question of using the SCAD as a standoff weapon would not go away. Edgar Ulsamer, writing in *Air Force Magazine* in November 1972, insisted that it "makes no sense to substitute a small, subsonic, relatively inaccurate missile for the ballistic missile. . . . The air force is determined to make SCAD meet these [decoy] goals, but SCAD is not, and never was meant to be, a new strategic weapons family."

In April 1973, the Defense System Acquisition Review Council (DSARC) ordered the air force to prepare proposals for the parallel development of both decoy and standoff SCADs. However, the resulting plans arrived against the backdrop of mushrooming costs in the project, and in June, the Defense Department canceled the SCAD program in its entirety.

As so often happens in the circuitous lives of strategic concepts, the idea behind SCAD did not die with it, but merely lay dormant. The decoy was dead, but it would be just half a year before much of what had gone into the project would be resurrected as the Air-Launched Cruise Missile (ALCM).

TERCOM

As had been the case with previous cruise missiles, an important element in the awakening ALCM program was the very factor that had condemned so many earlier cruise missiles to failure: guidance.

Autonomous navigation using a prerecorded terrain map combined with a radar altimeter, which measures height over the terrain rather than absolute altitude, originated in 1952. As described in chapter 2, this was the Goodyear Aircraft Corporation Automatic Terrain Recognition and Navigation (ATRAN) system that was first used operationally in the Mace cruise missile.

However, ATRAN was limited to places for which there were accurate and detailed prerecorded maps, and these required the route to have been previously flown by a reconnaissance aircraft. Missiles using ATRAN and successor systems were also limited by the amount of map data that could

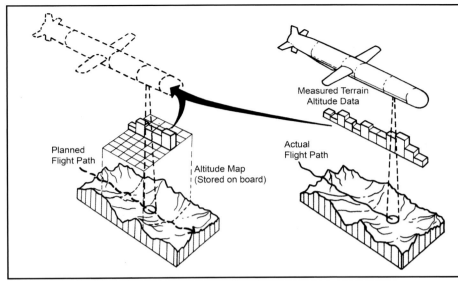

Planned
Flight Path

Altitude Map
(Stored on board)

Measured Terrain
Altitude Data

Actual
Flight Path

In-flight under TERCOM, a radar altimeter measured the actual elevations and then, at each waypoint, matched that sequence with the digital map stored in the computer. As air force historian Kenneth Werrell explained, the computer checked three maps, and if one was found to disagree with the other two, the odd reading was disregarded. The system was based on assumptions that the mapping information was available and accurate, that unique land contours could be used, and that the radar altimeter and computer could do their jobs. (DOD)

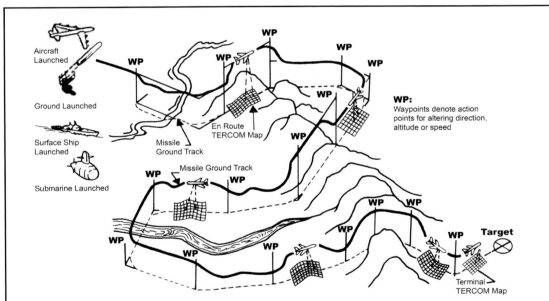

Aircraft
Launched

Ground Launched

Surface Ship
Launched

Submarine Launched

WP

WP

WP

WP

WP

WP

WP

WP

WP

WP

WP

WP

WP

WP

WP

WP

WP

Target

En Route
TERCOM Map

Missile
Ground Track

Missile Ground Track

Terminal
TERCOM Map

WP:
Waypoints denote action points for altering direction, altitude or speed

In the original cruise missile operational concept, the missile's inertial navigation system was "corrected," or updated, after launch at a series of waypoints by numerous en route TERCOM fixes. The last, or terminal, TERCOM fix was a short distance from the target. In developing the TERCOM system, engineers divided a terrain map into a matrix of cells that ranged in size from 100 feet to 3,200 feet on a side. The original E-Systems matrix consisted of 64 cells, each 400 feet on a side, yielding a 4.9-nm strip map. Engineers assigned each cell an average elevation derived from a contour map or satellite reconnaissance map, and this information was stored in the system's computer. (DOD)

be stored *internally*. It is here that one points out that the data storage capability found in the average smart phone memory card once required rooms with the square footage of gymnasiums filled with vintage computers.

Through the years, as the physical space required by both data storage and computing power shrank, it became possible to field subsequent generations of Terrain Referenced Navigation (TRN) systems. These have gone by such names as Low Altitude Contour Matching (LACOM), Rapid Contour Matching (RACOM), and Recursive All Weather Contour Matching (also RACOM).

The definitive system,

however, is Terrain Contour Matching (TERCOM), which originated with Chance Vought prior to that company's merger into the Ling-Temco-Vought (LTV) conglomerate in 1961. LTV-Electro Systems (or E-Systems) further developed the program for the nuclear ramjet-powered Supersonic Low Altitude Missile (SLAM), which was supposed to have flowed from Project Pluto, but which never did. Originally patented under the name "Fingerprint," the system became formally known as TERCOM, and the patent rights have long since been assigned to the U.S. Air Force.

As described by Kenneth Werrell in 1985, "In the TERCOM system, engineers divided a terrain map into a matrix of cells which have ranged in size from 100 feet to 3,200 feet on a side. Thus, each map measures a number of miles. The E-Systems matrix consists of 64 cells, each 400 feet on a side, yielding a 4.9-nm strip map. Engineers assign each cell an average elevation derived from a contour map or satellite reconnaissance map, and this information is stored in the system's computer. In flight, a radar altimeter measures the actual elevations and then at checkpoints matches that sequence with the digital map stored in the computer. Here, 'voting' takes place; that is, the system checks three maps and if one is found to disagree with the other two, the odd reading is disregarded. . . . The system is based on assumptions that the mapping information is available and accurate, unique land contours can be used, and the radar altimeter and computer can do their jobs."

In fact, TERCOM was based on a series of three maps, each with a different scale, called landfall, en route, and terminal area. Each was more detailed than the previous map. The terminal area map had greatly reduced navigation margins to permit a high degree of accuracy.

In the early days, access time was still on the slow side, and large volumes of space were required for data storage. It was not possible to store data for an entire flight, so smaller segments were stored and used to periodically update a conventional inertial navigation system in what was called a TERCOM-Aided Inertial Navigation System (TAINS). In TAINS, the inertial guidance system navigated the missile from one TERCOM checkpoint to the next, with the computer updating the inertial guidance system and correcting the missile's course. Processing speed to compare altimeter data to the terrain map was also a limiting factor.

The advent of the Global Positioning System (GPS) galaxy of navigation satellites, first launched by the Department of Defense in 1973, was destined to revolutionize TERCOM navigation. Today, of course, we take GPS for granted in our daily lives, and it is hard to imagine what life must have been like without it, even for those of us who experienced that bygone era.

The Development Process

Technical breakthroughs, such as TERCOM, were only part of the reason for the renewed interest in cruise missiles in the early 1970s. Often overlooked is the political dimension. The time frame of the early development of cruise missiles coincided with the signing in May 1972 by

The AGM-109 was competition for the Boeing AGM-86 from the Convair Division of General Dynamics. (Author's collection)

Chairman of the Joint Chiefs of Staff (and former Air Force Chief of Staff) General George Scratchley Brown discusses the Air-Launched Cruise Missile (ALCM) program with Deputy Secretary of Defense William Perry "Bill" Clements, who was a strong advocate of the ALCM. Before he left office in 1977, Clements cautioned against the "one-size-fits-all" requirements then proposed for adapting a single system for the air force and navy. (USAF)

The Convair AGM-109 Air-Launched Cruise Missile is displayed with a full-scale mockup of a B-52 Stratofortress at the General Dynamics Convair Division facility in San Diego, circa 1978. (Author's collection)

Leonid Brezhnev and Richard Nixon of the Strategic Arms Limitation Treaty (SALT), officially known as the Interim Agreement Between the United States of America and the Union of Soviet Socialist Republics on Certain Measures with Respect to the Limitation of Strategic Offensive Arms.

The SALT Treaty (later known as SALT I after the second agreement was signed) limited the respective arsenals of Intercontinental Ballistic Missiles (ICBM) and Submarine-Launched Ballistic Missiles (SLBM); however, it did not *mention* cruise missiles, which were seen at the time as embodying outdated and discredited technology, and therefore deemed irrelevant and unimportant. This left a loophole through which U.S. Secretary of Defense Melvin Laird was encouraged to fly the new weapon.

As SALT gave life to the interest in a standoff weapon that still simmered at the Defense Department, back on the technical side, the demise of the SCAD program left a great deal of half-finished engineering work that could be exploited. Recognizing both the political and technical issues, Deputy Secretary of Defense William Clements proposed in December 1973 that the Defense Department pick up the pieces and make a fresh start toward building an Air-Launched Cruise Missile (ALCM).

In February 1974, the former SCAD contractors were instructed by the Defense Department to pick up where they had left off and proceed with the standoff weapon, which was designated as AGM-86A. Boeing continued as the airframe contractor, while Williams International was selected to provide its F107 series turbofan engine as the powerplant. Founded by pioneer inventor Sam Barlow Williams, the company had been developing and building compact turbofan engines since the 1950s.

As with SCAD, the air force was accepting but

A full-scale rotary launcher was installed inside Convair's in-house B-52 mockup so that the company could demonstrate its use with their AGM-109 Air-Launched Cruise Missile. (Author's collection)

An artist's conception of the Convair AGM-109 being launched from a B-52 Stratofortress. (Convair Division)

The Convair AGM-109 Air-Launched Cruise Missile's first flight on 19 July 1979 was part of a flyoff with the Boeing AGM-86. (Convair Division)

A Boeing AGM-86B Air-Launched Cruise Missile in flight over the Utah Test and Training Range in 1980. (DOD photo by R. L. House)

unenthusiastic. The Vietnam War was winding down and the defense budget was shrinking. Chief of Staff General George Scratchley Brown had two very large strategic development programs on his plate and he was reluctant to add another for fear of jeopardizing the first two in the fragile funding environment. The B-1 bomber and the "MX" ICBM, which later became the LGM-118 Peacekeeper, were in their early stages of development and required a substantial slice of his budget and his attention.

Concurrent with the air force's simmering level of interest in the cruise missile concept through SCAD and the tentative steps toward ALCM, the U.S. Navy had been thinking similar thoughts, and it had initiated its Submarine-Launched Cruise Missile (SLCM) program. This would mark a return to the concept abandoned with the last sail of the Regulus a decade earlier and would eventually lead to the General Dynamics cruise missile that was designated as BGM-109 and later named Tomahawk (see chapter 7).

So many axioms come to mind, but the one about not realizing how much you miss something until it's gone is certainly apt. In 1975, when Congress defunded the air force's ALCM program, but *kept* the navy's Tomahawk in the defense budget, the air force position suddenly changed.

As SAC's Colonel Buddy Brown candidly admitted in 1976, "SAC's position [regarding the armed ALCM concept] has mellowed, because of the political atmosphere, and is in line with higher echelon [Defense Department] thinking."

Funding was restored in 1975, shortly after it was taken away, and the first AGM-86A ALCM was rolled out by the end of the year with plans for it to be fully tested and operational by 1980. It was 13 feet 11 inches long with a wingspan of 10 feet 5 inches, and it had a gross weight of 2,082 pounds.

The vehicle made its first powered flight on 5 March 1976, three weeks ahead of the navy's General Dynamics Tomahawk. The first AGM-86A flight using the TERCOM guidance package came six months later, on 9 September, and saw the missile flying as low as 30 feet. The failures suffered in the fifth and sixth flight tests were attributed to gyro failure and engine failure rather than to the TERCOM. At the White Sands Missile Range on 21 June 1978, the missile was flown for the first time with journalists looking on. Bernard Weintraub of the *New York Times* recorded that the military representatives were "elated" with the demonstration.

An Unexpected Flyoff

Though AGM-86 funding had been restored, it was clear that in the penny-pinching, post-Vietnam environment, the same fingers on the purse strings that deleted it once, could take it away again. As there had been three decades earlier with the air force Matador and navy Regulus, there was talk in defense circles about terminating the AGM-86 and acquiring the navy's Tomahawk for the air force's ALCM mission. According to a 1976 Government Accountability Office (GAO) study, picking the Tomahawk over the AGM-86 could "save $165 to $373 million. But the dollar savings had to be weighed against a loss of performance," and that the "SLCM was not optimal for the ALCM role."

There was definitely an "apples and oranges" aspect to two missiles that had originally been designed for *distinctly different* launch environments (airborne launches up to 40,000 feet for ALCM and underwater launches for the SLCM). However, the Tomahawk *seemed* like a more flexible system. It was already being adapted for surface-launch applications, such as land and surface ships. This was reflected in the designation that it was assigned. The "B" in

On 25 March 1980, Secretary of the Air Force Hans Mark announced that the Air-Launched Cruise Missile contract would go to Boeing for the AGM-86. An aerospace engineer by training, Mark later served as Deputy Administrator of NASA. (USAF)

Thornton Arnold "T" Wilson joined Boeing in 1943, became company president in 1968, chief executive officer in 1969, and chairman in 1972, where he served until 1986. He presided over some of the company's greatest achievements of the later twentieth century, from the 747, 757, and 767 jetliners to the Air-Launched Cruise Missile. In 1980, the ALCM contract was the biggest defense contract issued since the Vietnam War. (Boeing)

BGM-109 stood for "multiple" launch environments, while the "A" in AGM-86 stood for "air."

The move toward a jointly developed common cruise missile flowed directly from a meeting of the Defense Systems Acquisition Review Council (DSARC) on 6 January 1977. DSARC recommended proceeding with both the air force ALCM and navy SLCM to the Full-Scale Engineering Development (FSED) stage and then conducting a flyoff between the Boeing and General Dynamics missiles to settle the question of whether the Tomahawk could serve as an air-launched system.

Deputy Secretary of Defense William Clements had cautioned that "a common airframe for all applications may impose unnecessary and unwarranted performance compromises on both weapons systems." His words were pro-phetic. Nevertheless, he signed off on the common cruise missile approach only eight days later. Soon after the Carter administration took office on 20 January, it was mandated that the two services develop a single cruise missile.

In September 1977, the Joint Cruise Missiles Project Office (JCMPO) was established under Captain (later Admiral) Walter Locke. In the 1982 Rand Corporation study *The Joint Cruise Missiles Project*, E. H. Conrow, G. K. Smith, and A. A. Barbour noted that "Locke was also directed to achieve maximum commonality among the various missiles, specifically by using common engine and land-attack guidance systems." In fact, the two missiles were already both powered by a Williams F107-series turbofan engine and both used TERCOM guidance.

Final assembly of AGM-86B Air-Launched Cruise Missiles at the Boeing Space Center in Kent, Washington, on a cold winter day circa 1982, around the time of the author's first visit to this facility. (Courtesy William A. Rice, Boeing)

A Boeing Aerospace Company technician assembles an AGM-86B Air-Launched Cruise Missile (ALCM) at the company's production line at the Boeing Space Center in Kent, Washington, circa 1983. This missile was 1 of 40 produced each month at that time. (Courtesy William A. Rice, Boeing)

The missile crew from the 416th Bombardment Wing positions AGM-86B ALCMs for mounting to the pylon of a B-52G at Griffiss Air Force Base in September 1981. (U.S. Air Force photo by Tech Sergeant Pablo Marmolejo)

According to the General Accounting Office in Volume 58 of the comptroller general's report, McDonnell Douglas held the "prime contract with the Department of Defense (DOD) for the design, development, and furnishing of AN/DSW-15 Cruise Missile Land Attack Guidance Sets and Navigation/Guidance Equipment for the AGM-86B Air-Launched Cruise Missile." The Guidance and Control Systems Division of Litton Industries, meanwhile, was the subcontractor for design and production of the LN-35 inertial navigation system and a Honeywell radar altimeter. The ALCMs would also carry extensive electronic countermeasures (ECM) systems to help them defeat Soviet defenses.

The AN/DSW-15 was also used in the Tomahawk family of cruise missiles (see chapter 7). For both ALCM and Tomahawk, it was upgraded to the McDonnell Douglas AN/DPW-23 system in the 1990s.

In June 1977, meanwhile, the Carter administration canceled the B-1 bomber program. This stunned air force leadership and left SAC without one of the important weapons systems upon which it hoped to rely in the future, and for which it had been planning for years. The loss of the B-1 greatly increased the importance of the B-52 Stratofortress, especially when armed with an ALCM, to the future of the air force.

In September 1977, the director of Defense Research and Engineering (DDRE), William Perry (later secretary of defense), issued a memo to the secretaries of the air force and navy in which he asserted that "it is a matter of highest national priority, especially in light of the B-1 decision, to develop an air-launched cruise missile with optimum performance and minimum cost and schedule delays. I believe we can best accomplish those program objectives by conducting a competitive flyoff between Boeing and General Dynamics to determine which of their missiles will be the

ALCM to be flown on the B-52 and, as appropriate, other cruise missile carriers."

During the ALCM's conceptual development, the air force considered adapting large aircraft other than the B-52 as cruise missile platforms. In May 1978, the Senate Armed Services Committee approved a $41 million request to study converting aircraft such as commercial Boeing 747s and McDonnell Douglas DC-10s, which could each potentially carry dozens of ALCMs. It was meanwhile decided that JCMPO would continue to manage the program and conduct the ALCM flyoff, but that this program would also include operational tests by SAC crews.

To prepare for the flyoff, both General Dynamics and Boeing went back to the drawing board to develop a missile specifically tailored to the missions to be evaluated. The former created the AGM-109 variant of the BGM-109. Boeing produced a new AGM-86B (aka "ALCM-B"), a substantial redesign of the original concept. Meanwhile, an ALCM Extended Range Vehicle (ERV) variant was designed,

Crews from the 92nd Bombardment Wing load AGM-86B ALCMs aboard a B-52G during the November 1985 Strategic Air Command Combat Weapons Loading Competition at Ellsworth Air Force Base. (USAF photo by Staff Sergeant Rose Reynolds)

AGM-86C Conventional Air-Launched Cruise Missile (CALCM)
Subvariant Evolution *(USAF)*

Block 0: The original baseline CALCM, with a first-generation GPS navigation system and a blast fragmentation warhead.

Block I: The Improved CALCM, with a second-generation GPS navigation system, an improved blast fragmentation warhead, and production improvements.

Block IA: The Precision Accuracy Retrofit, with a third-generation GPS anti-jam navigation system with precision strike accuracy and steep terminal dive capability.

Block II MWS: Hard Target Capability through the Multiple Warhead System (MWS), plus a third-generation GPS anti-jam navigation system with precision strike accuracy.

Block II AUP-3M: Hard Target Capability through the Advanced Unitary Penetrator (AUP-3M), plus a third-generation GPS anti-jam navigation system with precision strike accuracy.

considered, and abandoned by Boeing in favor of the larger AGM-86B. Half again bigger than the AGM-86A, it was 20 feet 9 inches long with a wingspan of 12 feet. As with the AGM-86A, the wings were folded into the fuselage and designed to be deployed "switchblade" style when the missile was ejected from its launcher.

Externally, the larger AGM-86B differed from the pre-production test models in that the duck-like nose was changed to a new all-metal "whale-shaped" nose that was intended to reduce its radar cross section. There were notable improvements. Thanks to the work of the team headed by Boeing ALCM's Chief Engineer Henry Runkel, the 28 metal forgings used in the AGM-86A were reduced to a mere 4 in the AGM-86B, which in turn reduced weight, assembly

time, and cost. To reduce production costs, Boeing had also replaced the steel-forged elevon housing for one machined from a titanium casting, and aluminum elevons had been replaced by ones made of graphite epoxy.

The AGM-86B weighed 3,200 pounds and was powered by a Williams F107-WR-100 or F107-WR-101 turbofan engine delivering 600 pounds of thrust as well as a cruising speed of around 550 mph. It had a range of about 1,500 miles, double that of the Hound Dog. For the flyoff, the air force stipulated that the engines be fueled with high-density JP-9, rather than the typical JP-4 fuel.

As the program progressed, the second Strategic Arms Limitation Treaty (SALT II) was negotiated. Signed by Jimmy Carter and Leonid Brezhnev in Vienna in June 1979

AGM-86C Conventional Air-Launched Cruise Missiles (CALCM) on the production line at the Boeing Space Center in Kent, Washington. (Boeing)

on the eve of the ALCM flyoff, SALT II specifically limited Air-Launched Cruise Missiles to a range of no more than 2,500 kilometers (1,553 miles). The range of the AGM-86B was specifically taken into consideration in developing the stipulations.

Nearly three years passed between the last test flight of an AGM-86A and the first flight of the AGM-86B. The ALCM flyoff began on 19 July 1979 with the first AGM-109A launch and proceeded with the AGM-86B debut on 3 August 1979. General Dynamics was perceived to be more than just those 15 days ahead of its rival because the BGM-109 Tomahawk program had more than 37 flight hours under its belt, while the AGM-86A had fewer than 3 flight hours. The Tomahawk was also ahead of the ALCM because of the lengthy development time required for the new AGM-86B variant, though General Dynamics had expended extra development time of its own adapting an air-launched AGM-109 variant from the BGM-109 base model.

"Boeing and General Dynamics each made 10 test flights," reported *Time* magazine correspondent Jerry Hannifin, who witnessed the tests. "Most of them were held over the bleak wastelands of the Utah Test and Training Range, near Dugway, Utah. The missiles were programmed to sprint at 500 mph round and round an aerial race course 100 miles long by 30 miles wide. In later tests, some cruises were dropped from B-52s 60 miles out in the Pacific and

programmed to fly back over California and Nevada to Utah. Air force F-4 Phantom chase planes closely followed to observe and take over the missiles by radio control if anything went wrong."

Hannifin spoke of watching a "missile belting along at 500 mph across the desert about 10 feet above the ground." He went on to say that "the flights were not without their hair-raising moments. As the military looked on, the two companies' project managers pushed the weapons to fly tighter and tighter maneuvers, lower and lower, in order to test the equipment. Both suffered four crashes, but General Dynamics clearly came out the worse. Two of its missiles slammed into some isolated California scrubland during overland flights. . . . On another faulty flight, the wings failed to unfold and the missile plunged into the Pacific like a rock. Boeing's flops were far less dramatic: two stemmed from communications foul-ups with the chase planes, one from programming errors, and one from engine failure after 2½ hours of intricate maneuvering."

The bottom line, from Hannifin's point of view, was that "Boeing fundamentally won the contest on the basis of superior engineering. The Boeing missile was able to fly closer to rough terrain without any loss of target accuracy than its competitor. It had a better aerodynamic design for air launchings than the torpedo-like General Dynamics entry, which was a modification of a Submarine-Launched Missile

Technicians at work on the Air-Launched Cruise Missile production line at the Boeing Space Center in Kent, Washington. (Courtesy of William A. Rice, Boeing)

that the company had already made for the U.S. Navy."

Each missile had six successful flights and four failures, with Boeing logging 31.7 flight hours to 22.2 for General Dynamics. Both contractors managed to recover two of the flight test missiles, though Boeing made five attempts to do so. After the 10th Tomahawk flight in February 1980, the matter went to the Source Selection Evaluation Board (SSEB), comprised of officers from both services.

Time reported that "the rivalry between Boeing and General Dynamics also involved executive-suite maneuvering. Last December, in the middle of the competitive flyoffs, Oliver C. Boileau, president of Boeing's aerospace division and the official directly responsible for the missile, resigned to become president of General Dynamics. He thus ended up on both sides of the race. One of the first congratulatory calls received at Boeing headquarters last week after the contract winner was announced was from the versatile Boileau."

Given that Walter Locke, an admiral, was in charge at Joint Cruise Missiles Project Office (JCMPO), there had been those at both Boeing and the air force who feared that the navy's General Dynamics missile might have an inside track, but this was not to be the case. As Hannifin observed and as SSEB confirmed, while both missiles met the performance goals set by the air force, the mission failures suffered by General Dynamics were more serious and the AGM-86B had the potential for lower maintenance costs.

In turn, it did not take long for the Source Selection Advisory Council (SSAC), comprised of even higher-ranking officers, to conclude unanimously that the AGM-86B had won the flyoff. On 25 March 1980, Secretary of the Air Force Hans Mark announced that Boeing was to be awarded a contract for 3,418 AGM-86B ALCMs.

Mark said that the AGM-86B was picked because its guidance system was more accurate, its aerodynamic qualities were better for terrain following, and it was more easily maintained in the field.

In a 7 April *Time* magazine cover story, Hannifin and Joseph Kane wrote that "it was the biggest single Air Force contract since the Vietnam War, and it is almost certain to be remembered as the arms deal that propelled the U.S. into the weapons-bristling decade of the 1980s. The prize was the $4 billion [over $11 billion in current dollars] air-launched, cruise missile system that the U.S. is counting on to maintain a strategic edge over the Soviet Union for much of the remainder of the 20th century."

Indeed, it would be.

As noted previously, McDonnell Douglas, with Litton Industries as its subcontractor, was already part of the ALCM program for guidance system development. The company would now together earn about $1.4 billion for the navigational electronic package, while Teledyne and Williams would split the $1 billion of the powerplant budget.

Later in April 1980, Isham Linder, the director of Defense Test and Evaluation (DDTE) at the Defense Department, observed with less hyperbole that "the ALCM air vehicle is potentially capable of meeting operational requirements. There were no major problems found in the basic design, [therefore] there are no test-related issues which preclude commitment to production of the AGM-86B."

Meanwhile, the Air Force Testing and Evaluation Center (AFTEC) continued to evaluate the AGM-86B. In a round of tests from June 1980 through January 1982, test objectives included comparability with the Offensive Avionics Systems (OAS) of a B-52, the Electronic System Test Set (ESTS), and reliability and maintainability issues. Under "store and forget," the missiles were loaded on pylons for 36 months between ESTS tests, which included the altimeter, the con-

A specially designed remote control hydraulic trailer is used to attach a pylon carrying six AGM-86B ALCMs to the wing of a B-52G at Fairchild AFB in May 1984. (U.S. Air Force photo by Staff Sergeant Bob Simons)

trols, and the guidance system. On a 30-month rotation, missiles were returned to the factory for an engine change and a fuel check.

During the 1980–1982 operational test round, the AGM-86B amassed 48.5 hours of flight time and a 93-percent success rate compared to a 60-percent success rate in the flyoff.

Nevertheless, in September 1981, AFTEC concluded that "based on testing to date, operational effectiveness and operational suitability are both rated deficient when measured against the test thresholds established by the user," noting deficiencies in terrain-following and reliability, and being too heavy for its wing area and engine power. The latter resulted in a large turning radius and limited climbing ability.

Cold Warrior Deployment

The first B-52G bomber equipped with fixed ALCM pylons arrived at Griffiss Air Force Base in New York on 15 August 1981 and was assigned to the 416th Bombardment Wing. The plan at the time was to spend $650 million to convert 168 Stratofortresses at the Oklahoma City Air Logistic Center at Tinker Air Force Base.

The first 13 AGM-86Bs were delivered two weeks later. The 416th, which had operated light and medium bombers during World War II, had been reactivated as a Strategic Air Command B-52 unit in 1963. Griffiss was selected in part based on the existence of TERCOM maps of the route between there and Soviet targets. The first SAC ALCM squadron, the 668th Bombardment Squadron of the 416th Wing, was declared operational in December 1982.

During the next few years, subsequent deployments were with the 7th Bombardment Wing at Carswell Air Force Base in Texas, the 92nd Bombardment Wing at Fairchild Air Force Base in Washington, the 97th Bombardment Wing at Eaker Air Force Base in Arkansas, the 319th Bombardment Wing at Grand Forks Air Force Base in North Dakota, and the 379th Bombardment Wing at Wurtsmith Air Force Base in Michigan. The payload for each missile was a 300-pound W80 thermonuclear warhead with a yield that was variable up to 150 kilotons.

To reduce operational costs, the air force authorized the use of JP-10 jet fuel instead of the high-density JP-9 fuel used in the flight test program. The cost savings was the current equivalent of more than $100 a gallon. The missiles were deployed fully fueled under a "store and forget" doctrine that had first been used by air force with the SRAM.

ALCM operational testing, which continued after deployment, included TERCOM flights over northern Canada because, in the words of Kenneth Werrell, "Canadian terrain and foliage resemble that of the Soviet Union; this test series will provide the most realistic test of the system."

The concept for a live operational mission would involve a B-52 departing from a SAC base on the northern tier of the United States, crossing the Arctic, and approaching the northern coast of the Soviet Union. At this point, the bomber would descend to a low-level approach to avoid Soviet ground control intercept radar.

This was similar to the scenario that would have been executed earlier in the Cold War with B-52s armed with nuclear and thermonuclear gravity bombs. The difference with the AGM-86B, as with the Hound Dog before it, was that the missile would be fired at standoff range, while

A May 1984 view of Staff Sergeant Craig Van Wagenen of the 92nd Bomb Wing at Fairchild AFB working at the left side station of a B-52G ALCM control panel. (U.S. Air Force photo by Staff Sergeant Bob Simons)

the bomber reversed course. For example, an attack on the Leningrad-Moscow-Kuybyshev-Sverdlovsk arc would involve a missile launch over the Barents Sea.

With their TERCOM and inertial navigation system continually updated, the AGM-86Bs would chart a circuitous, low-level dash to their designated and preprogrammed targets, avoiding Soviet air defenses as they went.

The plan was to modify selected B-52G and B-52H Stratofortress aircraft to each carry a dozen AGM-86Bs externally on two underwing pylons, adding about 25,000 pounds of weight. ALCM-capable internal Common Strategic Rotary Launchers (CSRL) were not initially compatible, but the plan was for AGM-86Bs to be installed gradually after the bombers were deployed with externally mounted missiles.

Eventually, 98 B-52Gs and all 96 existing B-52Hs were equipped to carry six ALCMs on each of two underwing pylons, and 82 B-52Hs were retrofitted to carry ALCMs on their internal rotary launchers. By 1994, though, the entire air force B-52G fleet had been withdrawn from service, leaving only the B-52Hs.

While the B-52 was clearly the obvious first choice for an ALCM launch platform, the air force considered many other large airframes, ordering Boeing to study its compati-

bility with existing Boeing jetliners such as the Models 707 and 747, as well as with existing military transports such as the C-141 and C-5. While large transports were not considered ideal platforms for penetrating enemy airspace, proponents cited their availability and the number of ALCMs that could be carried. The studies showed that a C-5 could carry up to 72 AGM-86Bs, while a 747 could accommodate between 48 and 90 depending on configuration. None of these ideas ever left the drawing board.

The B-1 bomber had been canceled in 1977 and was therefore not part of the strategic planning under which the ALCM was being developed. When the B-1 program was reinstated by the Reagan administration in 1981, and the new B-1B variant made its debut in 1984, SAC initially decided to use it as a penetration bomber and maintain only the B-52 in a standoff role with ALCMs. However, by 1987, the B-1B was being tested with ALCMs.

The first batch of 225 AGM-86Bs ordered in 1980 were followed by a series of additional purchases, with the last of a total of 1,715 missiles delivered through October 1986 when production ended.

In a pair of consecutive milestones, the AGM-86B ALCM survived the end of the Cold War in 1991 and the end of the Strategic Air Command in 1992, as SAC was merged into the U.S. Air Force Air Combat Command (ACC). When nuclear-capable assets of ACC were transferred to the new Air Force Global Strike Command (AFGSC) in 2009, these included the AGM-86Bs.

The Attack of the CALCM

Twice previously in this book, and so often in other readings about technology, we encounter situations that demand a piece of hardware that has never existed be created, situations where necessity is the mother of invention. So it was in the wake of Operation Eldorado Canyon in April 1986. A massive American air attack on terrorist lairs and military infrastructure inside Muammar Qaddafi's Libya had succeeded, but at the cost of a U.S. Air Force F-111F and its crew. This was the catalyst for the development of a conventionally armed standoff weapon that could have accomplished a mission of this type without the loss of American life.

By this time, the air force had launched 10 Navstar satellites, and the Global Position System (GPS) was revolutionizing global navigation for the U.S. armed forces (civilian access to the program was not yet available). It was now possible to achieve an accuracy in cruise missiles that could not have been imagined at any time in the history of these weapons stretching back to World War I.

In June 1986, under a secret air force contract (identified by the Federation of American Scientists as F34601-91-C-1156), Boeing began a conversion program under which the W80 thermonuclear warheads were removed from 105 AGM-86Bs and replaced with 2,000-pound high-explosive blast fragmentation warheads.

Redesignated as AGM-86C and known as Conventional Air-Launched Cruise Missiles (CALCM), these also incorporated a new guidance system in which a multi-channel GPS receiver was integrated with the LN-35 inertial navigation system.

A tight lid of secrecy was screwed down onto the CALCM program specifically because the positions of the small number of GPS satellites were known, and potential enemies could perhaps use that information to jam the CALCMs. According to Boeing, even before the flight tests began in August 1987, the "program successfully met schedule, cost, and missile-performance goals. Engineering design for the conventional configuration was developed at an accelerated pace, with hardware and software critical design reviews conducted after only five and seven months, respectively, from program go-ahead. Successful flight test occurred within the first year of the program, and the first four production missiles were delivered within 13 months of contract go-ahead."

The CALCMs were quietly placed in bomb-proof storage igloos at Barksdale Air Force Base in Louisiana, pending possible future use. Boeing notes that "operational capability was achieved in January 1988," though the air force would not officially declare the CALCMs operational until three years later, and their existence remained undisclosed until 1992. Indeed, the CALCM program was to remain an officially classified program for a year past its baptism of fire in January 1991 during Operation Desert Storm.

In August 1990, when Iraq's Saddam Hussein decided to send his army to occupy Kuwait and to threaten Saudi Arabia, the outside world responded with a massive military buildup, which the United States, the largest contributor of forces, designated as Operation Desert Shield. After discour-

A close-up view of eight AGM-86B Air-Launched Cruise Missiles loaded on the rotary launcher in the bomb bay of a B-52G Stratofortress aircraft. (USAF)

aging the anticipated invasion of Saudi Arabia, the next step would be a military campaign aimed at liberating Kuwait. As part of its arsenal, the U.S. Air Force decided to break out and break in the CALCM.

General Buster Glosson, the director of Desert Shield and Desert Storm campaign plans at U.S. Central Command Air Forces (CENTAF), later commented, "We stood them up on alert because we were trying to give the National

Command authorities some options." Indeed, this was exactly the mission for which the CALCMs had been created.

The strike mission, the first American offensive cruise missile operation since World War II, was assigned to the 2nd Bombardment Wing's 596th Bombardment Squadron at Barksdale, commanded by Lieutenant Colonel Jay Beard. One of his crews had been involved in the CALCM flight test program, but the others had to be trained, and trained quickly because in August 1990, no one knew when Iraqi forces might invade Saudi Arabia.

Because the CALCM was then so deeply classified, its name could not be spoken, so the air force code named it "Senior Surprise." Code names with that prefix had long been associated with programs involving secret aircraft. For example, "Senior Trend" was related to the F-117A Nighthawk while "Senior Bowl" and "Senior Crown" were associated with the SR-71.

So secret was Senior Surprise in 1990, personnel involved in using it had to adopt a code name for the code name! The AGM-86Cs were nicknamed "Secret Squirrels" after the 1960s Hanna-Barbera cartoon character of the same name. As Major Steve Hess, the chief weapon system officer for the 596th, told John Tirpak of *Air Force Magazine* in 1994, "We couldn't say the real code name out loud, and [Secret Squirrel] had the same initials."

The list of targets was continuously updated through fresh digital maps that were brought in from SAC headquarters. By the middle of January, the list was narrowed down to eight. These involved Iraq's electrical grid and communications nodes, mainly around Baghdad, but also included a telephone exchange in Basra and powerplants in Mosul.

On the rainy afternoon of 16 January, 7 B-52Gs with 57 aircrewmen and 39 Secret Squirrels took off from Barksdale on a marathon, nonstop, 14,000-mile round-trip flight to Iraq. Each bomber carried a relief pilot and an additional navigator, and the crews took turns napping on two air mattresses that had been brought aboard each Stratofortress.

"It wasn't really sleeping," Hess told Tirpak. "It was more like lying down and dehydrating for two hours."

While the AGM-86B remained on nuclear alert, the AGM-86C was going to war. Refueling over the Azores and the Mediterranean, the bombers reached the war zone at mid-morning on 17 January, timing their arrival to follow the first wave of strike aircraft that had flown from in-theater bases throughout the morning. From a launch point over northern Saudi Arabia, the missiles, except four that suffered software glitches and were held back, were launched in a staggered sequence.

The expectation for the Secret Squirrels had been that they would take out 80 percent of the assigned targets, but post-strike reconnaissance and analysis indicated a success rate of between 85- and 91-percent accuracy. It was certainly a far cry from what had been achieved in most of the pre-GPS cruise missile testing that had been done through the previous decades.

After suffering severe weather that seriously complicated aerial refueling on the return trip, the bombers finally reached Barksdale at dusk on 17 January, 35 hours after departing. This concluded what was, at the time, the longest strike mission in the history of aerial warfare.

The crews were admonished to say nothing about their epic mission, and nothing was said publicly about the CALCM. As Boeing points out in its CALCM briefing paper, "Since the CALCM missile conversion was a Special Access program, it was not until January 1992 that the Department of Defense publicly acknowledged its existence" with the release of the *Final Report to Congress: Conduct of the Persian Gulf War*. The Defense Department confirmed that on the 16–17 January mission, the 7 B-52Gs had launched 35 AGM-86C CALCM cruise missiles against "military communications sites and power generation and transmission facilities" in southern Iraq. The terms "Senior Surprise" and "Secret Squirrels" were still not revealed.

"It's incredible what people say in hindsight," General Glosson said in response to media suggestions that the 35-hour mission was somehow a publicity stunt. "Had my interest been to just demonstrate a new capability, I would have done it two or three times and not kept the program secret afterward. We used those weapons because . . . it seemed the logical thing to do. Plain and simple . . . it saved lives. If we had lost a half dozen [manned tactical aircraft] attacking those targets, it would have been unforgivable."

Saddam Hussein's regime would feel the sting of the CALCM again later in the decade. In response to his brutal repression of an uprising by the Kurdish minority around Urbil in northern Iraq, the United States launched a series of air attacks as part of Operation Desert Strike. In this mission, two B-52Hs from the 2nd Bombardment Wing flew

An air-to-air front view of a B-52G Stratofortress from the 416th Bombardment Wing armed with AGM-86B Air-Launched Cruise Missiles. (USAF)

another nonstop, 14,000-mile round-trip flight, this time from Andersen Air Force Base on Guam to attack air defense sites in southern Iraq with 13 AGM-86C CALCMs on 3 September 1996.

Two years later, during Operation Desert Fox, the U.S. Air Force 2nd and 5th Bombardment Wings operating out of Diego Garcia in the Indian Ocean flew 3,500 miles to strike Iraq. On the night of 17 December 1998, a dozen B-52Hs launched 74 CALCMs against targets that included Republican Guard barracks, command and control facilities, and some of Saddam's own palaces. On 18 December, a pair of B-52Hs returned to launch 16 CALCMs.

In 1999, under NATO's Operation Allied Force, CALCM-armed B-52Hs from the 2nd Bombardment Wing at Barksdale AFB, staging through RAF Fairford in Britain, deployed in support of actions taken against Serbia and Ser-

bian forces in Kosovo. On 24 March, as NATO launched its air operations, the roughly 210 American aircraft included B-52Hs armed with CALCMs. According to Benjamin Lambeth in *NATO's Air War for Kosovo* (Rand Corporation Report MR1365), "The AGM-86C CALCMs launched against hardened enemy structures by six B-52s flying outside Yugoslav airspace. The latter were the first shots fired in the operation."

Whereas the success rate for the Secret Squirrels had been high during Operation Desert Storm, the same seemed not to be true for the opening night of Allied Force.

Citing reporting by John Morocco, David Fulghum, and Robert Wall in the 5 April issue of *Aviation Week and Space Technology*, Lambeth concluded, "The effectiveness of these initial standoff attacks was not impressive. During the first two weeks, no B-52 succeeded in launching all eight of its

A B-52H Stratofortress releases an unarmed AGM-86B Air-Launched Cruise Missile (ALCM) on 22 September 2014 over the Utah Test and Training Range during a Nuclear Weapons System Evaluation Program sortie. Conducted by airmen from the 2nd Bombardment Wing, Barksdale AFB, the launch was part of an end-to-end operational evaluation of Eighth Air Force capability to pull an ALCM from storage, load it aboard an aircraft, execute a simulated combat mission, and successfully deliver the weapon from the aircraft to its final target. (USAF photo by Staff Sergeant Roidan Carlson)

CALCMs. In one instance, six out of eight were said to have failed."

By the end of April, the bombers from Barksdale had been augmented by an additional aircraft from the 5th Bombardment Wing at Minot Air Force Base in North Dakota, which had deployed to Fairford on 29 April. According to a Defense Department briefing the same day, the B-52Hs were armed with CALCMs. The modest existing stocks of AGM-86Cs were largely depleted in April, so the majority of American cruise missile operations during Allied Force involved the use of shorter-range U.S. Navy Tomahawks (see chapter 9).

Throughout the 1990s, meanwhile, Boeing and the air force were continuing a series of further CALCM conversions as well as upgrades to those conversions. The original 105 baseline (later called Block 0) CALCM conversions were delivered through June 1993, and followed by June 1995 and March 1996 orders for a total of 200 Block I CALCM conversions. Delivered through 1997, these had a second-generation GPS system with improved accuracy as well as other improved systems. All these conversion and retrofit activities were conducted at various Boeing facilities,

including those at Oak Ridge, Tennessee, and St. Charles, Missouri.

In December 1996, Boeing demonstrated the precision the GPS-aided inertial navigation with a Block I CALCM that flew for 4.5 hours, performed a steep terminal dive, and impacted on a target within 2.5 meters [8 feet] of the aim point. As noted at the time, "a steep dive increases the effectiveness of penetrating warheads against a wide range of hard and deeply buried targets."

Based in part on this demonstration, the air force contracted with Boeing in April 1998 to upgrade existing Block 0 and Block I CALCMs with precision strike and vertical dive capability. These missiles, referred to as "Block IA CALCMs," were retrofitted with a "precision accuracy kit."

This kit employed a third-generation GPS Receiver Interface Unit/Precision (GRIU/P) with advanced navigation software built by Interstate Electronics Corporation, as well as a Harris Corporation GPS anti-jam electronics module and antenna for what Boeing called "a significant increase in jamming immunity."

The air force officially noted in 2010 that under the 1998 order, "upgraded avionics packages were retrofitted

An unarmed AGM-86B Air-Launched Cruise Missile maneuvers over the Utah Test and Training Range en route to its target on 22 September 2014. The test was managed by the then-new Air Force Nuclear Weapons Center's Air Delivered Capabilities Directorate (ND). (USAF photo by Staff Sergeant Roidan Carlson)

into all existing CALCM so all AGM-86C missiles are electronically identical."

After the AGM-86C with its blast fragmentation warhead came the AGM-86D with a "hard target" penetrating warhead. The catalyst was the "bunker-busting" requirement that arose from operations against Saddam Hussein's hardened command posts.

In 1997, a Foreign Comparative Test (FCT) program was undertaken to evaluate a British multi-stage warhead (MSW) for use in what would become the AGM-86D CALCM variant. Known as Bomb, Royal Ordnance Augmented CHarge (BROACH), the weapon has a two-stage warhead with a shaped charge in the lead to cut through armor, concrete, or dirt.

In 1999, it was decided that instead of BROACH, the CALCM would incorporate the 1,200-pound Lockheed Martin AUP-3 Advanced Unitary Penetrator warhead in the AGM-86D. The BROACH warhead was later incorporated into the Raytheon AGM-154C Joint Stand-off Weapon (JSOW), which was first deployed with the U.S. Navy in 2005.

The AGM-86D, also known as the CALCM Block II, was first flight tested by the air force in November 2001, being launched from a B-52H over the White Sands Missile Range in New Mexico. Two years later, it was first used in combat during Operation Iraqi Freedom. In operations taking place in Iraq between 19 March and 30 April, the U.S. Air Force launched 153 AGM-86C and AGM-86Ds, more CALCMs than had been used in all other previous operations against Iraq combined.

After the Strategic Air Command was disbanded in 1992, the ALCMs, along with SAC's bomber fleet, were reassigned to the arsenal of the U.S. Air Force Air Combat Command (ACC) until 2009. Because of an incident involving the transport of unguarded AGM-129s in 2007 (discussed in detail in chapter 10), all the air force's nuclear-capable assets were transferred from ACC in 2009 to the new Air Force Global Strike Command (AFGSC), an organization with a mission, and the official lineage and honors, of SAC. In turn, AFGSC is the air force component within the joint United States Strategic Command (STRATCOM).

According to a 2010 U.S. Air Force fact sheet, the service then possessed 1,142 nuclear-armed AGM-86Bs, 437 AGM-86Cs, and 50 AGM-86Ds. That the ALCM has a key ongoing role within STRATCOM is illustrated by comments by STRATCOM Commander Admiral Cecil Haney, who told the Pentagon press corps on 22 October 2015 that the military must change the culture so that every soldier, sailor, airman, marine, and civilian recognizes that "they're under attack all the time," adding that the ALCM will be "decades past its expected lifetime" before it is retired.

Chapter 7

BIRTH OF THE TOMAHAWK

For most of the Tomahawk test program, the U.S. Navy launched its missiles from the Pacific and recovered them in the Nevada desert. Here, a Tomahawk crosses the California coastline en route to the Tonopah Test Range. (U.S. Navy)

The Tomahawk family of missiles, still in service after four decades, is the most widely produced and widely used cruise missile type since the V-1. Through the end of the twentieth century, more than 4,000 had been built and 1,257 had been launched in combat operations through 2017.

The program originated out of an interest by the U.S. Navy in the development of sea-skimming anti-ship missiles. In the two decades after World War II, tactical missile development by the navy had focused mainly, albeit not exclusively, on their use against land or air targets. Anti-ship missile studies were already ongoing by 1967, both by the navy and by contractors, especially McDonnell Douglas.

The concept received an unexpected jumpstart in October of that year when the news came in of the sinking of the Israeli destroyer *Eliat* in 1967 by an Egyptian patrol boat firing a Soviet-made Raduga P-15 Termit anti-ship missile.

This incident breathed new life into anti-ship missile studies and led to the Harpoon missile program, a project so named because submarines, aka "whales," were an intended target of the planned weapon. In November 1970, the Defense System Acquisition Review Council (DSARC) authorized development by McDonnell Douglas of anti-ship missiles carrying a 250-pound conventional warhead that had a range of about 50 miles. Both air-launched and ship-launched Harpoons were to be developed under

During its early testing, the YBGM-109 was known simply as the "General Dynamics Cruise Missile." The name "Tomahawk" was not formally bestowed until it prevailed in its flyoff with the Ling-Temco-Vought YBGM-110 in 1976. (Convair Division)

the respective designations AGM-84 and RGM-84. In January 1972, submarine-launched UGM-84s were added to the program. The first Harpoon test flight came in July 1972, and the missiles became operational in 1977. Later variants remain in service to this day.

Defining the U.S. Navy Cruise Missile

As the Harpoon program was under way in the early 1970s, both the U.S. Navy and U.S. Air Force were beginning their parallel development of a new generation of cruise missiles with a much longer range and a nuclear warhead capability. As noted in chapter 6, both services had abandoned the cruise missile concept some years before, but now revisited it thanks to the wonders of Terrain Contour Matching (TERCOM) guidance.

As discussed in chapter 6, the road that led to the air force AGM-86 ALCM passed through a series of predecessor concepts such as SCAD, SCAM, and SCUD. Likewise, the navy was feeling its way toward the eventual Tomahawk.

A McDonnell Douglas RGM-84 Harpoon short-range anti-ship missile is launched from a canister launcher aboard the cruiser USS Leahy near the Pacific Missile Test Center in the Pacific Ocean off California in April 1983. The Harpoon was developed at around the same time as the Tomahawk, which was originally conceived as a long-range anti-ship missile. (DOD)

Several very diverse proposals began to take shape. An obvious consideration was a longer-range Harpoon variant because it would have been more quickly and easily achieved. An alternate program proposed in 1971 was the Submarine Tactical Anti-ship Weapons System (STAWS), a larger missile with a 500-mile range. In 1972, a new name and acronym for the conceptual missiles was coined by Secretary of Defense Melvin Laird: Submarine-Launched Cruise Missiles (SLCM).

Multiple proposals addressed how it would be stored and launched. In the beginning, the only launch platform under consideration was a submarine, but there was a question

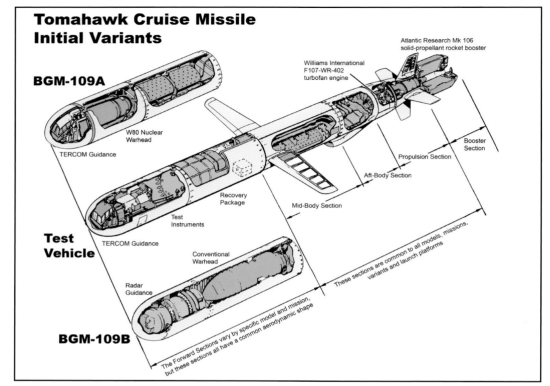

Tomahawk Cruise Missile Initial Variants

BGM-109A

Atlantic Research Mk 106 solid-propellant rocket booster

Williams International F107-WR-402 turbofan engine

W80 Nuclear Warhead

TERCOM Guidance

Booster Section

Propulsion Section

Aft-Body Section

Recovery Package

Mid-Body Section

Test Instruments

Test Vehicle

TERCOM Guidance

Conventional Warhead

These sections are common to all models, missions, variants and launch platforms

Radar Guidance

BGM-109B

The Forward Sections vary by specific model and mission, but these sections all have a common aerodynamic shape

of whether it should be launched horizontally like a torpedo or vertically like an SLBM.

There was also a question of whether existing attack or ballistic missile submarines should be converted or a new class of boats be built from scratch. A champion of the latter idea was Admiral Hyman Rickover, the so-called "father of the nuclear navy," who had pioneered nuclear propulsion for ships and who headed the United States Naval Reactors office from 1949 to 1982. The irascible and outspoken admiral saw the SLCM as an opportunity to expand his nuclear submarine fleet.

Against a backdrop of ambiguity about the launch scenario arose a wide spectrum of proposals. To note some examples of missiles designed to be retrofitted into Poseidon SLBM launch tubes, Ling-Temco-Vought (LTV) proposed a 29.3-foot missile weighing 10,631 pounds, while the Lockheed proposal was 26.5 feet long and weighed 8,316 pounds. The offering of the Convair Division of General Dynamics was 28 feet long and weighed 7,775 pounds. All had a diameter of about 32 inches.

Other missiles encapsulated in newly designed tubes ranged from a 2,890-pound McDonnell Douglas missile with a 23-inch diameter to a 35-inch, 9,610-pound Convair weapon.

In November 1972, the U.S. Navy decided that the new SLCMs would be launched from existing torpedo tubes, *not* SLBM tubes. This, in turn, limited the size of the cruise missile to a 21-inch diameter and a length of around 20 feet.

After evaluating a number of proposals through the ensuing year, the U.S. Navy narrowed the field to two SLBM program finalists in December 1973. Convair would build a demonstrator missile under the designation BGM-109 that was powered by a Williams F107-WR-100 turbofan engine. Meanwhile, Ling-Temco-Vought would produce another missile as the BGM-110, with a Teledyne CAE 471-11DX turbofan. In the designation, the "B" stands for multiple launch environments, "G" for ground attack, and "M" for missile.

Each missile was designed with an innovative system to deploy the wings after launch. The BGM-109's wings were retracted into the fuselage, one slightly higher the other, then snapped out like the blades of scissors. The one-piece BGM-110 wing pivoted on its centerpoint to 90 degrees after launch.

A flyoff was to be conducted in which the two would be evaluated comparatively and a winner chosen. A parallel guidance system evaluation would take place between systems developed by McDonnell Douglas and by LTV's E-Systems, the original developer of TERCOM, with the winner being installed in the winning missile. The guidance systems were flight tested in manned aircraft, not in the missiles.

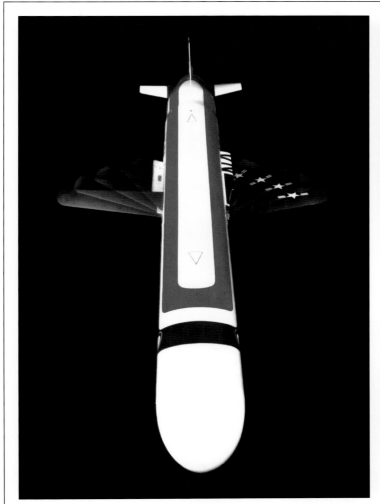

This time-lapse photo demonstrates how the wings of the General Dynamics Tomahawk fold out of the fuselage after launch. (Convair Division)

Convair's Grant Goulet studies a computer monitor as he works on a Tomahawk tail cone at the General Dynamics missile facility at Sycamore Canyon near San Diego in July 1986. At the time, the company was touting its "Paperless Factory of the Future," a "computerized work instruction system for cruise missile assembly at test operations." (Author's collection)

General Dynamics' technicians examine a Tomahawk forward fuselage section at the Convair Division facility at Kearny Mesa north of San Diego. (Author's collection)

A Convair Tomahawk cruise missile skims at low level over a desert landscape. Thanks to TERCOM, the Tomahawk could fly low and virtually undetectable. (Convair Division)

A rare photo of a Tomahawk being pursued by a Convair F-106B Delta Dart chase plane in the markings of the Air Defense Weapons Center at Tyndall Air Force Base in Florida. (Author's collection)

Independent of the flyoff, Chief of Naval Operations Admiral James Holloway had already signed off on the name "Tomahawk" for whichever missile won.

Two Flyoffs

Not one but two flyoffs marked the road to an operational Tomahawk, though the second one would lie on an unanticipated detour. First came the contest between the BGM-109 from the Convair Division of General Dynamics and the Ling-Temco-Vought BGM-110.

As Kenneth Werrell described, "The competition required each contractor to qualify its missile with one successful transition from underwater launch to inflight glide on two launches. Convair achieved success [in glide tests] on 13 and 15 February 1976. Vought did not fair so well. On the Vought missile's first test, the hydraulically actuated torpedo tube failed, a failure correctly charged to the Navy. On the second attempt on 24 February, the missile broached the surface but the wing did not deploy. The Navy scheduled another test for 24 March, but on 8 March, canceled the program."

Based on the test failures and problems with cost overruns, the navy chose Convair as the prime airframe contractor. Williams and Teledyne were picked as dual-source providers for the engine, while Atlantic Research and United Technologies were selected as dual sources for the Type 106 booster rockets. McDonnell Douglas was picked to build the guidance system. The first powered flight of the BGM-109 came on 28 March.

As the U.S. Navy's Submarine-Launched Cruise Missile (SLCM) program was making its way to the final selection of the BGM-109 as its cruise missile of choice, the U.S. Air Force was following a similar path en route to its AGM-86 Air-Launched Cruise Missile (ALCM). In fact, the two programs were so close that the Boeing AGM-86 had made its first powered flight only three weeks before that of the BGM-109.

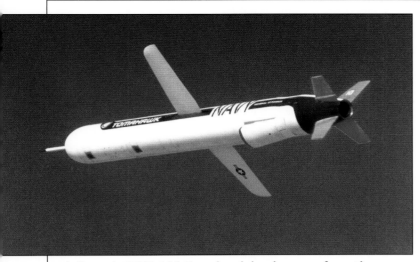

A Convair BGM-109 Tomahawk banks away from the camera plane during a test flight. (Convair Division)

As discussed in chapter 6, the Defense Systems Acquisition Review Council (DSARC) was meanwhile looking at the SLCM and ALCM through the same lens their predecessors of the 1940s had used to view the Regulus and Matador. Could not *one* of these cruise missiles be adapted to serve two masters? The move toward a jointly developed common cruise missile flowed directly from a DSARC meeting on 6 January 1977. The Carter administration, which took office that month, then mandated a single cruise missile for the two services. As noted in the previous chapter, the Joint Cruise Missiles Project Office (JCMPO) established in September 1977 had been directed to "achieve maximum commonality among the various missiles, specifically by using common engine and land-attack guidance systems."

As we have seen, the flyoff between the air force AGM-86 and the AGM-109 variant of the navy's BGM-109 began in 1979 and culminated in Boeing being awarded the ALCM contract in March 1980. In the meantime, both the navy and the air force briefly continued to look at air-launched Tomahawks under the general heading of the Medium-Range Air-to-Surface Missile (MRASM) program.

If a lesson had been learned from all these flyoffs, and it was learned only after MRASM was finally put to bed, it was that the AGM-86, designed from the start as an air-launched system, met the needs of the U.S. Air Force far better than any form of Convair AGM-109, and vice versa for the U.S. Navy.

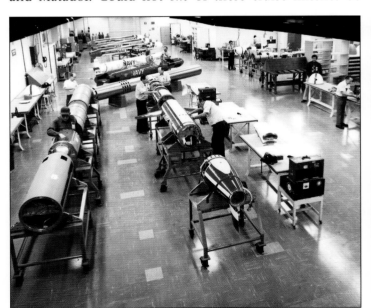

Early Tomahawk test birds with a variety of markings come together on the factory floor at the General Dynamics facility at Kearny Mesa. (Convair Division)

First Generation Tomahawk Variants

Before and during the ALCM evaluation in 1979, Convair continued to develop the BGM-109 Tomahawk for a variety of U.S. Navy applications. Originally conceived as a submarine-launched missile, it would be adapted for a wide array of surface ships. The erstwhile Submarine-Launched Cruise Missile (SLCM) had now become the *Sea*-Launched Cruise Missile. The acronym remained unchanged, but the spectrum of launch platforms and potential mission scenarios broadened considerably.

In service, the Tomahawks used for the original sea-launched, anti-ship mission were known as Tomahawk Anti-Ship Missiles (TASM), while three other variants, which were adapted for use against targets ashore, were all categorized as Tomahawk Land Attack Missiles (TLAM).

In the early years, the basic Tomahawk was configured into four visually similar variants, developed in parallel. The BGM-109A and BGM-109B were considered Block I missiles, and the BGM-109C and BGM-109D were Block II missiles, though they were all basically the same except for their payloads and guidance packages. The distinction was generally chronological, as the Block I missiles entered service by 1984 and the Block II missiles from 1986. All four variants were powered by the Williams International F107-W-400 turbofan engine, which delivered 600 pounds of thrust.

As they entered service, the designation prefix for these four missiles changed from BGM to RGM for surface-launched missiles, and from BGM to UGM for submarine-launched missiles. As noted previously, the AGM prefix denoted air-launched missiles. Through the years, these were extensively tested in several variations but not operationally deployed.

The RGM/UGM-109A was the Tomahawk Land Attack Missile-Nuclear (TLAM-N). Armed with a W80 thermonuclear weapon, it entered service in 1984, one year after the AGM-109B TASM. The RGM/UGM-109A had a range of up to 1,550 miles. With its booster, it weighed 3,180 pounds in its surface-launch configuration, and 3,260 when arming a submarine. Originally, 758 TLAM-Ns were planned, but only 350 were manufactured.

After the flyoff in which the BGM-109 was selected over the BGM-110, the first navy variant to be flight tested and to enter service was the BGM-109B TASM. The first TASM test

A Grumman A-6E Intruder armed with a Tomahawk at the Pacific Missile Test Center (PMTC) at NAS Point Mugu in California. The idea of an air-launched Tomahawk was briefly revived in 1983 under the Medium-Range Air-to-Surface Missile (MRASM) program. (Author's collection)

flight came on 6 December 1976. This was nine months after the first flight of a Tomahawk prototype, and more than two years before the flight testing of the air-launched variant. Coincidentally, however, for the first three flight tests, the TASM was air-launched from a U.S. Air Force B-52. The reason was to run tests of the missile without its booster. The first submarine launch of a BGM-109B was made from the USS *Barb* on 2 February 1978.

Despite early promise, the test program was not without glitches. On 25 July 1978, the press was invited to join Defense Secretary Harold Brown off California's San Clemente Island to watch two Tomahawks launched from the USS *Guitarro*, a Sturgeon class nuclear attack submarine. Also in attendance was Admiral Walter Locke, the JCMPO chief, as well as Admiral Donald Davis, the Pacific Fleet commander.

As Jack Jones of the *Los Angeles Times* reported, the missiles "tumbled ignominiously into the sea." Brown responded with what Jones called "a stiff smile," commenting, "This demonstrates what happens in a test program. It has its successes as well as its failures." Though Brown said, "This does not change my view of the cruise missile," he added that the Tomahawk "needs work."

The RGM/UGM-109B TASM first started rolling off the assembly line in 1982, entered service in 1983, and reached its full rate of production the following year. The payload

This artist's conception shows an air-launched Medium-Range Air-to-Surface Missile (MRASM) program Tomahawk releasing submunitions during a strike on a Warsaw Pact airfield. The MRASM was never deployed. (Convair Division)

was a 1,000-pound WDU-25B blast fragmentation warhead of the type originally developed for the AGM-12 Bullpup ground attack missile. The TASM weighed in at 3,190 pounds in its surface-launch configuration, and 3,270 when submarine-launched. The RGM/UGM-109B had a range of 300 miles.

The RGM/UGM-109C Tomahawk Land Attack Missile-Conventional (TLAM-C) was similar to the RGM/UGM-109A TLAM but armed with a 1,000-pound conventional WDU-25B unitary warhead like that of the RGM/UGM-109B TASM instead of a nuclear payload. The surface-launched TLAM-C weighed 3,435 pounds, while the submarine-launched variant weighed 3,300 pounds.

The navy's conventionally armed TLAM-C, like the air force AGM-86C CALCM, was kept under wraps. Though it was operational by 1986, it was not widely known to exist. Indeed, the public knew nothing about it until the fall of 1987. In the *New York Times* on 24 October, Richard Halloran wrote "The Navy has quietly created a new mission for submarines—firing cruise missiles with high-explosive, nonnuclear warheads at military targets ashore, according to Pentagon officials. Today, Department of Defense officials indicated, American attack submarines armed with cruise missiles carrying conventional warheads are on patrol near the Persian Gulf. . . . Submariners said the range and accuracy of cruise missiles had progressed further than they thought possible a few years ago. In the near future, officials in the cruise missile program said, pinpoint accuracy would be achieved at 3,000 miles. The submariners said that the range and accuracy would be improved by having a submarine fire a cruise missile, the guidance of which would then be picked up by a surface vessel, an aircraft, or a satellite equipped with advanced sensors and long-range control devices."

In 1980, under the Medium-Range Air-to-Surface Missile (MRASM) program, the idea of the air-launched Tomahawk was briefly and quixotically revived. Test vehicles were built and tested, air-dropped by A-6E Intruders, in 1983 by the Pacific Missile Test Center (PMTC) at NAS Point Mugu. Part of the idea was for a less expensive missile with a price tag about 60 percent that of existing TLAMs. Part of the savings would have been accomplished by replacing the Williams F107 turbofan with a less expensive Teledyne CAE J402-CA-401 turbojet. As part of MRASM, the U.S. Navy considered adapting TLAM-C for air launching under the designation AGM-109C, but the program never evolved.

Entering service in 1988, the RGM/UGM-109D Tomahawk Land Attack Missile-D (TLAM-D) was derived from the TLAM-C and is very similar to it except that it is armed with a warhead containing 166 BLU-97 submunitions called Combined Effects Bomblets (CEB). Each CEB weighed 3.6 pounds and was 6.6 inches by 2.5 inches in size. The surface-launched TLAM-D weighed 3,230 pounds, while the submarine-launched variant weighed 3,300 pounds.

A submarine-launched UGM-109 Tomahawk Land Attack Missile (TLAM) uses an air-burst explosion to destroy a decommissioned North American Aviation A-5 Vigilante during a 1 April 1986 test strike on San Clemente Island off the coast of California. (DOD)

According to a press briefing conducted by Lieutenant Commander Don Lewis on 26 August 1987, the first ocean-launched, submunition-deploying flight test of the TLAM-D had occurred the day before. Operational evaluation of the TLAM-D variant began in 1988, two years after its first successful flight, and it became operational in 1991.

The RGM/UGM-109E designation was reserved for an improved variant of the RGM/UGM-109B anti-ship TASM, but this project never went forward and the "E" designator was revived in the twenty-first century for the Block IV Tactical Tomahawk (see chapter 11).

The BGM-109F designation was set aside for a variant that was to have been armed with anti-airfield submunitions. This concept went nowhere as the BGM-109F but was revived briefly as the AGM-109H. (The BGM-109G designation went to the U.S. Air Force Ground-Launched Cruise Missile discussed in chapter 8.)

The AGM-109H was another MRASM concept, the air-launched air force equivalent of the navy's BGM-109F. Known as the Tomahawk Anti-Airfield Missile (TAAM), the AGM-109H would have been armed with the AVCO BLU-106B Boosted Kinetic Energy Penetrator (BKEP) submunitions. The BKEP dispenser, loaded into a full AGM-109H mockup carried by an A-4D Skyhawk was tested in early 1983 at the Mojave Test Range. The air force had already rejected an air-launched Tomahawk, and the navy never proceeded with the TAAM on its own.

The AGM-109I designator was reportedly used in connection with an MRASM concept of an inexpensive Tomahawk with a scaled down TERCOM structure and an imaging infrared terminal seeker. This MRASM could have served both as a land-attack and anti-ship missile.

The AGM-109J would have been an inexpensive MRASM armed with a submunition dispenser like that of the RGM/UGM-109D TLAM-D. Once again, however, as had been proven in flyoff between the AGM-86 and the AGM-109,

The General Dynamics BGM-109D (TLAM-D) was the variant armed with BLU-97 Combined Effects Bomblets. It is here seen on display at the annual Navy League Sea-Air-Space Exposition in Washington, DC, in April 1986. (Convair Division)

the MRASM program showed that the true calling of the Tomahawk was *not* as an air-launched weapon.

A Second Source

The July 1978 test failure that led Defense Secretary Harold Brown to observe that the Tomahawk "needs work," was highly indicative of its early teething troubles. As Kenneth Werrell pointed out in 1985, "The navy considered Tomahawk's 68-percent test success rate inadequate compared with their standard of 90 percent. While some claim there was no pattern to the failures, others focus on quality control."

Though the Convair Division of General Dynamics had originated the Tomahawk, McDonnell Douglas was brought in as a second-source supplier in 1982 by the Joint Cruise Missile Program Office. Werrell believed that second sourcing, which Convair despised, "gave [the] joint [cruise missile] program its particular character as well as many of its problems."

In June 1982, JCMPO issued a Method D quality control warning to Convair. This is the strongest measure possible short of a stop work order and was the only Method D that had been issued since 1945. As Barbara Bry reported in the *Los Angeles Times* a month later, JCMPO's Robert Holsapple had indicated that "if the poor work continues, General Dynamics could lose the contract."

Heads rolled. In August, only one day before the navy informed the press, Rear Admiral Walter Locke was ousted as head of JCMPO, a post he had held for more than a decade, and

replaced by Rear Admiral Stephen Hostettler. Werrell recalled that Secretary of Defense Caspar Weinberger told the House Appropriations Defense Subcommittee that "quality control was a central issue to Locke's removal." Meanwhile, Leonard Buchanan, who had been the general manager of the General Dynamics Convair Division, was reassigned and replaced by Richard Adams from the company's Aerospace Division.

In December 1982, under Hostettler, the navy lifted the Method D from General Dynamics, and as Werrell recalled, "In 1983, the Tomahawk's test failures were less visible. While some problems continue, the program appears [circa 1985] to be coming along."

After the dual-source deliveries began in 1984, the proportion of orders given to the two firms fluctuated. For example, McDonnell Douglas received a 60-percent slice of the pie for fiscal years 1985 to 1987, but Convair was given 70 percent in the following two fiscal years.

The Tomahawk in Detail

The TERCOM guidance package was a key feature that the TLAM variants all had in common. According to the *Introduction to the Scene Matching Missile Guidance Technologies*, approved for public release by the National Air Intelligence Center more than a decade later, and data plates visible in manufacturing photos, the original Tomahawk guidance system was the McDonnell Douglas AN/DSW-15. It had a precision of between 40 and 425 feet. The package included the Honeywell AN/APN-15 pulsed, range-tracking radar altimeter. The system was run by a 16-bit LC-4516C digital computer developed by the Guidance and Control Systems Division of Litton Industries. The LC-4516C had 30 kb of memory; amazingly scant by today's standards, but impressive in the early 1980s.

As noted in chapter 6, the AN/DSW-15 was also used in the AGM-86B ALCM, and Litton, as the principal subcontractor for the guidance package, contributed its LN-35 inertial navigation system for both missiles. By the 1990s, the TERCOM had been upgraded to the McDonnell Douglas AN/DPW-23 system and incorporated into both.

The TERCOM guidance system incorporated into the TLAM variants was not used in the TASM. Because it was designed to operate over the ocean surface, there are no terrain features for a TERCOM system to use for reference.

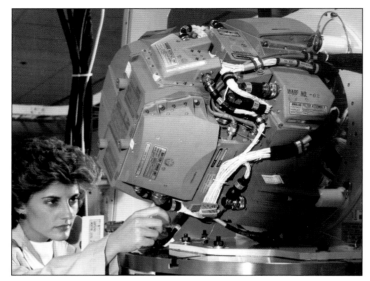

At work on the Tomahawk's McDonnell Douglas AN/DSW-15 guidance system. With a precision of between 40 and 425 feet, it incorporated a Honeywell AN/APN-15 pulsed, range-tracking radar altimeter. By the 1990s, the TERCOM had been upgraded to the McDonnell Douglas AN/DPW-23 system, which was also used in the air force AGM-86 cruise missile family. (Convair Division)

A close-up look at the Tomahawk's McDonnell Douglas AN/DSW-15 guidance package. The system was run by a 16-bit LC-4516C digital computer developed by Litton Guidance and Control Systems. The LC-4516C had 30 kb of memory, negligible by today's standards, but remarkable in the early 1980s. (Convair Division)

Instead, it used radar guidance to fly its mission at very low, sea-skimming altitude. This system incorporated the Texas Instruments AN/DSQ-28 active radar seeker that also aided the Harpoon anti-ship missile to acquire and strike its targets.

While the contents of the forward section containing the guidance and payload differed greatly from variant to variant, the TASM and three TLAMs all had a common aft section that contained the aerodynamic surfaces. All Tomahawk missiles were 20.4 inches (McDonnell Douglas literature of the 1980s lists 20.5 inches) in diameter, necessary for the torpedo tubes of one launch scenario, and 18 feet 3 inches long without the solid-fuel rocket booster, or 20 feet 6 inches with it. The wingspan, with the folding wings deployed, was 8 feet 9 inches.

Each Tomahawk was (and still is) packaged as, and thought of in terms of being, an All-Up-Round (AUR) system. The AUR includes the missile itself, its booster, and the pressurized container that protects it during transportation and storage. This container, a canister in the case of sur-face ships or capsule aboard submarines, also functions as the launch tube. All Tomahawk missiles are packaged and launched with their wings folded into their fuselage. Spanning 8 feet 9 inches, these unfold immediately after launch.

The launch sequence begins with vertically launched Tomahawks being ejected by gas pressure, and submarine-launched missiles being ejected horizontally through a torpedo tube by water impulse. The Type 106 rocket booster is then fired for a few seconds of airborne flight. Meanwhile, the airscoop is deployed and the missile transitions to cruising flight under the power of its Williams International F107-WR-400 turbofan engine. The cruising speed is up to Mach 0.75. The range and weight vary by mission and payload.

DSMAC

Beginning in 1987, the TERCOM navigation system of the TLAM family of cruise missiles was augmented by the addition of the Digital Scene Matching Area Correlator

Checking out a Williams International F107-WR-402 turbo-fan engine prior to it being installed in the tail cone of a Tomahawk Land Attack Missile. (Author's collection)

(DSMAC), which takes over for the terminal phase of the flight, the final dash to the target, to eliminate TERCOM and inertial navigation errors and ensure pinpoint precision, even at night or in adverse weather.

As DSMAC was explained by the General Dynamics/Convair fact sheet, "TERCOM generates position fixes by sampling terrain height using a radar altimeter, and then correlating the elevation profile against a digital elevation map in the missile guidance system's memory. DSMAC performs a correlation between a stored image and snapshot of the terrain beneath the missile to generate a position fix."

In fact, multiple target images are taken from different directions and angles. From these images, navigational and targeting maps can be produced for TERCOM and DSMAC so that the National Command Authority can direct strategic goals, strategic and regional commanders can develop contingency plans in response to developing strategic situ-

Terrain Contour Matching (TERCOM), utilizing a prerecorded contour map of the terrain compared with measurements made during flight by an onboard radar altimeter permits much higher accuracy than an inertial navigation system (INS). The Digitized Scene-Mapping Area Correlator (DSMAC), when combined with TERCOM as a terminal guidance system, allowed an even more accurate point attack, which was useful with conventional warheads. (DOD)

ations, field commanders can direct the mission, and strike planners can pick and coordinate TLAM strikes.

To provide a comprehensive database of imagery to operational commanders, the Defense Department created the National Imagery and Mapping Agency (NIMA) in October 1996. In November 2003, NIMA was redesignated as the National Geospatial-Intelligence Agency (NGA).

According to the agency fact sheet, it "was formed to bring together our nation's most capable imagery and geospatial assets into a single agency. Influenced by lessons learned from Operations Desert Shield and Desert Storm, NIMA brought together the Defense Mapping Agency, Central Imagery Office, Defense Dissemination Program Office, and National Photographic Interpretation Center, and also incorporated parts of the Central Intelligence Agency, Defense Airborne Reconnaissance Office, Defense Intelligence Agency, and National Reconnaissance Office." This repository became the resource for which DSMAC guidance data would be derived and navigational mapping produced.

When it achieved operational capability, the system was designated as DSMAC-2 to distinguish it from the prototype DSMAC that was designated without a suffix.

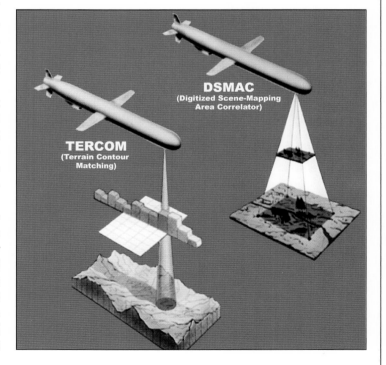

TOMAHAWK CRUISE MISSILE VARIANT CUTAWAY VIEWS

	Guidance Section	Forward Section	Mid-Body Section	Aft-Body Section	Propulsion Section	Booster Section
BGM-109A TLAM-N (Also RGM-109A and UGM-109A)	TERCOM guidance system	**Payload** (W80 Thermonuclear Warhead) / Fuel tanks	• Fuel tanks • Wing and Wing Slots and actuation systems / Wing Slot Doors open during wing deployment and close afterward to provide a clean aerodynamic fuselage.	Fuel tank and Mission Control Module / Extendible scoop intake	Williams F107 turbofan engine / Pneumatically deployed fins	Solid-fuel rocket booster (Atlantic Research or United Technologies)
BGM-109B TASM (Also RGM-109B and UGM-109B)	Active Radar Homing guidance system	**Payload** (WDU-25B Unitary Blast Fragmentation Warhead)	• Fuel tanks • Wing and Wing Slots and actuation systems / Wing Slot Doors open during wing deployment and close afterward to provide a clean aerodynamic fuselage.	Fuel tank and Mission Control Module / Extendible scoop intake	Williams F107 turbofan engine / Pneumatically deployed fins	Solid-fuel rocket booster (Atlantic Research or United Technologies)
BGM-109C TLAM-C (Also RGM-109C and UGM-109C)	INS / TERCOM plus DSMAC guidance • Fuel tank • DSMAC illuminator	**Payload** (WDU-25B Unitary Blast Fragmentation Warhead)	• Fuel tanks • Wing and Wing Slots and actuation systems / Wing Slot Doors open during wing deployment and close afterward to provide a clean aerodynamic fuselage.	Fuel tank and Mission Control Module / Extendible scoop intake	Williams F107 turbofan engine / Pneumatically deployed fins	Solid-fuel rocket booster (Atlantic Research or United Technologies)
BGM-109D TLAM-D (Also RGM-109D and UGM-109D)	INS / TERCOM plus DSMAC guidance • Fuel tank • DSMAC illuminator	**Payload** (BLU-97 Combined Effects Bomblets)	• Fuel tanks • Wing and Wing Slots and actuation systems / Wing Slot Doors open during wing deployment and close afterward to provide a clean aerodynamic fuselage.	Fuel tank and Mission Control Module / Extendible scoop intake	Williams F107 turbofan engine / Pneumatically deployed fins	Solid-fuel rocket booster (Atlantic Research or United Technologies)
TLAM Block III Upgrades	GPS / RPU guidance system / Fuel tank	**Payload** PBXN-107 Explosive Warhead	• Fuel tanks • Wing and Wing Slots and actuation systems / Wing Slot Doors open during wing deployment and close afterward to provide a clean aerodynamic fuselage.	Fuel tank and Mission Control Module / Extendible scoop intake	Williams F107 turbofan engine / Pneumatically deployed fins	Solid-fuel rocket booster (Atlantic Research or United Technologies)

Chapter 8

THE CRUISE MISSILE THAT WON THE COLD WAR

The Ground-Launched Cruise Missile (GLCM) was not a new idea, but one that had been discarded and now was about to be reborn. As discussed in chapter 2, the U.S. Air Force had fielded ground-launched Matador and Mace tactical nuclear cruise missiles in Europe in the 1950s. However, various issues, such as fragile and unreliable guidance systems, had led to the systems being withdrawn in the 1960s and not replaced.

Secretary of Defense Donald Rumsfeld had less than a month left in office when he sat down for a 21 December 1976 meeting with Edward C. "Pete" Aldridge, director of the Department of Defense Planning and Evaluation, and Malcolm Currie, director of Defense Research and Engineering (DDRE), to talk about the future of the cruise missile. According to air force historian Kenneth Werrell, who was closely monitoring the subject in those days, Rumsfeld "expressed special interest in a ground-launched version of the cruise missile."

A test firing of a BQM-109G Ground-Launched Cruise Missile (GLCM) painted in early development colors. This launch utilized an operational-type MAN tractor truck to pull the Transporter-Erector-Launcher (TEL) unit. (Author's collection)

The early two-tube GLCM proof-of-concept launch system is seen here pulled by a standard M35 truck on maneuvers with a pair of M60 tanks at the U.S. Army's Dugway Proving Ground, circa 1981. (Convair Division)

With this, they adjourned for the holidays. When they returned after New Year's, their discussions culminated in a 6 January 1977 meeting of the Defense Systems Acquisition Review Council (DSARC) that Werrell called "probably the most important decision point in the evolution of the weapon."

Two weeks later, Rumsfeld left office as Gerald Ford handed the reins of the presidency to Jimmy Carter, but he had helped set a course for the incoming administration. A great deal would happen in the defense establishment during the next 24 years until Rumsfeld resumed the office of Defense Secretary in 2001.

Defining the Ground-Launched Cruise Missile

Operational cruise missiles launched from air and sea flowed from the 1977 "decision point," but so, too, did the Ground-Launched Cruise Missile (GLCM), in a program that built upon work that the Convair Division of General Dynamics already had been doing on a potential variant of its Tomahawk.

The *idea* of a next generation ground-launched tactical nuclear cruise missile was alive in the 1970s, but it had been pushed to a distant back burner. After the DSARC decision point meeting, the U.S. Air Force gave Convair a green light for development work on a ground-launched variant of the BGM-109.

In discussing the meeting, Kenneth Werrell added that "in the wake of Jimmy Carter's defeat of President Gerald Ford in November 1976, many believed that any basic decision should be postponed so that the incoming president would have maximum latitude."

Indeed, the new president was the most reluctant since World War II to pursue new weapons system programs. In the post-Vietnam and post-Watergate era, the idealistic Carter had come to office perceived as one who followed a moral high road. While previous presidents had pursued policies of emphasizing America's nuclear arsenal as a counterbalance to Soviet numerical military superiority, especially in conventional ground forces, Carter favored an emphasis on disarmament.

It was the Europeans, living in the shadow of the massive Soviet and Warsaw Pact forces, who were most anxious to see the United States maintain a robust tactical nuclear deterrent in Western Europe. In an October 1977 speech to the International Institute of Strategic Studies in London, West German Chancellor Helmut Schmidt pointed out that the Soviet Union now had a superiority in tactical nuclear weapons in *Eastern* Europe and insisted that the United States address this imbalance in the West. The 1972 SALT Treaty had addressed parity in *strategic* nuclear weapons, but not *tactical* nuclear weapons.

Schmidt and other European leaders were especially worried about the deployment into Eastern Europe by

Launching a GLCM precursor from the two-tube launch system at the Dugway Proving Ground in 1981. (Convair Division)

the Soviets of more than 200 RSD-10 Pioneer mobile Intermediate-Range Ballistic Missiles (IRBM). Known as the SS-20 Saber in NATO nomenclature, the Pioneer's 3,000-mile range could easily deliver a nuclear strike against any target in Western Europe and each missile had three independently targetable warheads.

Deployed in 1977, the SS-20 was a costly gamble. In his book *Autopsy for an Empire*, Russian historian Dmitri Volkogonov wrote that "astronomical amounts of money were spent" on the missile, which Soviet leadership, including General Secretary Leonid Brezhnev, hoped would drive the detente-anxious West to concessions in future arms control discussions. Instead, the move backfired. As Volkogonov pointed out, "The short-sighted Soviet strategists had handed the Americans a knife with which to cut the Soviet throat."

Instead of bowing to Soviet intimidation, the United States, pressed by NATO partners, decided in 1979 to embrace the knife handed to them. The Carter Defense Department, headed by Defense Secretary Harold Brown, decided to deploy *two* nuclear-armed missile systems to Europe: the Martin Marietta MGM-31 Pershing II solid-fuel Medium-Range Ballistic Missile (MRBM) and the Ground-Launched Cruise Missile that Convair was developing.

Kenneth Werrell reports that because the Department of Defense "could not choose between the Pershing and GLCM, it used a traditional bureaucratic solution, adopting both with the rationale that they complemented each other."

Convair's missile was designated as BGM-109G, and to distinguish it from its similar sibling, the sea-launched Tomahawk, it

When the Convair Division built its first prototype Transporter-Erector-Launcher (TEL) unit, circa 1981, it sent the TEL out for field testing with a film crew and an M35 low-mobility 6 x 6 tractor trailer truck. (Convair Division)

Building the missile tube assembly Transporter-Erector-Launcher (TEL) trailers at Air Force Plant 19, part of the Convair Division complex at San Diego's Lindbergh Field. (Author's collection)

was officially named "Gryphon." However, it would become best known by its acronym, GLCM, pronounced as "Glick-Em" or "Glick-Um."

The GLCM was the same size as the Tomahawk and used generally the same guidance and propulsion systems. It was armed with a W84 thermonuclear warhead with a variable yield between .2 and 150 kilotons. This compared to the selectable yield of between 5 and 150 kilotons in the W80 warhead used in the TLAM-N.

The Pershings would be manned by the U.S. Army, which had a long history with tactical *ballistic* missiles, but Werrell added that the army had refused the GLCM because of the large support structure, especially personnel, that the system required. A typical flight of 16 GLCMs required 74 people: a commander and assistant commander, as well as 8 launch control officers, 19 enlisted maintenance personnel, 1 medic, and 44 security police. Having previously deployed the Mace and Matador cruise missiles, the U.S. Air Force would manage the manpower-intensive GLCMs.

In December 1979, NATO formally signed off on a plan by which 108 Pershing IIs would be deployed, along with 464 GLCMs.

The full strongback trailer assemblies for the GLCM Transporter-Erector-Launcher (TEL) system take shape at Air Force Plant 19, part of the Convair Division complex at San Diego's Lindbergh Field. Three of the TELs are open, and one is closed and erected. Ahead of it is a Launch Control Center (LCC) trailer. Two TELs were built for each LCC. (Author's collection)

An aerial view of a completed Transporter-Erector-Launcher (TEL) system on the left, parked nose to nose with a Launch Control Center (LCC) trailer on the right. Both are mated with their MAN M1014 tractors. They are posed in front of Air Force Plant 19, within the Convair Division complex at Lindbergh Field in San Diego. (San Diego Air and Space Museum)

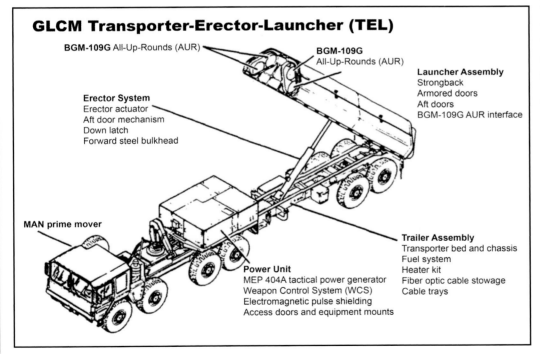

GLCM Transporter-Erector-Launcher (TEL)

BGM-109G All-Up-Rounds (AUR)

BGM-109G
All-Up-Rounds (AUR)

Launcher Assembly
Strongback
Armored doors
Aft doors
BGM-109G AUR interface

Erector System
Erector actuator
Aft door mechanism
Down latch
Forward steel bulkhead

MAN prime mover

Power Unit
MEP 404A tactical power generator
Weapon Control System (WCS)
Electromagnetic pulse shielding
Access doors and equipment mounts

Trailer Assembly
Transporter bed and chassis
Fuel system
Heater kit
Fiber optic cable stowage
Cable trays

The Soviets were especially concerned about the GLCMs based in Germany. Kenneth Werrell wrote in 1984 that "the Russians appear to be genuinely fearful of the missile, especially in German hands, sometimes calling GLCM the 'German-Launched Cruise Missile.'"

The Germans had been the most eager to have GLCMs based on their soil, but Belgium and the Netherlands remained reluctant through the fall of 1979, fearing that the weapons might make them targets for Soviet nuclear strikes.

Some doubt was expressed by Western Europeans that year, notably by Klaas de Vries, the chairman of the defense committee in the Dutch parliament, that the United States would actually *use* tactical nuclear weapons to defend its allies. This same opinion had been expressed by Charles DeGaulle of France in the 1950s.

Meanwhile, plans were also made for deploying GLCMs to South Korea. An advance planning staff was assigned to Pacific Air Forces (PACAF) headquarters, but this proposal was canceled.

Of the latter, 160 would be based in the United Kingdom, 112 in Italy, 96 in West Germany, and 48 each in Belgium and the Netherlands. The Pershings were all based in West Germany near Neu Ulm and Schwabish Gemund. The plan was that the GLCMs would be operationally deployed in Europe beginning in December 1983.

Developing the Ground-Launched Cruise Missile

Because the basic missile already existed as the Tomahawk, the GLCM development and test phase focused mainly on working out the launch scenario. The first platform launch of a BGM-109G GLCM came in February 1981, one of three flights by Convair crews before the system was turned over to the air force. There were eight successful launches out of nine attempts between February 1982 and June 1983. The tests were conducted at the Dugway Proving Ground, a U.S. Army facility in the Utah Desert. As with their navy cousins, the Tomahawks, the air force GLCMs were recoverable after test flights. The last missile fired in this phase was recovered after a 700-mile flight on 27 July 1983. A second round of 13 test launches, designated as Follow-on Test and Evaluation Phase II, took place at Dugway in the winter of 1985–1986.

In the meantime, GLCM crews were reporting to the 868th Tactical Missile Training Group (TMTG) at Davis-Monthan Air Force Base in Arizona, where they were trained to operate the missile and to do so in a ground combat environment. Convair, meanwhile, assigned Integrated Logistics Support (ILS) teams to Davis-Monthan.

Because the GLCM was to be mobile, as a fixed launch location would make it more vulnerable to attack, a mobile launch vehicle was developed. This brought back memories of the big MM-1 Teracruzer prime mover created three decades earlier for the TM-76 Mace. Whereas the Teracruzer was built in Wisconsin, its equivalent for the GLCM was built in Germany by the German truckmaker Maschinenfabrik

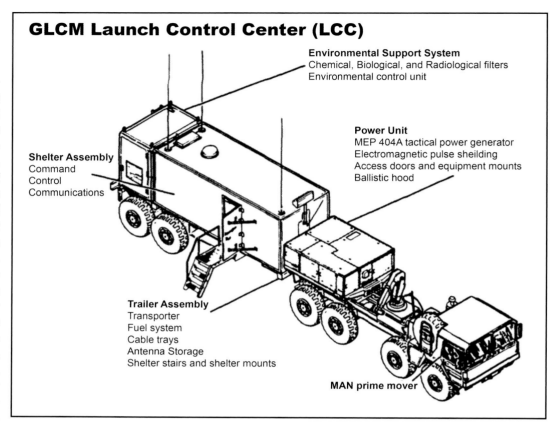

GLCM Launch Control Center (LCC)

Environmental Support System
Chemical, Biological, and Radiological filters
Environmental control unit

Power Unit
MEP 404A tactical power generator
Electromagnetic pulse sheilding
Access doors and equipment mounts
Ballistic hood

Shelter Assembly
Command
Control
Communications

Trailer Assembly
Transporter
Fuel system
Cable trays
Antenna Storage
Shelter stairs and shelter mounts

MAN prime mover

Augsburg-Nürnberg (MAN). This vehicle, which would be the prime mover for both the GLCM and for the Pershing II, was a 10-ton, eight-wheeled all-wheel-drive V10 diesel tractor. This vehicle was originally developed as a high-mobility, off-road vehicle for the German army. Known as Kategorie-1 (Kat 1) by the Bundeswehr, it was designated as M1014 by the U.S. armed forces.

The GLCM's M1014 pulled a trailer on which was mounted on a "strongback" launch assembly. This in turn carried four missiles and elevated to an angle of 45 degrees for launch. In the early proof-of-concept stage of the program, the idea for the GLCM was demonstrated with a two-tube launcher, from which Tomahawk cruise missiles could be launched.

The strongback trailer was built by the Convair Division at Air Force Plant 19, part of the Convair complex at Lindbergh Field in San Diego. When the MAN and strongback were mated, they constituted an overall vehicle known as the Transporter-Erector-Launcher (TEL). It was 56 feet long and 8 feet wide, and it weighed 40 tons. The first TEL "production article" was delivered to the 868th TMTG on 4 October 1982, and six more were delivered by the end of the year.

The M1014 tractor trucks were not initially available, so the early strongback trailers were mated with standard M35 diesel 6x6 tractors. Later field exercises that took place in the United States used MAN M1001 vehicles nearly indistinguishable from the M1014s that were used when the GLCMs were operationally deployed.

Each pair of TELs was accompanied by a Launch Control Center (LCC) trailer. This trailer, about the same size as the TEL strongback, supported the control center itself, which was located within a bullet-proof box with approximately 120 square feet for its four-person

A launch of a BGM-109G Gryphon Ground Launched Cruise Missile (GLCM) from a Transporter-Erector-Launcher (TEL) system at Dugway Proving Ground in November 1982. (USAF)

crew. Also built by Convair in California, the LCC was mounted on a four-wheeled trailer and pulled by an M1013 MAN vehicle similar to the M1014 used for the TEL. The LCC was shielded from chemical, biological, and radioactive agents, but in the worst-case scenario, there was an escape hatch in the floor. The LCC was linked to the TEL by fiber optic cables. The MAN tractors for both TEL and LCC carried a power unit containing an MEP-404A turbine generator.

GLCM flights, built around four TELs and a pair of LCCs, were supported by 16 other vehicles, though deployments usually found the flight splitting into two cells of roughly equal size that maintained independent launch capability. These included a heavy-duty MAN wrecker, as well as 5 sup-

ply vehicles and 10 security vehicles, many of which pulled additional trailers.

This resulted in a convoy of substantial size, but it would allow for continued operation independent of the main operating base for resupply and logistical support if the flight's base was destroyed.

Deploying the Ground-Launched Cruise Missile

In 1983, as the GLCM was becoming operational, production outpaced that of Tomahawks. Convair reported at year's end that it had delivered 42 GLCMs, compared to 36 Tomahawk SLCMs. Through the early 1980s, the BGM-109G

Major James Blondin, an instructor with the 868th Tactical Missile Training Squadron, in the missile launch commander's position in the GLCM training simulator at Davis-Monthan AFB. He is going over missile-status checking procedures and the environmental control board during GLCM training. (U.S. Air Force photo by Tech Sergeant Rob Marshall)

GLCM force gradually took shape, as five tactical missile wings became operational with three numbered air forces within the U.S. Air Forces in Europe (USAFE) command. The first was the 501st Tactical Missile Wing at RAF Greenham Common, 50 miles west of London in the United Kingdom, which became operational in December 1983. The Pershing II, meanwhile, first became operational in West Germany that same month, deployed with the 1st Battalion of the U.S. Army's 41st Field Artillery Regiment.

The second GLCM wing, and ultimately the largest, was the 487th TMW at Comiso Air Base on the island of Sicily, which became operational in March 1984. Thereafter, at least a year passed between GLCM wing activations. The 485th TMW at Florennes Air Base in Belgium became operational in March 1985, the 38th TMW at Wüschheim Air Base in Germany became operational in March 1986, and the 303rd TMW at RAF Molesworth in the United Kingdom became operational in December 1987. As it had with the 868th TMTG in the United States, Convair dispatched Integrated Logistics Support (ILS) teams to the overseas loca-

tions where the GLCMs were assigned. The teams supported the missiles and the TELs and LCCs, which were both built by Convair.

The 501st TMW at RAF Greenham Common in the United Kingdom, and the 487th TMW at Comiso AB both received their full complements of 96 GLCMs in six flights and 112 in seven flights, respectively. The 485th TMW at Florennes AB received only 16 of its planned 48 and was activated with only one flight. The 38th TMW at Wüschheim Air Base, which had the legacy of having been a Matador and Mace unit three decades before, received 64 of its planned 96 GLCMs and was able to operate four flights. The 303rd TMW at RAF Molesworth was scheduled for 64 GLCMs but received just 16 for a single flight.

Some sources report differing data for these deployments, but we rely on information appearing in *United States Air Force Ground Launch Missiles: A Study in Technology, Concepts and Deterrence*, an Air War College report by Lieutenant Colonel Randall Lanning. He joined the GLCM Initial Operational Test and Evaluation Team in 1980, deployed to Europe with the 501st TMW in 1982, and in 1985, transferred to the Directorate of GLCM Operations at Headquarters, USAFE.

Further deployments were suspended by the terms of the INF Treaty (discussed in this chapter). As of 9 December 1987, the number of operational GLCMs was frozen at the 288 that had already been deployed. The 176 GLCMs still in the pipeline never made it overseas, and three of the five operational GLCM wings never received all their intended missiles. The 486th TMW at Woensdrecht AB in the Netherlands never became operational as the sixth GLCM location. Indeed, enthusiasm within that country for the missile had never been strong. Although the Dutch parliament approved the deployment in December 1979, a later shift of the balance of power in that body made deployment politically difficult for the Dutch government.

Airmen load an inert BGM-109G Gryphon into a Transporter-Erector-Launcher (TEL) during their pre-deployment training program. (USAF photo by Tech Sergeant Bill Thompson)

On the ground, the GLCM flights were each housed in a Ready Storage Shelter (RSS) when neither deployed nor on maneuvers. At each base with multiple flights, several RSSs were concentrated inside a secured GLCM Alert and Maintenance Area (GAMA) that also contained a wing command post and living quarters for a launch crew who was on Quick Reaction Alert (QRA). In the event of a launch order, the QRA crew would mount up, roll out of the GAMA to a predetermined launch site, and execute its launch against advancing Soviet armies.

Soviet Reaction

In 1980, after the United States countered the SS-20 with two missile types, the opposing sides, then led by Jimmy Carter and Leonid Brezhnev, agreed to enter negotiations known as the Intermediate-Range Nuclear Forces (INF) talks. After 1981, the Reagan administration proposed a "Zero Option," agreeing to halt deployment of the GLCM and Pershing II *if* the Soviets eliminated their SS-20 as well as SS-4 (R-12) and SS-5 (R-14) missiles. In February 1983, Soviet Premier Yuri Andropov, who succeeded Brezhnev in 1982, explicitly rejected Reagan's "Zero Option" plan, calling the plan "patently unacceptable."

Beginning with the 1979 NATO decision on deployment, a wave of opposition began to trickle across Western Europe that was unlike that which had previously greeted nuclear weapons systems on the continent. It was as though it emerged out of nowhere, but of course, it had not. Oleg Gordievsky, the Soviet KGB station chief in London, who had been turned by British intelligence as a double agent in 1974, later reported that the KGB was ordered to mobilize an anti-missile propaganda effort in the West, though this was something that their opposite numbers at the CIA had known about early on.

In the 1983 report Soviet Strategy to Derail U.S. INF Deployment: An Intelligence Assessment, which is still only partially declassified, CIA analysts wrote that "a key goal in Moscow's security policy since 1979 has been to derail NATO's plans to deploy the Pershing II Medium-Range Ballistic Missile (MRBM) and the Ground-Launched Cruise Missile (GLCM). By blocking these deployments, scheduled to begin in late 1983, the USSR would retain its current predominance in Intermediate-Range Nuclear Forces (INF) as well as further its long-term objective of weakening NATO and dividing Western Europe from the United States. . . . The Soviets see the new U.S. systems as an effective counter to their SS-20 IRBM force and may believe that the scale of NATO's deployments would nullify the advantage in escalation control that they had planned to secure with that force."

It is further noted that "the Soviets have actively promoted the European 'peace movement' through aggressive propaganda and covert activities. They have focused their efforts primarily on those countries scheduled to base the new NATO missiles. . . . Moscow has instructed West European Communists and the leaders of pro-Soviet international organizations to make the anti-INF campaign their foremost concern and has provided funding and political guidance for their peace movement activity."

Taking the show on the road with the MAN M1014 in the lead. When deployed to Europe, GLCM units trained by moving launch cells to various locations in the countryside to simulate an actual launch scenario. The convoy for each launch cell included a TEL with four GLCMs plus around eight other support vehicles. Here, members of the 485th Tactical Missile Wing from Florennes AB roll down a country lane in Belgium. (USAF photo by Sergeant Scott Stewart)

The Soviets encouraged vocal and often violent demonstrations across Europe. As John Vinocur reported in the *New York Times* of 26 July 1983, "the Danish and Swiss governments have exposed attempts by ostensible Soviet diplomats, actually KGB officers, to influence or buy their way into groups trying to block deployment of new medium-range missiles in Western Europe."

Echoing the assessment of the CIA analysts, Vinocur quoted Stanislav Levchenko, a KGB defector, who pointed out that "the Soviet Union does exert influence in the West through Western Communist parties. . . . The degree of Soviet success so far has been great. The buildup of criticism on nuclear weapons by these [anti-missile] groups had gone basically in only one direction—against NATO."

Meanwhile, the Soviets had given the anti-missile demonstrators a useful catchword into which to package their movement. In March 1982, Brezhnev had announced that the Soviet Union would be in favor of "freezing," albeit not *reducing*, the number of Soviet nuclear missiles in Eastern Europe. The term "nuclear freeze" quickly entered the media lexicon and was suddenly on editorial pages and college campuses across the United States and Europe. The idea of a "freeze" was, as Brezhnev intended, that Soviet intermediate-range missiles would stay, but American missiles would not be deployed. With a freeze as their goal, the various "peace" movements targeting the American missiles were silent when it came to the Soviet deployment of SS-20s and other missiles.

Many European politicians, worried about this particularly vocal sliver of public opinion, were swept up in the fuss over the freeze, but most remained aligned with the idea of matching the SS-20 deployment.

As elections came and went, notably in Britain and West Germany in 1983 at the height of the freeze excitement, the political parties advocating GLCM deployment remained in power. Also in 1983, and again in 1984, Italy's Socialist Premier Bettino Craxi, as well as the Italian parliament, renewed that country's commitment to the GLCM. When the matter of a delay reached the Belgian parliament in 1985, the vote was to deploy the missiles on schedule. Even in the Netherlands, where the GLCM became especially unpopular, the endorsement of the NATO agreement to deploy the missiles was confirmed by parliament in 1985.

As West German Defense Minister Manfred Woerner said in April 1983, "Whoever demonstrates for *unilateral* disarmament is making mutual, evenhanded disarmament impossible."

Amid the demonstrations, perhaps the most visually prominent peace movement activity took place outside RAF

Members of the 487th Tactical Missile Wing at Comiso AB on the island of Sicily raise the launch tubes of a GLCM launcher during a field training deployment in November 1983. (USAF photo by Tech Sergeant Rob Marshall)

Greenham Common in England. Beginning during the summer of 1982, even before the GLCMs arrived, congregations of various counterculture organizations began to come and go here. Soon a tawdry tent city known as the "Greenham Common Women's Peace Camp" sprang up. Protesters ensconced themselves on the base perimeter for several years after the missiles arrived in December 1983. This transient population waned in the winter and waxed in the warmer months, with numerous failed attempts to block access to the base and to harass crews during off-base training exercises.

The camp-dwellers proved to be a nuisance. In a 2002 interview with Peter Grier of *Air Force Magazine*, Colonel Doug Livingston, who served with the 501st TMW, said, "It was tough. We had to 'protester proof' the vehicles [with safety wiring over the gas caps and protecting parts of the vehicles against objects being thrown]. They may have slowed us down a bit, but there were never any serious accidents."

Though this would continue for several years, the peak of the anti-GLCM and anti-Pershing disturbances and demonstrations came and went in 1983. By the spring of 1984, after the missiles were deployed, the movement was unraveling.

"At Mutlangen in southern Germany, a knot of forlorn figures stand in the snow outside an American Pershing 2 missile base, bearing placards predicting nuclear doom," wrote James Markham in the *New York Times* of 11 March 1984. "On slow news days, West German television crews occasionally shoot footage of these doughty remnants of the lost campaign against the deployment of medium-range missiles in Western Europe. Otherwise, they are ignored. The coalition that spearheaded the anti-missile movement last fall has retreated to its winter quarters. When it re-emerges in the spring for traditional

The 303rd Tactical Missile Wing became operational here at RAF Molesworth in England in December 1987. This aerial photo was taken in January 1989. (USAF photo by Master Sergeant Patrick Nugent)

At a field location somewhere in Germany, the launcher on the strongback of the Transporter-Erector-Launcher (TEL) has been raised to 45 degrees and air force personnel are going through the steps required for a launch that would never come. (USAF photo by Master Sergeant Paul Hayashi)

New York Times visited Florennes, the Belgian town 40 miles south of Brussels near where the 485th TMW had just become operational with the GLCM. Mayor Louis Timermans told him that "the antimissile people say that the population is resigned to the missiles. The truth is that they never did anything to express any ideas against them. . . . There were foreigners who came here. On Saturday, they held a demonstration, but when they marched, the streets were empty. Nobody from Florennes was there."

Documents recovered from Soviet archives after the end of the Cold War, as well as memoirs of those who were there in the 1980s, show that Soviet leadership reacted to the GLCMs and the Pershing II with an unusually high level of concern. Aleksander Savelyev and Nikolay Detinov in their book *The Big Five: Arms Control Decision-Making in the Soviet Union* write that Andropov became obsessed with the capabilities of the two American missiles. The Pershing could fly at a speed exceeding Mach 8 and could not be stopped, while the TERCOM of the GLCM allowed it to fly so low that detecting and intercepting it would have been virtually impossible.

Easter marches, it seems likely to be considerably more divided and uncertain of its targets. Many militants are disillusioned. . . . Events have conspired against those who had predicted apocalypse when the first Pershing 2s went into Mutlangen in November. Instead of worsening, relations between West Germany and Communist East Germany have improved in the post-deployment months."

"I've noticed an incredible weakening of the peace movement," Petra Kelly, the founder of the German Green Party told Markham that winter, recounting how only 60 people had showed up for a recent rally in Bonn.

In October 1984, William Stivers of the *New York Times* wrote, "One year ago this month, close to a million demonstrators took to the streets of West Germany to protest the approaching deployment of United States cruise missiles. . . . One year later, quiet prevails, and the peace movement seems dispirited and unfocused."

Local enthusiasm for the protests appeared to be thin to nonexistent. In March 1985, Richard Bernstein of the

In a February 1983 document that Oleg Gordievsky leaked to the British, the Soviets recognized that with ICBMs, "The time required for determining the direction of their flight in fact leaves roughly 20 minutes reaction time. This period will be considerably curtailed after deployment of the Pershing II missile in [West Germany], for which the flying time to reach long-range targets in the Soviet Union is calculated at four to six minutes."

Markus Wolf, the head of the foreign intelligence branch of the East German Ministry of State Security, the notorious "Stasi," wrote in his autobiography, *Man Without a Face*, that "with the U.S. rearmament program and the advent of the aggressive Reagan administration, our Soviet partners had become obsessed with the danger of a nuclear missile attack."

Training for a launch under combat conditions in a Belgian forest in August 1987. An airman of the 485th Tactical Missile Wing from Florennes AB wearing an M17 gas mask maintains his security position as a Transporter-Erector-Launcher (TEL) for BGM-109G GLCMs stands in raised position. (USAF photo by Sergeant Scott Stewart)

After the Cold War, Gordievsky wrote that the Soviet Union greeted the deployment of the missiles, especially the GLCMs, almost as a strategic checkmate. In an interview with author David Hoffman, he admitted that Soviet leaders "knew they would be the first to die, and [they] didn't want to die."

The GLCM Legacy

As Soviet and peace movement propaganda painted the American missile systems as the specific precursors of nuclear Armageddon, many in the West nervously succumbed to that notion and the idea that the nuclear freeze was the answer to the superpower tensions that settled over Europe in the 1980s.

In the United States, Paul Warnke, who had been director of the Arms Control and Disarmament Agency under the Jimmy Carter administration, became a convert to the freeze movement. He insisted in a counterintuitive *Washington Post* op-ed piece later cited by *Air Force Magazine*

that the United States unilaterally halt deployment of the GLCM, regardless of the Soviet deployment of the SS-20. His alternative to such a freeze would mean that "the United States will face a further deterioration in its relations with the Soviet Union, and Western Europe's confidence in American leadership will decline."

Warnke was right about the fact that the Soviet Union *was* angry about the GLCM, but the result was just the opposite of what he predicted. When Warnke complained that the GLCM had "no military justification," he could not have been further from the truth. The nuclear checkmate afforded by GLCM compelled the Soviet Union to go to the bargaining table for the talks.

In March 1985, Mikhail Gorbachev succeeded Andropov, bringing to the Soviet hierarchy a new desire to negotiate toward a de-escalation of the continuing nuclear showdown. Accepting Reagan's Zero Option in principle, the Soviets came back to the INF talks, and Gorbachev met face-to-face with President Ronald Reagan in summit conferences in 1985 and 1986. On 8 December 1987, the two met in Washington to sign the Intermediate-Range Nuclear Forces Treaty, which called for the elimination of *all* short- and intermediate-range nuclear-capable missiles from Europe by June 1991.

During the same week the treaty was signed, Howell Raines of the *New York Times* visited the "peace camp" outside the fence line at Greenham Common. He spoke with Jane, "a pale young woman who, following the protesters' protocol inherited from the 1960s, declines to use her last name."

"Maybe they're just hoping we're going to go now," Jane told him. "A lot of people will say about us, 'Why are they still there?' But until it's ratified, we're going to stay. That means a couple of years more or five years more."

Raines wrote that she was "one of a cheerless remnant of about 25 women who remain in the four primitive tent-camps that were set up here in 1981, at the time of the announcement of plans to put United States–made land-based cruise missiles at Greenham. In the heyday of the British anti-nuclear movement, hundreds of people sometimes occupied a half-dozen camps. . . . They cite distrust of Mr. Reagan as their reason [for remaining at the camps], but some of the younger women, who live on unemployment payments and the daily hot meal brought in by support groups, suggest that they really have no place to go."

Under the INF Treaty, the United States destroyed 846 missiles and the Soviet Union scrapped 1,846. Each side was permitted to send inspectors to monitor this process on the other side. The first GLCM unit deactivated was the 486th TMW in the Netherlands, which pulled out in 1988. The last two to go were the 487th TMW in Sicily and the 501st TMW at Greenham Common, which both stood down in 1991.

By this time, the peace camp had devolved into a gradually shriveling New Age theme park, decaying relics of which still remain in the fields near the base, which became a public park in 1997.

The missiles were withdrawn to Davis-Monthan AFB, where they were cut up under the watchful eyes of Soviet

inspectors. By terms of the treaty, the United States kept eight deactivated GLCMs along with their launchers as museum displays at locations such as the National Museum of the U.S. Air Force in Ohio.

An aerial view taken in January 1989 of the Ground-Launched Cruise Missile facilities at Florennes AB in Belgium, home of the 485th Tactical Missile Wing. (USAF photo by Master Sergeant Patrick Nugent)

General Secretary Mikhail Gorbachev of the Soviet Union and President Ronald Reagan of the United States sign the Intermediate-Range Nuclear Forces Treaty (INF) in the East Room of the White House on 8 December 1987. The number of Ground-Launched Cruise Missiles was frozen at 288, and they were eliminated by 1991 along with Soviet intermediate-range missiles deployed in Europe. (National Archives)

Chapter 9

THE TOMAHAWK GOES TO SEA

On 10 May 1983, the USS New Jersey became the first battleship and the second surface ship to fire an RGM-109 Tomahawk. The launch, from one of the eight armored box launchers aboard the ship, came while the New Jersey was under way off the coast of Southern California. The Tomahawk traveled approximately 500 miles to its target at the Tonopah Test Range in Nevada. (U.S. Navy)

The Tomahawk was destined to become a cornerstone of the Reagan administration's ambitious plan for a "600-Ship Navy." President Ronald Reagan entered office in January 1981 determined to rebuild the armed forces of the United States, which had declined steeply since the end of the Vietnam War. Articulated specifically as one of the key elements of this plan was "naval superiority."

Secretary of the Navy John Lehman immediately undertook a program that involved both new shipbuilding and reactivating the four battleships of the Iowa class, the largest surface ships in the U.S. Navy. These included the USS *Iowa*, USS *New Jersey*, USS *Missouri*, and USS *Wisconsin*. Each was earmarked to become a launch platform for Tomahawks.

The first Tomahawk launch from a surface ship, the

A BGM-109D Tomahawk Land Attack Missile (TLAM) during a development flight, circa 1987. (Author's collection)

USS *Merrill*, took place on 19 March 1980. A Spruance class destroyer, the USS *Merrill* was a new ship, having been commissioned into the fleet in March 1978; it had been selected to serve as the test platform for the Tomahawk Cruise Missile Program. For the submarine fleet, the USS *Guitarro* served as the first test platform. On 29 April 1983, the USS *La Jolla*, a Los Angeles–class fast attack submarine, was the first to fire a Tomahawk while submerged. The battleship USS *New Jersey*, recommissioned in December 1982, became the second surface ship to fire a Tomahawk on 10 May 1983.

Tests typically involved launches from the Pacific Ocean off Naval Air Station Point Mugu in California's Ventura County, home of the Pacific Missile Test Center (PMTC). Many of the sea-launch test Tomahawks made the 500-mile flight to the Tonopah Test Range, north of the Area 51/Groom Lake complex in the Nevada Desert, where they were recovered. The fact that the Tomahawks could be recovered and reused set them apart from the air force ALCM. Going back to the days of the Regulus, the navy had favored recoverable cruise missiles for testing.

Live fire tests were also conducted, from which there was obviously no recovery. Some were against test targets on San Clemente Island, part of the Naval Air Systems Com-

mand (NavAir) test range off the coast of California. Others were against ships at sea. On 18 July 1982, for example, a Tomahawk fired from USS *Guitarro* sank the decommissioned destroyer USS *Agerholm*.

As part of the 600-ship program, the Tomahawk would be installed across the fleet, on submarines, as originally intended, as well as on Spruance-class destroyers and existing guided missile cruisers, such as the USS *Long Beach* and members of the Virginia class and Ticonderoga class. They would be included in the armament of the recommissioned battleships and would be standard armament on the new Arleigh Burke–class destroyers that were to be built as an element in the 600-ship plan. The missiles deployed included the RGM/UGM-109B Tomahawk Anti-Ship Missile (TASM), and later the various Tomahawk Land Attack Missile (TLAM) variants.

In 1983, the Tomahawk became active with the fleet, though full operational capability was postponed for two years. As Deputy Defense Secretary Frank Carlucci told John Tower, the chairman of the Senate Armed Services Committee on 30 December 1982, "a major reevaluation and restructuring of the Joint Cruise Missile Program" would be pushed back until 1985.

Beginning with the test ships, the USS *Merrill* and the USS *Guitarro*, the TLAMs gradually made their way into service. As they were recommissioned, the four Tomahawk-armed battleships became the centerpieces of Battleship Battle Groups (BBBG), aka Surface Action Groups (SAG), that comprised a cruiser, two destroyers, and three frigates with a battleship. In 1986, the USS *New Jersey* and the USS *Merrill* deployed to the western Pacific together as part of Battle Group Romeo, the first Tomahawk-armed BBBG deployed.

In addition to the Tomahawk missiles themselves, the deployed components of the operational Tomahawk Weapon System (TWS) included the Theater Mission Planning Center (TMPC) and Afloat Planning System (APS) as well as a Tomahawk Weapon Control System (TWCS)

By November 1986, the floor space devoted to Tomahawk production at the Tomahawk Contractor Maintenance Assembly (CMA) in Building 5 at Convair's Kearny Mesa had doubled to 26,000 square feet. (Author's collection)

for surface ships, or a Combat Control System (CCS) for submarines.

The TWCS/TMPC of 1983 was later superseded by the Advanced Tomahawk Weapon Control System (ATWCS) of 1994, by the Tactical Tomahawk Weapon Control System (TTWCS) of 2003, and by the Next Generation TTWCS in 2006.

In the beginning, the Tomahawks were housed in Mark 143 Armored Box Launchers (ABL), each of which contained four missiles that were ready to fire. The number of ABLs per ship ranged from two aboard the Spruance-class destroyers to eight for the recommissioned battleships, which had 5-inch gun mounts removed to make room.

Over time, the ABLs were superseded in new installations by the Mark 41 Vertical Launching System (VLS), a canister launch system providing a rapid-fire capability. Originally developed in the 1960s for the RIM-66 Standard Missile, the VLS can hold different types of missiles, permitting more mission flexibility. The VLS is installed in eight-cell modules that share a common exhaust system located between two rows of four launch tubes. The Zumwalt-class destroyers, first commissioned in 2016, will use the improved Mark 57 Guided Missile Vertical Launching System (GMVLS) that can accommodate newer missile systems.

On attack submarines, Tomahawks can be stowed in torpedo rooms and launched from torpedo tubes, but some attack submarines had VLS cells installed forward, external to the pressure hull. Capsule Launch Systems (CLS) were later used in

A submarine launch of a UGM-109 Tomahawk during the early 1980s. The nuclear-powered attack submarine USS Guitarro was the dedicated test sub at the time. (U.S. Navy)

On 18 July 1982, the attack submarine USS Guitarro launched the UGM-109B Tomahawk Anti-Ship Missile (TASM) that sank the decommissioned Gearing-class destroyer USS Agerholm off Point Mugu, California. (U.S. Navy)

Los Angeles–class and Virginia-class submarines. In the early twenty-first century, the improved Block IV Composite Capsule Launching Systems (CCLS) began to replace the existing CLSs.

While all four of the Tomahawk variants were available to arm both surface ships and submarines, under the 1994 Nuclear Posture Review, the Clinton administration made the decision to delete nuclear-armed missiles from the surface fleet, so all RGM-109A TLAM-Ns were removed, leaving the UGM-109A TLAM-N aboard nuclear attack submarines.

By March 1984, after a year in service, Convair delivered its 100th Tomahawk. The milestone missile was considered sufficiently significant to warrant a visit from Rear Admiral Stephen Hostettler, head of the Joint Cruise Missiles Project Office (JCMPO). Convair Cruise Missile Division head Mike Keel ceremonially turned the missile over to Hostettler at the company's Building 5 at Kearny Mesa, north of downtown San Diego, a facility known to those working on the program as "Tomahawk Country." The company achieved the 400-Tomahawk mark in November 1985, and 500 production series missiles had emerged from Tomahawk Country by May 1986.

The Tomahawk Goes to War

The baptism of fire for the Tomahawk came during Operation Desert Storm in January 1991. As with the U.S. Air Force AGM-86C CALCM, also first used against Iraqi targets in the Gulf War, the combat debut of the U.S. Navy's RGM/UGM-109C TLAM-C came very soon after it first became operational.

It was with the Gulf War that the ability of cruise missiles to strike high-value targets without risking the loss of aircraft or aircrews really came into focus in both the popular media and in strategic planning. In the predawn darkness of 17 January, nine ships in the Mediterranean, Persian Gulf, and Red Sea fired the first TLAMs of Desert Storm. The guided missile cruiser USS *San Jacinto* fired the first Tomahawk from the Red Sea, while the guided missile cruiser USS *Bunker Hill* fired the first from the Persian Gulf. The first wave of Tomahawks also included missiles launched from the battleships USS *Missouri* and USS *Wisconsin*. The TLAMs reached Baghdad at around 2:37 a.m. local time.

In total, 52 Tomahawks were launched the first day of Desert Storm, targeting command, control, and communications centers, as well as air defense sites; 51 hit their targets. They were launched so that two missiles would strike each target in succession, with the second achieving greater penetration. Some of the missiles were adapted TLAM-Ds that unspooled long carbon fiber wires across electrical substations, causing devastating short circuits in the Baghdad power grid. By the end of 18 January, 216 Tomahawks had

been launched. On the third day, the fast attack submarines USS *Louisville* and USS *Pittsburgh* were the first boats to fire Tomahawks in combat while submerged.

During the six weeks of Operation Desert Storm, the U.S. Navy fired 288 TLAMs, mainly from surface ships, but also from submarines, accounting for roughly a third of the existing inventory. Of these, only six failed to successfully transition to cruise flight after launch.

Some Tomahawks were lost to Iraqi ground-based anti-aircraft artillery, but the navy found "no evidence that surface-to-air missiles contributed to Tomahawk kills." The limited number of routes used by Tomahawks to approach Iraqi targets and the tactics employed to ensure coordination with tactical aircraft missions are believed to have contributed to missile losses. Because the usable routes into Iraq were, according to the navy, "so limited, multiple Tomahawks were launched along the same route. Thus, Iraqi gunners might have come to expect that once a Tomahawk was sighted, others would soon follow along the same path."

In April 1995, the General Accounting Office published its Report GAO/NSIAD-95-116, an evaluation of cruise missile combat operations. This document reported that "according to studies conducted by the Center for Naval Analyses and the Defense Intelligence Agency and the GAO of Gulf War Air Power Survey data, Tomahawks and CALCMs hit their intended aim points with success rates approaching those of manned precision strike aircraft."

Quoting navy officials, the GAO said that "the 38 target complexes that Tomahawks attacked were all heavily defended and lent themselves to attack by an accurate, unmanned weapon such as the Tomahawk. Many of these targets were similar to those struck by manned aircraft. In many cases, the Tomahawk and manned aircraft not only struck the same categories of targets but also the same complexes. . . . In addition, Tomahawk missiles were the only weapons that struck targets in the downtown Baghdad area during daylight for most of the campaign. Even though the air force's F-117As attacked Baghdad-area targets at night

The battleship on which the surrender of the Japanese Empire was signed at the end of World War II fired the first Tomahawk of Operation Desert Storm. Here, a TLAM climbs away from the USS Missouri *on 17 January 1991, bound for Iraq. The* Missouri *and its sister ship USS* Wisconsin *were both operational with RGM-109 TLAMs during the 1991 Gulf War. (U.S. Navy)*

throughout the campaign, attacks by other aircraft were stopped after Iraqi ground defenses shot down two F-16s on the second day of the conflict."

Also cited was the Tomahawk's unrefueled range, which permitted it to strike targets flying from launch points in the Mediterranean Sea, the Red Sea, and the Persian Gulf. Manned aircraft flying from bases in southern Saudi Arabia were refueled on all missions.

The GAO reported that the Gulf War experience demonstrated the Tomahawk's "performance under arduous conditions. The flat, featureless terrain gave mission planners perhaps the most difficult task possible in creating the TERCOM and DSMAC scenes needed. The hot Middle East climate meant that the Tomahawk's engine was operating under the harshest possible conditions as well."

In his own assessment, General Colin Powell, Chairman of the Joint Chiefs of Staff, said he was "very pleased" with his Tomahawks. Vice President Dan Quayle visited Tomahawk Country at the Convair Kearny Mesa facility on 8 February 1991 to tell an assembly of workers that "it was your Tomahawk that led the charge. . . . The American workforce made this happen."

On the first morning of Desert Storm, as the news of the Tomahawk's role came in, Convair's Jack Isabel told Chris Kraul, the San Diego business editor of the *Los Angeles Times*, that "there is a sense of pride and satisfaction from people

An RGM-109 TLAM is launched toward a target in Iraq from the port side Mk.143 Armored Box Launcher on the stern of the nuclear-powered guided missile cruiser USS Mississippi during Operation Desert Storm in January 1991. (U.S. Navy photo by MMCS Henderlite)

during the Gulf War, while 240 were ordered from McDonnell Douglas, the second source supplier. Six months later, Convair received a $180.7 million contract to produce 208 Tomahawks, while the parallel McDonnell Douglas order was for 70 missiles.

In 1993, TLAMs were once again used against targets in Iraq that were considered unacceptably dangerous to strike with manned aircraft. On 17 January, the second anniversary of the opening day of Desert Storm, TLAMs were launched against the Zafraniyah Nuclear Fabrication Facility outside Baghdad in response to Iraq's refusal to cooperate with UN nuclear inspectors. The attacking ships included the cruiser USS *Cowpens* and the destroyers USS *Hewitt* and USS *Stump* in the Persian Gulf, and the destroyer USS *Caron* in the Red Sea. Of the 46 launched, 42 successfully transitioned to level flight after launch and reached the target.

On 26 June, the guided missile cruiser USS *Chancellorsville* successfully fired nine TLAMs from the northern Persian Gulf, while the destroyer USS *Peterson* launched 14 from the Red Sea in a coordinated night attack against the Iraqi Intelligence Service headquarters in Baghdad in retaliation for their having planned and executed an unsuccessful plot to assassinate former President Bush, his wife, Barbara, two of their sons, and former Secretary of State James Baker during a visit to Kuwait.

According to the 1995 GAO study, "The success rate was about 26 to 35 percent higher for the Zafraniyah raid, and 20 to 29 percent higher for the raid on Iraqi Intelligence headquarters than the success rate during Desert Storm." This was attributable in no small measure to Block III upgrades (discussed in this chapter), especially to navigation systems.

Through the end of the twentieth century, TLAMs were used in two additional air campaigns against Iraq, which was under a "no-fly" restrictions as a result of the Gulf War. Operation Desert Strike in 1996 was largely in response to Iraqi violations of UN Resolution 688 prohibiting genocidal actions against Kurdish minorities, while Operation Desert Fox in 1998 was aimed at Iraqi missile and weapons of mass destruction programs.

On 3 and 4 September 1996, during Desert Strike, TLAMs were fired in two waves of 27 and 17 as part of a coalition air campaign against Iraq. The missiles were fired from the cruiser USS *Shiloh*, the submarine USS *Jefferson City*, and from the destroyers USS *Hewitt*, USS *Laboon*, and USS *Russell*.

who had the opportunity to contribute to the system. It's totally different when you build a system and test it from when it's used and [it] works as well as it was reported to have worked by our government today."

On 31 January, Kraul reported that Convair was issued a contract for 160 more Tomahawks to replace those expended

On 1 June 1989, the Convair Division of General Dynamics delivered its 1,000th Tomahawk. The ceremony took place at the company's Building 5 at Kearney Mesa, known to insiders as "Tomahawk Country," but the actual missile was delivered from the Sycamore Canyon plant. Rear Admiral William Bowes, the guest speaker, said, "We cherish this piece of history, but we can't look back." (Convair Division)

The targets included Iraqi Republican Guard concentrations in the vicinity of Kut, Iskandariyah, Nasiriyah, and Talil, as well as Iraqi surface-to-air missile sites and air defense command and control sites in southern Iraq.

Operation Desert Fox saw the largest TLAM combat operation of the twentieth century, with 325 missiles launched on 19 December 1998, the opening day of a massive four-day air campaign that also involved 600 sorties by manned combat and support aircraft. The air force, meanwhile, expended 90 ALCM-Cs.

President Bill Clinton and the Joint Chiefs of Staff declared "victory" in Operation Desert Fox, but Secretary of State Madeleine Albright admitted, "I don't think we're pretending that we can get everything, so this is . . . I think . . . we are being very honest about what our ability is. We are lessening, degrading his ability to use this. The weapons of mass destruction are the threat of the future." Indeed, fear of them would lead to war in 2003.

Also in 1998, TLAMs were the sole weapon used in Operation Infinite Reach, the first major United States operation targeting Osama bin-Laden and the al-Qaeda terrorist gang. President Bill Clinton ordered the strikes in response to al-Qaeda's 7 August bombings of American embassies in Kenya and Tanzania, which had killed 224 people. On 20 August, two coordinated attacks were launched.

First, the guided missile cruisers USS *Cowpens* and USS *Shiloh*, along with the destroyers USS *Elliott* and USS *Milius* and the fast attack submarine USS *Columbia*, fired 73 Tomahawks into the Zhawar Kili al-Badr al-Qaeda terrorist training camp in Afghanistan's Khost Province. A barrage of TLAM-Cs was followed by another of TLAM-Ds with the idea being that as al-Qaeda personnel came out to inspect the aftermath of the first waves, the submunitions released by the second wave would amplify the number of enemy killed or wounded. Osama bin Laden, who was thought to be present, turned out to be elsewhere.

In the second strike that day, the destroyers USS *Briscoe* and USS *Hayler* launched six TLAMs against the al-Shifa pharmaceutical plant near Khartoum, Sudan. The plant was believed to contain chemicals used in the making of VX nerve gas for the al-Qaeda network. Subsequent investigations concluded that this was probably not the case.

A UGM-109 breaks the surface of the Pacific during a test launch. (U.S. Navy)

Tomahawk Block III

Initiated in 1988, the Tomahawk Block III upgrade program involved a broad spectrum of improvements that were to be incorporated into future production and retrofitted into many existing RGM/UGM-109B Tomahawk Anti-Ship Missiles (TASM) as well as TLAM-C and TLAM-D missiles. The individual missile designations did not change. It was announced that 1,085 new Block III missiles would be produced through 1998.

For Block III, McDonnell Douglas Missile Systems Company was given the engineering and development contract. As had been the case with earlier Tomahawks, dual-source production was split between the McDonnell Douglas plant in Titusville, Florida, and the General Dynamics Convair Division facilities around San Diego, California, where Tomahawks were first built. As a point of comparison,

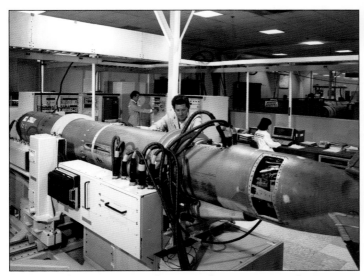

Running diagnostics on the propulsion section of a Tomahawk Land Attack Missile. Convair maintained parallel production operations at both Kearny Mesa and Sycamore Canyon in San Diego County. This Sycamore Canyon is not to be confused with the coastside Sycamore Canyon where the company test fired missiles such as the Atlas ICBM. (Author's collection)

Convair technicians mate the midbody section with the payload section (right) of a Tomahawk Land Attack Missile at the General Dynamics Sycamore Canyon plant. (Author's collection)

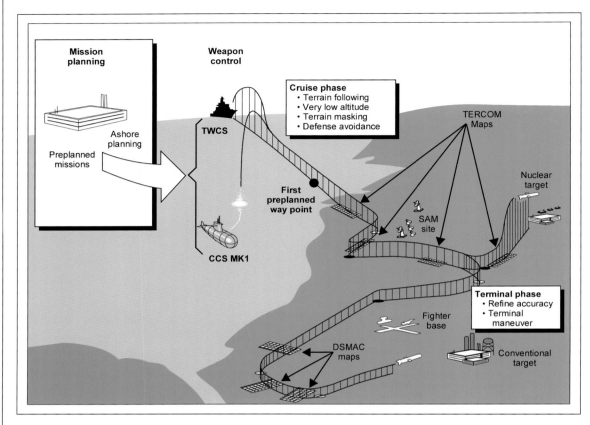

Mission planning · Preplanned missions · Ashore planning

Weapon control

TWCS

CCS MK1

First preplanned way point

Cruise phase
• Terrain following
• Very low altitude
• Terrain masking
• Defense avoidance

TERCOM Maps

SAM site

Nuclear target

Terminal phase
• Refine accuracy
• Terminal maneuver

Fighter base

DSMAC maps

Conventional target

The Tomahawk's flight profile is illustrated in this graphic from an April 1995 report from the National Security and International Affairs Division of the General Accounting Office. During the initial portion of its flight, the missile navigates by its Terrain Contour Matching (TERCOM) system. A radar altimeter aboard the missile periodically scans the terrain over which the missile is flying. The onboard computer then compares the resulting terrain elevation profile to its profile of the predicted route to the target, which was stored in the computer before the missile's launch. The computer then adjusts the missile's course so that it is following the planned route to the target. The Tomahawk navigates with its Digitized Scene-Mapping Area Correlator (DSMAC) during the terminal leg of its flight to the target. Preplanned missions are handled by a Combat Control System (CCS) aboard a submarine or a Tomahawk Weapon Control System (TWCS) aboard a surface ship. (U.S. Navy graphic via GAO/NSIAD, color added by author)

Convair produced its 1,000th Tomahawk in May 1989, while McDonnell Douglas achieved this production milestone in July 1991. As Convair pointed out, machinists and other specialties earned around 40 percent less in Florida than they did in California. Operations in the Golden State were nearing an end.

In May 1992, Hughes Missile Systems acquired the General Dynamics Convair Division missile activities for a reported $450 million. In turn, Tomahawk production ceased in California and was shifted to Arizona, where Hughes had excess capacity at its 2.2-million-square-foot plant in Tucson. General Dynamics closed its historic Convair Division permanently in 1996.

Shortly after Hughes entered the picture, the Defense Department went to a single source of new manufacturing and remanufacturing of older missiles. McDonnell Douglas was that sole source until 1994, when it was outbid by Hughes. In 1997, Raytheon acquired the aerospace and defense business of Hughes Aircraft Company from Hughes Electronics Corporation, then a subsidiary of General Motors. Raytheon remains the prime Tomahawk contractor to this day.

While new Block III Tomahawks were being delivered to the U.S. Navy, the United Kingdom became the first Tomahawk export customer. The agreement to sell 65 submarine-launched TLAM-Cs was reached in 1994, and the

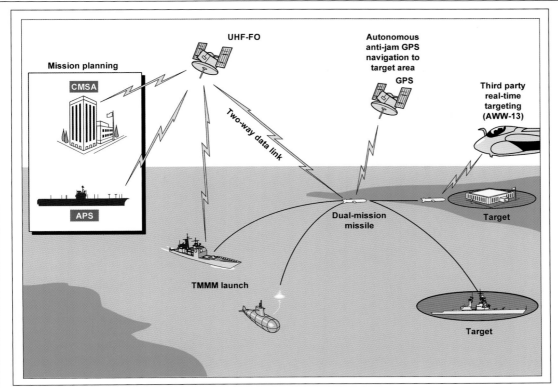

The Block IV Tomahawk Multi-Mission Missile (TMMM) Data Link Concept of Operations as illustrated in a graphic from an April 1995 report from the National Security and International Affairs Division of the General Accounting Office. Through a satellite data link, command authorities at either the Cruise Missile Support Activity (CMSA) ashore or an Afloat Planning System (APS) could abort a missile from its mission if success was in doubt, lessening the chance for unintended collateral damage. The Ultrahigh Frequency Follow-On (UHF-FO) satellite data link also allows commanders to divert the missile to an alternate target if tactical considerations dictate. (U.S. Navy graphic via GAO/NSIAD, color added by author)

first missiles were delivered and tested by the Royal Navy in its Astute-class submarines in 1998.

To date, the United Kingdom is the only international customer for the Tomahawk. Early in the twenty-first century, both the Netherlands and Spain expressed interest in acquiring the Tomahawk but decided not to do so. Also in the twenty-first century, Japan has occasionally been mentioned as a potential customer.

A key feature of the Tomahawk Block III program was the addition of a jam-resistant Global Positioning System (GPS). With GPS, navigation and mission planning was no longer dependent on terrain features, so it could be used over water and coastal targets. With GPS, mission planning time was also reduced. After GPS testing that continued through July 1994 using both TLAM-C and TLAM-D variants, the U.S. Navy initiated a fleetwide upgrade.

The DSMAC-2 was also improved, with added capability to process half again as many images, and the ability to process images with low visual contrast and complex visual textures. This improved system was known as DSMAC-2A.

Block III also involved the retrofit of more compact WDU-36B conventional warheads, which were designed and developed at Naval Air Station China Lake in California. The new warhead included an improved-technology PBXN-107 explosive, an FMU-148 fuse, and a BBU-47 fuse booster. Block III TLAMs were first used operationally in Bosnia during Operation Deliberate Force in September 1995.

Meanwhile, the ongoing Operational Test Launch (OTL) program evaluated Tomahawk performance through realistic test scenarios, including BBBG operations, for missiles launched from both surface ships and submarines. The OTL program expended an average of six TLAM-C and TLAM-D missiles, along with about two unarmed TLAM-N missiles each year during the 1990s. In 1995, the navy initiated a parallel five-year TLAM performance study to statistically verify such aspects as accuracy and reliability.

An improved Williams F107-WR-402 turbofan engine, offering a 10-percent increase in thrust, was installed in

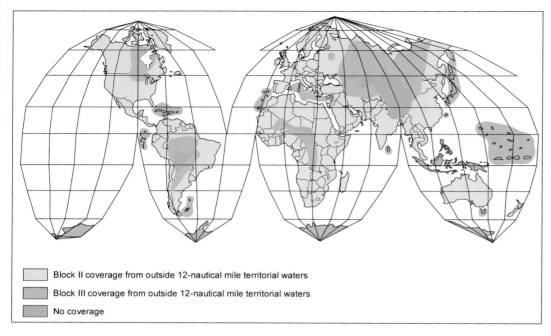

World areas covered by the range of Block II and Block III TLAM-C missiles, circa 1995. More potential targets were within reach of the Block III TLAM-C because of its greater range, as shown here. The additional range also allows the Tomahawk-equipped ships or submarines to remain farther out from shore, increasing the distance from potential shore-based threats. (U.S. Navy graphic via GAO/NSIAD, color added by author)

Block II coverage from outside 12-nautical mile territorial waters

Block III coverage from outside 12-nautical mile territorial waters

No coverage

the Block III Tomahawks. Submarine-launched Tomahawks were now fitted with higher-thrust Type 111 booster rockets. As with the Type 106 rockets, they were built by Atlantic Research and United Technologies.

The first Block III test flight occurred on 15 January 1991, less than two days before the Block III Tomahawks first went to war in Operation Desert Storm. The first flight with a live WDU-36B came after an at-sea launch from aboard the destroyer USS *David R. Ray* off the coast of California on 13 November 1991. All upgrades were complete and the Operational Test and Evaluation of the Block III Tomahawk Weapon System (TWS) concluded in 1994.

Wars in the Balkans

The collapse and disintegration of Yugoslavia in the 1990s saw the most serious armed conflict in Europe since the end of World War II. Yugoslavia itself was a mismatched collection of dissimilar, ethnically based regions that was patched together after World War I from remnants of the collapsed Ottoman and Austro-Hungarian empires combined with previously independent Serbia. These regions became technically autonomous constituent republics,

though Serbia emerged as the most powerful constituent republic within Yugoslavia. Except under Axis domination from 1941 to 1945, Yugoslavia had existed as an entity from 1918 to 1982, held together only by a succession of powerful central governments. (Serbia, however, would continue to call itself the "Federal Republic of Yugoslavia" until 2003.)

The unraveling of Yugoslavia involved the falling away of other constituent federated republics from the Serbian core. Naturally, that Serbian core, ruled by the dictator Slobodan Milosevic, opposed this, and a series of conflicts ensued. This quickly involved serious ethnic violence, especially between Christians and Muslims, that included mass murder and widespread "ethnic cleansing" on a staggering scale.

The first major conflict within the "former Yugoslavia" was the Bosnian War of 1992–1995 that occurred generally within what became the Republic of Bosnia-Herzagovina. Bosnian Serbs wished to remain part of Serbia, but other Bosnians wished to be separate. This complicated conflict also spread to involve Croatia and ethnic Croatians. Because of its military superiority, Serbia and its ethnically Serbian allies maintained the upper hand, though not a decisive one. The United Nations established so-called "safe areas"

The nuclear attack submarine USS Santa Fe in February 1994, with the doors of its Mk.36 Vertical Launch System for UGM-109 Tomahawk missiles in the open position. (U.S. Navy photo by OS2 John Bouvia)

to protect civilians from the violence, but these, too, were threatened.

In 1993, the UN declared a "no fly" zone for Serbian military aircraft that was enforced by NATO under Operation Deny Flight. Limited strikes against ground targets that began in 1994 led to Operation Deliberate Force, a major offensive air campaign that began on 30 August 1995. It turned out that Serbia had amassed a very effective anti-aircraft capability, including both anti-aircraft artillery and surface-to-air missiles. NATO losses led to many NATO air missions being devoted to suppressing this threat.

A major focus of the air campaign was the ethnically Serbian area around the city of Banja Luka in the northern part of Bosnia-Herzagovina. As U.S. Air Force Colonel Robert C. Owen wrote in his study *Deliberate Force: A Case Study in Effective Air Campaigning*, intelligence assessments had concluded that the Serbs had redeployed "their entire SAM system" into this area and "air planners expected the region to pose formidable risks to NATO aircraft."

On 7 September, U.S. Air Force General Michael E. Ryan, commander of the Sixteenth Air Force and Allied Air Forces Southern Europe in Italy, who directed the NATO air combat operations in Bosnia-Herzagovina, contacted Admiral Leighton W. Smith, commander in chief of Allied Forces Southern Europe about the use of TLAMs. Owen wrote that Ryan and his staff "recognized the danger that Serb air defenses posed to NATO aircraft in this area, [so] he wanted to soften the area before sending in manned aircraft in large numbers."

A salvo of 11 TLAMs was launched at around midnight on 10 September from the USS *Normandy*, a Ticonderoga-class guided missile cruiser. As Owen later wrote, the TLAMs "proved remarkably accurate." Seven struck the operations building and bunkers at the early warning radar site at Lisina, achieving direct hits. Others targeted the radio relay station, which post-strike reconnaissance photos showed as "completely destroyed, with debris scattered throughout the site."

Many sources state that all 13 TLAMs used during Deliberate Force were fired on the first night, but Owen clarifies that 2 were fired on 13 September. These hit the Lisina radio-relay and television transmitter, and "analysts said that damage to these targets ranged from 'severe' to 'destroyed.'"

An RGM-109 Tomahawk launches from the bow of the USS Philippine Sea, headed for a target in Kosovo on 24 March 1999. The cruiser was operating in the Adriatic Sea in support of NATO's Operation Allied Force. (U.S. Navy)

The flash of this Tomahawk launch brightly illuminated the deck of the destroyer USS Gonzalez in the early morning hours of 4 April 1999. (U.S. Navy)

Brought to a climax by the allied air campaign, the conflict in Bosnia-Herzagovina was formally concluded by the Dayton Peace Accords in December 1995, though NATO peacekeepers remain in the area.

In 1999, another trouble spot in the former Yugoslavia boiled over as a result of Slobodan Milosevic's cleansing of ethnic Albanians from Kosovo, then a semiautonomous part the Federal Republic of Yugoslavia, which now consisted mainly of Serbia and smaller areas such as Kosovo and Montenegro within the Serbian shadow.

Once again, NATO airpower was unleashed in an effort to curb the actions of the brutal Milosevic and to extricate Serbian forces from Kosovo. The campaign, which NATO called Operation Allied Force and the United States called Operation Noble Anvil, began on 24 March 1999.

The first U.S. Navy TLAMs were launched from the Ticonderoga-class cruiser USS *Philippine Sea* at 6:50 p.m. local time. Tomahawks emerged from the British submarine HMS *Splendid* soon after. Other U.S. Navy TLAM-capable ships in the Adriatic Sea during the ensuing 78-day campaign included the destroyers USS *Stout*, USS *Nicholson*, and USS *Thorn*.

It was a much more extensive bombing campaign than had occurred under Operation Deliberate Force, and it included strategic bombing attacks on the Serbian/Yugoslav capital of Belgrade. Many of these were undertaken by Tomahawks because the robust air defense system around the capital made such attacks dangerous for allied pilots.

Among the attacks in which Tomahawks were used were the strikes on the nights of 29–30 April and 7–8 May that heavily damaged the Yugoslav Ministry of Defense building on Nemanjina Street. Today, the former mansion of Slobodan Milosevic in the Dedinje neighborhood stands gutted after what locals still describe as a failed "assassination attempt" by three TLAMs on the night of 22 April.

On 10 June, the bombing campaign ended after Milosevic agreed to withdraw his forces from Kosovo. Arrested by his own government on corruption and abuse of power charges in 2000, the former dictator was turned over to the International War Crimes Tribunal. He died of a heart attack in 2006 while his trial was ongoing.

The book *Jane's Strategic Systems* reports that 181 of 218 TLAMs fired by the U.S. Navy during Allied Force found their targets, and that 17 of 20 fired by the Royal Navy scored successful hits.

Chapter 10

THE TROUBLED LIFE OF THE ADVANCED CRUISE MISSILE

An AGM-129 Advanced Cruise Missile during an early test flight. The missile made its first flight in July 1985. (McDonnell Douglas)

During the early 1980s, while much attention was given to the AGM-86B ALCM entering service and the B-1 bomber program being revived, things were happening behind the scenes in the undisclosed "black" world of U.S. Air Force systems acquisition. Rumors circulated of "stealth" technology, a means of obscuring aircraft from enemy radar. Rumors also suggested that stealth aircraft were in the works, though few people had yet been read into the top secret and untested programs that led to the Northrop B-2 "stealth bomber" or the Lockheed F-117 "stealth fighter."

With advances in Soviet radar, stealth technology was thought to be vitally important. Because of the advent of "look-down/shoot-down" radar capability in Soviet interceptors, it was perceived that low-flying cruise missiles, which once had a reasonably good chance of evading Soviet radar, were now vulnerable.

With this came the perceived need for a stealthy cruise missile. As with the manned stealth aircraft, the early devel-

opment of this missile occurred secretly in that mysterious black world.

At Lockheed, the Skunk Works Advanced Development Projects component had been working on a stealthy cruise missile since the early days of the Have Blue aircraft, predecessor to the F-117. Known as "Senior Prom," this vehicle utilized the same faceted surface design as Have Blue to reduce its radar cross section. The program had begun in 1977 and the vehicle had been tested at the secret test range near Groom Lake in Nevada that was known in CIA nomenclature as Area 51.

In 1982, when the U.S. Air Force undertook its Advanced Cruise Missile (ACM) program, Senior Prom was ready, but it was reportedly rejected because it was not compatible with the internal rotary launcher designed for the AGM-86B. Instead, in 1983, the contract went to the Convair Division of General Dynamics, which was then building the Tomahawk family for the U.S. Navy and the air force GLCM.

Ordered under the designation AGM-129A, the ACM

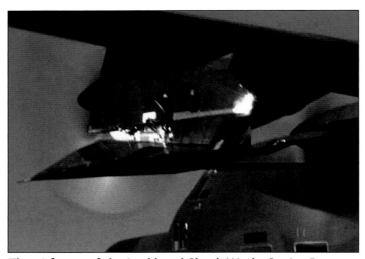
The airframe of the Lockheed Skunk Works Senior Prom vehicle was based on the Have Blue aircraft, the precursor to the F-117 Nighthawk stealth fighter. (Tony Landis collection)

The Lockheed Senior Prom vehicle was airdropped from a Lockheed DC-130 Hercules mothership, as were the CIA's Ryan Model 147 Lightning Bug reconnaissance drones over Vietnam in the 1960s. (Tony Landis collection)

was 20 feet 10 inches long with a fuselage diameter of 2 feet 5 inches. Spanning 10 feet 2 inches, the folding wings were forward swept to help reduce the radar signature. The powerplant was a Williams F112-WR-100 turbofan engine that permitted a range of up to 2,300 miles. Guidance was a combination of inertial navigation and Terrain Contour Matching (TERCOM), the latter being updated in flight by a Light, Imaging, Detection, and Ranging (LIDAR) system using pulsed laser beams to conduct three-dimensional scanning. The warhead for the missile was the same W80 variable-yield nuclear weapon that was installed in the AGM-86B.

As the program evolved, consideration was given to the possible development of an AGM-129B variant. According to the Department of Defense document DOD 4120.15-L, entitled *Model Designation of Military Aerospace Vehicles*, the B-model would have been an AGM-129A "modified with structural and software changes and an alternate nuclear warhead for accomplishing a classified cruise missile mission." With the conventionally armed AGM-86C in service, there was also some talk of a conventionally armed AGM-129C, but neither the "B" nor the "C" variant ever materialized.

First flown in July 1985, the prototype ACM was seen as a key element of the Reagan administration's nuclear modernization program. President Ronald Reagan person-

ally announced in May 1986 that the still classified program would be accelerated in a partial response to what was alleged to be Soviet cheating on the still unratified second Strategic Arms Limitation Treaty (SALT II) agreement that had been signed in 1979. The plan was that the air force would eventually replace its entire fleet of 1,461 AGM-86Bs at a rate of 200 per year as soon as that level of production could be reached.

ACM manufacturing was centered at Air Force Plant 19 in San Diego, rather than at Kearny Mesa, where the Convair Division of General Dynamics produced the Tomahawk cruise missile. Here, the ACM program was under tight wraps, with rigorous security inspections occurring at contractor facilities. Strict orders were issued to *never* write down the combinations to safes holding ACM data.

Nevertheless, production problems complicated the ACM program and the schedule unraveled. On 21 April 1988, R. Jeffrey Smith of the *Washington Post* wrote that knowledgeable undisclosed sources had told him that the program was "at least three years behind schedule and will ring up $2 billion in cost overruns," and that House Armed Services Committee Chairman Les Aspin had called the ACM "a 'procurement disaster' because of low-quality production and inept air force and contractor supervision."

Said Aspin, a staunch Defense Department critic, "High classification is no barrier to bad management. These black programs are supposed to get high-order . . . attention. If this one did, it didn't do much good."

The air force officially replied that "testing revealed design and manufacturing concerns that required correction . . . [and] the air force and General Dynamics have taken steps to remedy these problems through improved management oversight, increased design margins, and enhanced testing."

Aspin added, "The air force, despite a concerted effort, also has not met a 1986 congressional demand that it conduct at least six successful test flights of the missile before beginning full-scale production. Missiles supplied by General Dynamics, the principal contractor, have failed and crashed 'randomly' during recent flight tests, one source said, although the defects appear to be in parts produced by subcontractors."

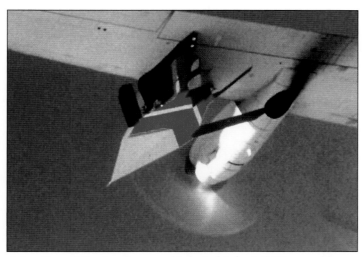

A Lockheed Senior Prom vehicle in high visibility markings, its wings folded back. (Tony Landis collection)

Technicians swarm over an AGM-129 on the factory floor of the General Dynamics Convair Division factory in San Diego. (Convair Division)

Avionics assembly for the AGM-129 program in Building 33 at the General Dynamics Convair Division factory in San Diego. (Convair Division)

In May 1987, Lieutenant General Bernard Randolph had admitted to a closed hearing of the House Appropriations Committee that General Dynamics had done "less than a perfect job in managing their subcontractors."

The General Accounting Office (GAO) was called in to investigate, and its report on the Advanced Cruise Missile program, published in September 1990, was scathing.

"The initial program plans provided for the first operational missile to be delivered in late 1986," the report noted. "Test failures, production problems, and other program changes resulted in slippage of the first operational missile delivery until 1990. However, the air force continued to provide logistics support using original delivery schedules because logistics program plans were not officially changed. The air force did not change logistics plans until after Congress eliminated production funds for fiscal year 1989. Even after Congress eliminated production funds, over one year passed before the air force changed the logistics program plans."

GAO went on to point out that because of this "spares were purchased too early, and limited quantities are becoming unusable as design changes are made and about $30 million was spent for Advanced Cruise Missile facilities at an [unnamed and classified] air force base that was deleted

from basing plans for the missile. In addition, the air force paid $7.2 million for contractor repair services through 1989, even though no operational missiles were repaired. Furthermore, air force personnel trained to work on the missiles at K. I. Sawyer Air Force Base were reassigned or separated before working on an operational missile, which was delivered about 3½ years later than originally planned."

It was also observed that the air force had spent $6.4 million on 27 spare guidance sets that were in inventory three years before the missiles in which they were to be used had arrived.

The GAO pointed out that purchasing parts earlier than necessary would "increase inventory holding costs, lead to excessive inventories, and increase the probability of obsolescence, especially in concurrent programs. Obsolescence results in additional costs to modify parts or to replace parts that cannot be modified. For example, because of system design changes, three parts are now obsolete and must be modified to fit the newest missile configuration."

In November 1987, because of numerous schedule delays and quality problems affecting the program, the air force chose McDonnell Douglas Missile Systems Company as a second production source. GAO noted that General Dynamics remained as "the design agent (i.e., responsible for

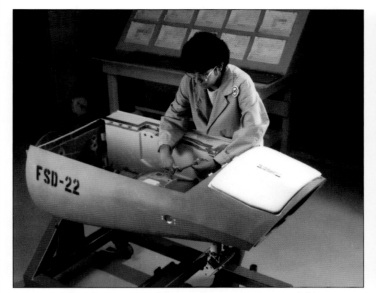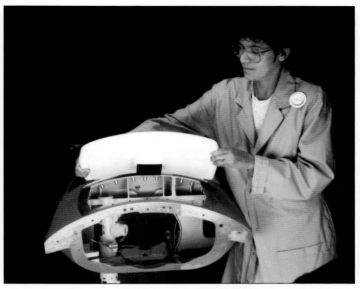

Forward fuselage assembly work ongoing in Building 51 at Lindbergh Field, part of the General Dynamics Convair Division complex in San Diego. (Convair Division)

managing and controlling design changes to the missile)."

The air force procured AGM-129 missiles from both companies, with the total quantity split unevenly between the two. In March 1992, it was announced that Convair was under contract for 420 and McDonnell Douglas for 100.

The first missile, which was referred to as "preoperational" because it did not meet contract specifications, was delivered to Sawyer in June 1988. GAO reported that a total of 25 preoperational missiles were delivered to K. I. Sawyer AFB in Michigan for use in "validating operating procedures, providing on-the-job training, conducting ground testing, and repairing missiles." According to the air force, the missiles were to be returned to General Dynamics to be reconfigured to the latest system design standards.

The first "operational" missile was finally delivered in June 1990, 42 months behind schedule. The ACM was first displayed to the public in October 1991 by the air force at an Air Force Association function in Washington, and by Convair/General Dynamics at their cruise missile facility in Kearny Mesa in California (even though the ACM was built in San Diego).

Even as the first operational missiles were finally being deployed, both the test flight and subsystem reliability levels were below the air force's reliability goals. GAO noted that this posed "significant concerns for the air force and General Dynamics . . . success frequency is below the required reliability levels. The sensor, guidance set, forward and aft avionics units, actuators, altimeter, and deployment system present significant reliability concerns for the missile system."

The air force correctly predicted that the flight reliability level would gradually increase, but just as the bugs were being wrung out, the need for the full inventory of 1,461 ACMs was fading. In January 1992, President George H. W. Bush undertook a massive restructuring of defense acquisitions in light of the end of the Cold War and the collapse of the Soviet Union. As part of this, the air force retained the AGM-86B and reduced its AGM-129A commitment to 460 units. Later that year, General Dynamics sold its missile business to Hughes Aircraft Corporation, and in 1997, Hughes divested its aerospace and defense business units to Raytheon.

Beginning in 1994, the Advanced Cruise Missile Program Office, which was established at Tinker AFB, home of the Oklahoma City Air Logistic Center, coordinated program management and technical support for the AGM-129A. In turn, this office was a component of the Missile Sustainment Division of the Air Force Nuclear Weapons Center at Kirtland Air Force Base near Albuquerque, New Mexico.

All depot support activities for the missiles and their systems were handled by the 309th Missile Maintenance Wing at Hill Air Force Base in Utah. The operational management of the AGM-129A fleet would be through the 410th Bombardment Wing at K. I. Sawyer AFB, and its B-52Hs would be the first bombers armed with them.

The treaty between the United States of America and the Russian Federation on Strategic Offensive Reductions (SORT), signed in Moscow by presidents Vladimir Putin and George W. Bush in 2002 and ratified by Russia and the United States in 2003, committed the two countries to each pair down their nuclear arsenals to between 1,700 and 2,200 operationally deployed nuclear warheads. Initially, the U.S. Air Force planned to retain a mix of AGM-86B and AGM-129A cruise missiles, and a Service Life Extension program (SLEP) was planned. However, reliability issues led the air force to a March 2007 decision to quietly phase out all 400 or so remaining stealthy ACMs. The AGM-129A managed to make one last ignoble appearance in the popular media as the centerpiece of a scandal not directly attributable to its own inherent shortcomings.

On 30 August 2007, 12 ACMs were loaded on a B-52H to be flown from Minot AFB in North Dakota to Barksdale AFB in Louisiana for decommissioning. The W80 nuclear warheads were supposed to have been removed from each, but after the bomber departed, only six could be found. The result was that a half-dozen thermonuclear weapons were unaccounted for in the American heartland for 36 hours.

After much wringing of hands, the missing weapons were found safe and sound, still installed in six AGM-129s at Barksdale. An official investigation of the incident ensued and heads rolled. In June 2008, Secretary of the Air Force Michael Wynne and Chief of Staff of the Air Force General T. Michael Moseley were asked for their resignations, which were given.

Installing the guidance package in the nose section of an AGM-129 Advanced Cruise Missile. To reduce electronic emissions, the system installed in the AGM-86B was superseded by an amalgam of inertial navigation and TERCOM, which was improved with exceedingly precise information supplied by a LIDAR Doppler velocimeter. LIDAR (Light Imaging, Detection, and Ranging) calculates the location of a target by illuminating it with a pulsed laser light and measuring reflected pulses with a sensor. (Convair Division)

AGM-129 Advanced Cruise Missiles on the underwing pylon of a B-52 Stratofortress. (USAF)

Grinning broadly, Brigadier General Garrett Harencak, commander of the Air Force Nuclear Weapons Center at Kirtland AFB, New Mexico, crushes an AGM-129A Advanced Cruise Missile at Hill AFB, Utah, after a demilitarization ceremony in April 2012. (USAF photo by Alex Lloyd)

In October 2008, in response to recommendations by a review committee, the U.S. Air Force removed all of its nuclear weapons, and the bombers, missiles, and personnel charged with their use, from the Air Combat Command (ACC), where they had resided since the demobilization of the Strategic Air Command in 1992. In 2009, as mentioned in chapter 6, the air force re-created SAC in the form of its new Air Force Global Strike Command (AFGSC) to control all U.S. Air Force nuclear assets. AFGSC then became the air force component within the joint United States Strategic Command (STRATCOM).

As they had managed and supported the AGM-129A through its operational lifetime, the Advanced Cruise Missile program office at Tinker AFB managed its decommissioning on behalf of the Missile Sustainment Division. Much of the "demilitarization" of the missiles, components, engines,

and training infrastructure was carried out by the 309th Missile Maintenance Wing, which had long been responsible for the careful maintenance of components that it now was scrapping.

In April 2012, Brigadier General Garrett Harencak, commander of the Air Force Nuclear Weapons Center, climbed aboard a hydraulic excavator at Hill AFB and ceremonially crushed the fourth to last AGM-129A. It had taken a little more than four years to raze the fleet. An official press release said that this had been accomplished "almost 17 months before the required deadline." Two decades earlier, the delivery of operational missiles had been 42 months behind schedule, but the demolition of those same missiles was *ahead* of schedule.

The last three AGM-129As survive as museum displays.

Chapter 11

TOMAHAWK IN A NEW CENTURY

By the turn of the century, 4,170 Tomahawk missiles of all variants and blocks had been delivered at a total program cost of $12.5 billion (in 2000 dollars), with a unit cost for the missiles alone of $1.4 million. Of these, more than 1,200 had been expended during combat operations, the majority of these against targets in Iraq.

At the beginning of the twenty-first century, three of the original four Tomahawk variants remained in service. These included the TLAM-N (RGM/UGM-109A) with its W80 nuclear warhead, the TLAM-C (RGM/UGM-109C) with its unitary conventional warhead, and the TLAM-D (RGM/UGM-109D) with its Combined Effects Bomblets (CEB). The RGM/UGM-109B Tomahawk Anti-Ship Missile (TASM) had been withdrawn from service after the end of the Cold War.

The Block III upgrade program had achieved its goals by 1994, but the Block III improvements continued. These included over-the-horizon detection, classification, and targeting enhancements. In 1998, a decade after the Tomahawk Block III upgrade program had gotten underway, Phase I work had already begun on the goals for the next major upgrade that would ultimately be known as Block IV.

Along the way to the new generation, there had been some false starts. The original Tomahawk Weapon Control System (TWCS) had been superseded in 1994 under Block III by the Advanced Tomahawk Weapon Control System (ATWCS), but this was soon in need of more upgrading. Evaluations of a system called the ATWCS Track Control Group Replacement (TCGR) were undertaken with great

The first Tomahawk combat launches of the twenty-first century came on 8 October 2001 as part of Operation Enduring Freedom. Here, an RGM-109 TLAM is launched from aboard the guided missile destroyer USS John Paul Jones *as part of a barrage against al Qaeda terrorist training camps and military installations of the Taliban regime in Afghanistan. (U.S. Navy photo by photographer's Mate 1st Class Ted Banks)*

The guided missile destroyer USS Porter launches an RGM-109 Tomahawk Land Attack Missile (TLAM) toward Iraq on 22 March 2003 during the initial stages of Operation Iraqi Freedom. (U.S. Navy photo by Lt. Christopher Senenko)

A Raytheon Block IV Tactical Tomahawk (TacTom) is launched from a vertical ground launcher during a contractor test and evaluation operation at Point Mugu, California, on 23 August 2002. (U.S. Navy)

promise, but TCGR was deemed not to be operationally suitable. Other problems included software issues and sluggish mission performance that required the development of time-consuming workarounds.

The system was replaced by the Tactical Tomahawk Weapon Control System (TTWCS) in 2003, only to be superseded by the "Next Generation" TTWCS in 2006.

Twenty-First Century Warrior

Also along the way to the Block IV upgrades, the existing conventional Tomahawks suddenly found themselves thrown into war. The 11 September 2001 attacks stunned the nation like no attack since Pearl Harbor, and invited a response. The enemy was al-Qaeda, and its safe haven was in the mountains of Afghanistan, where Tomahawks had flown just three years earlier in Operation Infinite Reach.

Operation Enduring Freedom, the campaign to eliminate Afghanistan as a safe haven for al-Qaeda began on 7 October 2001, with coalition air strikes against both al-Qaeda training camps and military installations occupied by the Taliban, the Islamic militant movement that had ruled most of Afghanistan since 1996.

"These carefully targeted actions are designed to disrupt

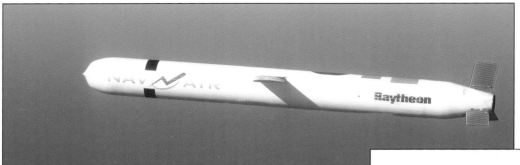

Achieving operational capability in 2004, Raytheon Block IV Tactical Tomahawk (TacTom) missiles are designated as RGM-109E when configured for shipboard launches or UGM-109E for the submarine launch environment. (Raytheon)

the use of Afghanistan as a terrorist base of operations, and to attack the military capability of the Taliban regime," President George W. Bush told Congress that day. "By destroying camps and disrupting communications, we will make it more difficult for the terror network to train new recruits and coordinate their evil plans."

The first TLAM strikes were launched early the following day from the guided missile destroyer USS *John Paul Jones* and the guided missile cruiser USS *Philippine Sea*. A week later, seven additional British and American Tomahawks struck targets near Kandahar, Mazar-i-Sharif, and Kabul.

As the war in Afghanistan dragged on (into its second, fifth, fifteenth year, and beyond) the Tomahawk was *no longer* a weapon of choice in that theater of operations. The illusive targets here proved more suitable to a new aerial weapon that few people had noticed before: the *armed* Unmanned Aerial Vehicle. Only about 50 Tomahawks were launched during all the years of Operation Enduring Freedom, fewer than the 79 used in the single day of Operation Infinite Reach in 1998.

By contrast, five years later, Operation Iraqi Freedom, the invasion of Iraq in March 2003, saw the largest number of Tomahawks used in any single military operation to date. The 802 TLAMs that were launched accounted for nearly half of all Tomahawks fired up to that time.

On 20 March, the invasion was covered by a massive cloud of air cover, with Tomahawks among the assets tasked with taking out command, control, and communications targets and air defense sites in Baghdad and in northern Iraq. In the predawn hours, TLAMs were launched by the Aegis destroyer USS *John S. McCain* and attack submarines USS *Columbia* and USS *Providence*, as well as by the British submarines the HMS *Turbulent* and HMS *Splendid*.

The guided missile destroyer USS Milius launches an RGM-109 Tomahawk Land Attack Missile (TLAM) toward Iraq on 22 March 2003 during Operation Iraqi Freedom. (U.S. Navy photo by photographer's Mate 1st Class Thomas Lynaugh)

The Tomahawk program is managed by the Tomahawk Weapons System Program Office (PMA-280) of the Naval Air Systems Command (NAVAIR). PMA-280 oversees both the Tomahawk Block III conventional variants (TLAM-C and TLAM-D), and the Block IV Tactical Tomahawk (TacTom or TLAM-E). The "PMA" initials stand for "Program Manager, Air." (U.S. Navy)

In this 2003 test, a Block IV RGM-109E Tactical Tomahawk (TacTom) missile was launched from aboard the destroyer USS Stethem, whereupon it traveled 875 miles to success-fully impact its intended target on San Clemente Island. Part of the Naval Air Systems Command (NAVAIR) test range in Southern California, San Clemente had been the target of Tomahawk live fire tests for a quarter century. (U.S. Navy)

As is typical in coalition warfare, each member had a separate operational code name. While the Americans used "Iraqi Freedom," the British used "Operation Telic."

In a 21 March Pentagon press briefing, chairman of the Joint Chiefs of Staff, Air Force General Richard Myers, confirmed that on the first day, "Coalition ships launched more than 20 Tomahawks against eight targets in Baghdad. One of the targets housed Saddam Hussein's Special Security Organization. Ten Tomahawks also hit three Iraqi Republican Guard targets in Kirkuk."

At a briefing on 1 April, Meyers displayed images of a remote terrorist camp in northeastern Iraq hit by coalition aircraft. "We struck this camp with several dozen Tomahawk missiles and precision air strikes, and initial estimates indicate that a significant number of terrorists were killed," Myers said. "Many of the deceased appear not to be Iraqis but members of Ansar al-Islam, al-Qaeda, or perhaps other international terrorist organizations."

In a 31 March Pentagon briefing, it was announced that more than 700 Tomahawks had been launched during the first 10 days of combat. In a briefing on 7 April, Meyers said that "since the war began we have fired 750 Tomahawks," indicating that the rate of TLAM operations had slackened to just 10 percent of the earlier rate. Nearly 90 percent of the Iraq War Tomahawk sorties were flown in the first three weeks.

The catalyst for Operation Iraqi Freedom had been an idea that proved to be a carefully crafted illusion. Shared by American and other Western strategic planners, as well as

The guided missile destroyer USS Sterett *launches an RGM-109E Tactical Tomahawk (TacTom) missile during weapons testing on 23 June 2010 while under way off the coast of Southern California. The ship was undertaking missile testing in preparation for an upcoming deployment. (U.S. Navy photo by Fire Controlman 1st Class Stephen J. Zeller)*

This artist's concept illustrates the conversion program involving four Ohio-class nuclear submarines, the USS Ohio, *USS* Michigan, *USS* Florida, *and USS* Georgia. *Previously ballistic missile submarines (SSBN), they had been armed with Trident missiles but were retrofitted between 2003 and 2007 to carry the Tomahawk as guided missile submarines (SSGN). The SSGNs could support and launch up to 154 UGM-109 Tomahawk missiles, a significant increase in capacity compared to other platforms. The 22 missile tubes also provided the capability to carry other payloads, such as unmanned underwater vehicles (UUVs), unmanned aerial vehicles (UAVs), and special forces equipment. This platform also provided the capability to carry and support more than 66 Navy SEALs and insert them clandestinely into potential conflict areas. (U.S. Navy)*

by the United Nations and even Iraqi military leaders, this was the misconception that Iraq possessed great stockpiles of Weapons of Mass Destruction (WMD): chemical and biological and possibly nuclear. Ultimately, it was ascertained that, although Iraq's WMD program had imploded and was no longer viable, Iraqi leader Saddam Hussein had maintained, as a self-preservation measure, the chimera that it still existed in its earlier robust form.

Following the invasion of Iraq on 20 March, coalition forces, mainly American and British, defeated the Iraqi armed forces in three weeks. This culminated in the capture of Baghdad and the collapse of Hussein's 24 years of rule on 9 April. Resistance by Saddam loyalists persisted through the year, but gradually the country devolved into the chaos of sectarian warfare and insurgency, which is well covered elsewhere. The majority of the Tomahawk operations occurred in the early weeks of the Iraq War.

On 8 May 2003, even as the Block III TLAMs were completing the biggest Tomahawk combat operation ever, the next technological step was taking place. In the calm, distant waters of the Pacific, an Arleigh Burke–class destroyer, USS *Stethem*, conducted the first launch of the Block IV Tomahawk from an operational surface ship.

The Arleigh Burke–class guided-missile destroyer USS Barry launches an RGM-109 Tomahawk to support Joint Task Force Odyssey Dawn. This Tomahawk was one of around 124 cruise missiles fired from American and British ships and submarines that targeted about 20 radar and anti-aircraft sites along Libya's Mediterranean coast. (U.S. Navy photo by Mass Communication Specialist 3rd Class Jonathan Sunderman)

Sailors and Civilian Mariners (CIVMARS) assigned to the submarine tender USS Frank Cable *lower a Capsule Launch System (CLS) Tomahawk cruise missile at Polaris Point, Guam, on 16 November 2012. The CLS and its Tomahawk were going aboard the Los Angeles–class fast-attack submarine USS* Oklahoma City. *(U.S. Navy photo by Mass Communication Specialist 1st Class Jason C. Swink)*

The Block IV TacTom

By the turn of the century, the next step in the technological evolution of the Tomahawk had begun. In 1998, a DOD contract was issued to Raytheon for a program that would be known by many names as it evolved. Among these were Tomahawk Baseline Improvement Program (TBIP), Baseline IV, and finally Tomahawk Block IV. Because these improvements effected the tactical TLAM variants, the new Block IV missile was also referred to as the "Tactical Tomahawk," or "TacTom."

The development project lay within the jurisdiction of the Tomahawk Weapons System Program Office within the Naval Air Systems Command, an organization cryptically designated as PMA-280 (for Program Manager, Air, 280). The navy had also maintained a parallel Cruise Missile Weapons Systems organization known as PMA-282 that became part of PMA-280 in 2005. PMA-280's overall objective was to create a missile that was more responsive and more flexible than current variants. Before and after this merger, PMA-280 would define and execute the objectives for the Block IV upgrade, both the systems and the systems integration. The former included the All-Up-Round (AUR) system of the missile, the booster and canister, and the control system.

In terms of striking power, the Block IV TacTom retained the WDU-36B warhead of the Block III missile, but fuse modifications, major structural changes, and altered terminal engagement limits were introduced to make it more lethal. In 2014, PMA-280 was evaluating the use of a new Joint Multiple Effects Warhead System (JMEWS) for the Block IV to improve performance against reinforced targets such as bunkers.

Many of the Block IV missiles would be produced by remanufacturing existing earlier-variant missiles, including mothballed RGM/UGM-109B Tomahawk Anti-Ship Missiles (TASM).

After a series of development delays, the debut surface launch of a Block IV test vehicle came in August 2002, followed by the first underwater launch three months later. Reviving a long-abandoned "E model" designation, the newly built Block IV missiles would receive the designation RGM-109E for those built for surface launch from existing Mark 41 Vertical Launching System (VLS) cells, while those that would be launched from submarines would be designated as UGM-109E.

Formal acceptance of the Block IV came in a Pentagon ceremony in October 2004, at which Captain Bob Novak, the PMA-280 program manager, called it a "great day for the Navy to formally celebrate the hard work of the Navy-Raytheon team that enabled the fleet introduction of this revolutionary weapon, whose flexible targeting and loitering capabilities build on the tremendous 32-year tradition and success of the legacy Tomahawk program."

Harry Schulte, vice president of Raytheon's Strike Product Line, added, "What makes this missile so revolutionary are the advanced capabilities it brings to the warfighter . . . which position Tomahawk to be a critical node of the network of the future integrated battle space."

Pointing out that this "missile so revolutionary" was also economical, Rear Admiral Brad Hicks, deputy for Surface Combat Systems and Weapons, bragged that the missile "provides a quantum leap in capability that will translate directly to greater success in combat when called upon. And all this at nearly half the cost of the previous [Tomahawk variant] missile."

The Block IV TacTom first became operational aboard the Arleigh Burke–class destroyer USS *Stethem* in May 2004, which had been the program's surface test ship. During the same month, the British Royal Navy placed its own initial order for the Tomahawk Block IV to be used in its submarines.

The Royal Navy Attack submarine HMS Astute *fires a Tomahawk during an exercise in the Gulf of Mexico on 8 November 2011. At the time, the vessel was the Royal Navy's newest submarine. (Royal Navy photo by Paul Punter released for reuse under the Open Government License)*

The launch systems for the submarine-launched UGM-109E TacToms were specifically upgraded. In 2007, Raytheon received a contract for 111 new Block IV Composite Capsule Launching Systems (CCLS) for submarines, as well as for 220 retrofit kits to replace the Capsule Launch Systems (CLS) that had been installed in submarines since the early days of the Tomahawk program in the twentieth century.

As noted previously in this chapter, the state-of-the-art system in control was now the Tactical Tomahawk Weapons Control System (TTWCS). It was said by the navy to be capable of "limited end-to-end mission planning aboard the launch platform," a rapid response procedure distinct from the complicated and protracted previous processes.

Under way in the Red Sea, the guided-missile destroyer USS Arleigh Burke *launches RGM-109 Tomahawk cruise missiles against Islamic State targets ashore on 23 September 2014. (U.S. Navy photo by Mass Communication Specialist 2nd Class Carlos M. Vazquez II)*

The TacTom was equipped with a greatly upgraded mission computer and a two-way satellite data-link, along with its jam-resistant GPS. The plan was to be able to divert a missile to a secondary target or rewrite the mission plan while in flight, attributes that were called "en route flex" and "in-flight retargeting."

This capability was evaluated in test flights run in February 2014 after launching from the Arleigh Burke–class destroyer USS *Sterett*. As the official release explained, the missile "flew a preprogrammed route while receiving updates from a simulated maritime operations center and from advanced off-board sensors updating the missile's target location. Throughout the flight, the missile maintained communications with all the command and control assets and provided updates on its location before hitting the target."

In October 2015, Raytheon demonstrated that a Tomahawk Block IV could be launched from one location, travel to a second area of operations, assess battlefield damage, communicate via a UHF SATCOM link with a third location halfway around the world, loiter, and then attack a target following analysis of the data evaluated by its operators, then transmitted back to the missile.

In 2012, with stocks running low after Operation Odyssey Dawn over Libya, the U.S. Navy began ordering substantial numbers of new Block IV Tomahawks. In June and July, Raytheon received two fixed-price contracts worth $383.7 million to deliver 238 RGM-109Es and 246 UGM-109E missiles. In December, the service committed $254.6 million for 132 RGM-109s and another 120 UGM-109s. The plan was for these missiles to be delivered on a schedule of 196 units annually.

The United Kingdom had initially ordered 64 submarine-launched Block IV Tomahawks in 2004, and added another 65 to the order books in 2014. The Royal Navy had also considered surface-launching Tomahawks from its Type 45 destroyers, which were equipped with French-built Systeme de Lancement Vertical (Sylver) launchers.

The U.S. Navy's Tomahawks were deployed on a wide array of ships. As of the closing years of the second decade of the twenty-first century, most were deployed aboard Ticonderoga-class cruisers and Arleigh Burke–class destroyers. The newest of the Virginia-class and "improved" Los Angeles–class attack submarines each are equipped with 12 launch tubes, while Seawolf-class and early Los Angeles submarines have to reduce their torpedo load to carry Tomahawks.

Meanwhile, the first four of the Ohio-class Ballistic Missile Submarines (SSBN), originally commissioned between 1981 and 1984, were completely remodeled and converted to dedicated TLAM/TacTom launch platforms (SSGN). In

Captured by incredible stop-action photography, this Block IV Tactical Tomahawk is a split nanosecond away from precisely impacting its target during a test flight. (Raytheon)

Members of the Explosive Ordnance Disposal Technology Division team at the Naval Surface Warfare Center in Indian Head, Maryland, prepare a Tomahawk missile for a functional ground test at the Large Motor Test Facility on 17 March 2015. (U.S. Navy photo by Monica McCoy)

the conversion, 22 of the 24 88-inch Trident ballistic missile tubes were modified to carry Vertical Launch Systems (VLS), with each of the former tubes replaced by a cluster of seven Tomahawk tubes. This configuration permits the carrying of up to 154 Tomahawk or other missile systems. The other two Trident tubes were converted to lockout chambers for deploying SEAL or other special operations troops.

The USS *Ohio*, USS *Florida*, and USS *Michigan* rejoined the fleet in active service in 2006, and the and USS *Georgia* followed in 2007. The plan was for them to remain operational in this configuration until the middle to late 2020s.

In January 2014, Raytheon announced the delivery of its 3,000th Tomahawk missile. The *Selected Acquisition Report DD-A&T(Q&A)823-289* issued by Defense Acquisition Management on 18 March 2015, reported that "as of 31 January 2015, a total of 3,433 TacTom missiles have been delivered, which includes 65 [Foreign Military Sales] missiles for the United Kingdom."

Raytheon announced in August 2017 that the 4,000th "TLAM for the U.S. Navy" had just been officially rolled out. In the meantime, Secretary of the Navy Ray Mabus had spoken publicly of a desire to maintain an arsenal of 4,000 Tomahawks to arm the fleet. Considering that more than 2,000 missiles had been expended by the time of the August 2017 delivery, Tomahawk production has a long future.

Continuing Combat Operations

In the eight years following the Iraq War of 2003, the Tomahawk saw little combat action. Only four were fired operationally. On 3 March 2008, two struck targets at Dobley in Somalia. *Jane's Defence Weekly* reported that the target was terrorist leader Saleh Ali Saleh Nabhan, who had masterminded attacks against an airliner and hotels in Kenya. He survived, only to be killed by U.S. Navy SEALs in 2009. Another two TLAMs were used on 17 December 2009, in another underpublicized strike, this time against an al-Qaeda camp in Yemen.

The next major combat campaign in which the Tomahawk played a role was the international intervention in a civil war in Libya. On 19 March 2011, following the passage of United Nations Resolution UNSCR 1973, American, British, French, and other allied forces established a no-fly zone over major cities and air bases near the Libyan coast. As usual, each of the involved countries adopted a separate operational code name. For the Americans, it was Operation Odyssey Dawn. For the British, it was Operation Ellamy, while the French called it Operation Harmattan.

The opening Tomahawk salvos fired by the U.S. Navy

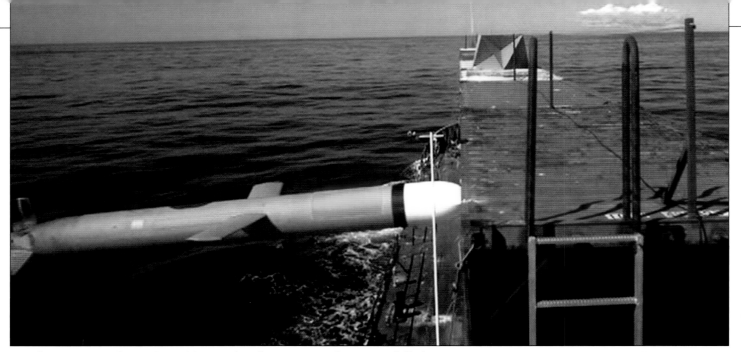

A video capture of an RGM-109 Tomahawk cruise missile successfully hitting a moving maritime target on 27 January 2015 after being launched from the USS Kidd *near San Nicolas Island off California. In this test, the missile altered its course toward the target after receiving position updates from a surveillance aircraft. (U.S. Navy)*

during Odyssey Dawn began on the evening of 19 March, with strikes made against Libyan military sites using both Block III and Block IV missiles. These were launched from the Arleigh Burke–class destroyers USS *Barry* and USS *Stout*, as well as the Los Angeles–class nuclear fast attack submarines USS *Providence* and USS *Scranton*. Also active in Odyssey Dawn, the USS *Florida* was the first of the recently converted Ohio-class guided missile submarines to launch a TLAM in combat.

Meanwhile, the Royal Navy's Trafalgar-class nuclear attack submarine HMS *Triumph* fired a dozen Tomahawks in the first three days of Operation Ellamy. On 23 March, writing in Britain's *Daily Telegraph*, Thomas Harding reported that the Royal Navy was now "running short of Tomahawk missiles," citing a unit price tag of £800,000 ($1.3 million).

Jeremiah Gertler of the Congressional Research Service of the Library of Congress detailed in a report to Congress on 30 March that the U.S. Navy had expended 184 Tomahawks during Odyssey Dawn, and noted a unit cost of $1.4 million.

The next major international challenge against which Tomahawks were deemed essential was the Islamic State.

Gunner's Mate 1st Class Derrick J. Evans (left) and Gunner's Mate 1st Class Zachary Lobao position a lifting adapter to connect to the forward end of a Tomahawk during certification trials in Guam on 31 March 2015. (U.S. Navy Photo by Mass Communication Specialist Seaman Apprentice Michael Doan)

The guided-missile destroyer USS Porter launches Tomahawk Land Attack Missiles (TLAM) against Shayrat Air Base in Syria on the night of 7 April 2017. (U.S. Navy photo by Mass Communication Specialist 3rd Class Ford Williams)

The organization behind this entity had been around since the turn of the century, known variously by names such as Islamic State of Iraq and Syria (ISIS) or the Islamic State of Iraq and the Levant (ISL) with "Levant" being a term for the eastern Mediterranean region centering on Syria, Lebanon, and Palestine.

The United States continued to downplay its strategic significance, even as Islamic State seized and controlled a contiguous "empire" of around 81,000 square miles in parts of Iraq and Syria that was roughly the size of Great Britain. Even as late as January 2014, after it had seized the major city of Fallujah from the Iraqi government, President Barack Obama continued to laugh it off as "a jayvee team."

In June 2014, Islamic State seized Mosul, Iraq's second largest city, and its leader, Abu Bakr al-Baghdadi, declared a worldwide Islamic caliphate. Only then did the United States initiate Operation Inherent Resolve, involving very limited air operations against areas of Iraq and Syria occupied by Islamic State. In September, however, the tempo increased and Tomahawks were brought into the mix. This turn was described in the October 2014 paper *The Air War Against the Islamic State*, by Anthony Cordesman, the Arleigh Burke

Chair in Strategy at the Center for Strategic and International Studies (CSIS).

He wrote that Tomahawks had been used "in the current air campaign in striking targets in Syria on 22–23 September 2014, although it is not clear that such a strike should be tied to the broader strategic goals of Operation Inherent Resolve. The U.S. launched 47 Tomahawk cruise missiles from U.S. Navy ships in the Gulf and the Red Sea. The two launched ships were the USS *Philippine Sea*, a guided missile cruiser in the Gulf, and the USS *Arleigh Burke*, a destroyer in the USS *George H. W. Bush* Carrier Strike Group in the [Persian] Gulf, a force whose carrier also played an important role in the [combat aircraft] strikes on the Islamic State."

As with Operation Enduring Freedom in 2001 and Operation Odyssey Dawn in 2011, all the Tomahawks used in Inherent Resolve were launched in the first few days of a lengthy campaign.

The next use of the Tomahawk in combat came in 2016 as a response to attacks on American ships by Iran-backed Houthi rebels based in Yemen who were using Chinese-built C-802 anti-ship missiles. The first Houthi attack, on 1 October, targeted the HSV-2 *Swift*, a hybrid catamaran vessel

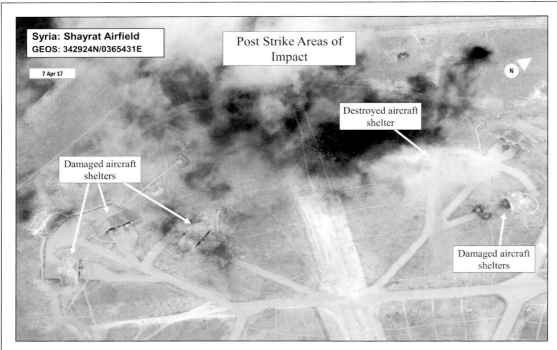

Syria: Shayrat Airfield
GEOS: 342924N/0365431E

7 Apr 17

Post Strike Areas of Impact

Destroyed aircraft shelter

Damaged aircraft shelters

Damaged aircraft shelters

N

Syria: Shayrat Airfield
GEOS: 342924N/0365431E

7 Apr 17

Post Strike Areas of Impact

Damaged aircraft shelters

N

Battle damage assessment images of Shayrat AB in Syria following Tomahawk Land Attack Missile (TLAM) strikes 7 April 2017 from the USS Ross and USS Porter. The United States fired Tomahawk missiles into Syria in response to a suspected chemical attack in the town of Khan Shaykhun in the Idlib Province. The attack on Khan Shaykhun was believed to have been launched from Shayrat. (U.S. Navy photo)

that had served with the U.S. Navy's Military Sealift Command, but which was under lease to the National Marine Dredging Company of the United Arab Emirates. Additional attacks were made between 6 and 12 October against the Arleigh Burke–class destroyer USS *Mason* and the amphibious transport ship USS *Ponce*. The *Swift* was hit and seriously damaged, while the others were untouched. Sam LaGrone of U.S. *Naval Institute News* wrote that "in at least one encounter on [9 October], *Mason* fired three missiles to protect the ship and its crew from attack."

Beginning at around 4:00 a.m. on 13 October, the USS *Nitze*, a sister ship of the *Mason*, retaliated with five TLAMs. According to a U.S. Navy statement, these were launched against radar

Streaking toward their targets at Shayrat AB in Syria are 3 of the 59 Tomahawk Land Attack Missiles (TLAM) launched by the U.S. Sixth Fleet guided missile destroyers USS Ross and USS Porter on 7 April 2017. (U.S. Navy photo by Mass Communication Specialist 3rd Class Ford Williams)

"installations along the Red Sea and north of the strait of Bab el-Mandeb [in English, "Gateway of Tears"]. . . . Initial assessments indicate that all three targets were destroyed. These radars were active during previous attacks and attempted attacks on ships in the Red Sea."

Pentagon spokesman Peter Cook said that "limited self-defense strikes were conducted to protect our personnel, our ships, and our freedom of navigation in this important maritime passageway."

The Reuters Newswire quoted "shipping sources" who said the "sites were hit in the Dhubab district of Taiz province, a remote area overlooking the Bab al-Mandab [strait] known for fishing and smuggling."

After the Obama administration deployed TLAMs in five separate operations, the first use of Tomahawks under the Donald Trump administration was against Syria on 7 April 2017. At 4:40 that morning, the Arleigh Burke–class guided missile destroyers USS *Porter* and USS *Ross* launched 60 TLAMs from their positions in the eastern Mediterranean. One of the missiles failed shortly after launch, and an official statement said that 58 out of the 59 remaining cruise missiles launched "severely degraded or destroyed" their

intended target. An independent bomb damage assessment conducted by ImageSat International counted hits on 44 targets, with some targets being hit by more than one missile.

The targets were at the al-Shayrat Air Base in Syria. The strike was in retaliation for a deadly attack on 2 April against the rebel-held town of Khan Sheikhoun by Syrian air force aircraft armed with chemical weapons, an attack that originated at al-Shayrat.

An unnamed Pentagon official told Megan Eckstein of U.S. *Naval Institute News* that "It's a fairly large airfield—that runway is almost 10,000 feet long. . . . Also, there's known chemical storage bunkers, and there's also surface-to-air self-defense missile systems that are on the outskirts of this airfield."

A U.S. Central Command press release stated that Tomahawk missiles hit "aircraft, hardened aircraft shelters, petroleum and logistical storage, ammunition supply bunkers, defense systems, and radars," adding that "approximately 20 planes" were destroyed. Syria's own *Al-Masdar News* reported that 15 fighter jets were damaged or destroyed and that the destruction of fuel tankers caused several explosions and a large fire. On 10 April, Secretary of Defense James Mattis said that the strike destroyed about 20 percent of the Syrian government's operational aircraft and the base had lost the ability to refuel or re-arm aircraft.

The 2017 Shayrat Tomahawk strike marked the first air strike of any kind conducted by the United States against Syrian government forces during that country's six years of civil war.

The End of TLAM-N

The nuclear-armed RGM-109A TLAM-Ns aboard U.S. Navy surface ships had been withdrawn from service back in 1994, leaving only the UGM-109As aboard nuclear attack submarines. By 2010, the TLAM-N arsenal had been reduced to 260 units from the original 350. In that year, the Obama administration's Nuclear Posture Review decided that the remainder of the inventory should be withdrawn from service. By 2013, this had apparently been done.

In keeping with its long-established policy of issuing no public statements about its nuclear weapons arsenal, the navy said nothing through the years about the TLAM-N, even going so far as to officially ignore its retirement after nearly three decades.

It was Hans M. Kristensen, the director of the Nuclear Information Project at the Federation of American Scientists, who deduced that the TLAM-N was no longer in service. In March 2013, he reported that "although the U.S. Navy has yet to make a formal announcement that the nuclear Tomahawk land-attack cruise missile (TLAM/N) has been retired, a new updated navy instruction shows that the weapon is gone. The evidence comes not in the form of an explicit statement, but from what has been deleted from the U.S. Navy's instruction *Department of the Navy Nuclear Weapons Responsibilities and Authorities (SECNAVINST 8120.1A)*. While the previous version of the instruction from 2010 included a whole subsection describing TLAM/N responsibilities, the new version published on 15 February 2013 contains no mentioning of the TLAM/N at all and the previous subsection has been deleted."

With this, he concluded that "the U.S. Navy is finally out of the non-strategic nuclear weapons business." He added, this came two decades after the navy retired the RIM-2 Terrier, UUM-44 SUBROC, and RUM-139 ASROC tactical nuclear missiles.

The Rebirth of TASM as MST

In September 2017, under its Maritime Strike Tomahawk program, the U.S. Navy awarded Raytheon a $119 million contract to develop an anti-ship variant of the missile. It will be recalled that the Tomahawk was originally conceived more than four decades earlier specifically as an anti-ship missile. The RGM/UGM-109B Tomahawk Anti-Ship Missile (TASM) first entered service in 1983 but was withdrawn after the end of the Cold War when the threat from the Soviet Navy diminished. By the second decade of the twenty-first century, though, the rapidly-expanding Chinese Navy was now seen as a potential threat.

It was announced that during January 2015 flight testing, a Tomahawk launched from the destroyer USS *Kidd* had successfully struck a "moving maritime target" near San Nicolas Island off the California coast. Citing this test, Deputy Secretary of Defense Bob Work said, "This is potentially a game changing capability for not a lot of cost. It's a 1,000-mile anti-ship cruise missile. It can be used practically by our entire surface and submarine fleet."

Sam LaGrone of the U.S. *Naval Institute News* explained that in the twentieth century the TASM's "sensor technology wasn't sophisticated enough for long-range target discrimination and the weapons were quickly converted [from] standard land attack variants. However, [the] 2015 NAVIAR test of a Block IV weapon, with external guidance, proved that a Tomahawk could hit a moving maritime surface target at range with more assurance than the old Tomahawk Anti-Ship Missile (TASM) sensors."

Captain Mark Johnson, the PMA-280 program manager, told LaGrone in August 2017 that Raytheon would develop and install a sensor that would convert Block IV TLAM/TacToms into the new Maritime Strike Tomahawk (MST) variant.

"We're upgrading the radio, the harnessing, and the antenna for the communication," Johnson said. "So every recertified missile will get an upgraded navigation and communication."

Raytheon's program manager, Dave Adams, told LaGrone that a multi-mode seeker with a mix of passive and active sensors might also be installed into Block IV missiles during their midlife recertification.

Chapter 12

TWENTY-FIRST CENTURY DEVELOPMENTS

Among the American cruise missiles flying in the twenty-first century are some that have roots reaching back into the final years of the twentieth century, and others that are the research aircraft roots of cruise missiles that will come later in the twenty-first century.

JASSM

The AGM-158 Joint Air-to-Surface Standoff Missile (JASSM) is a twenty-first century cruise missile with a chronology starting before the turn of the century and overlapping that of the troubled AGM-129 Advanced Cruise Missile (ACM). The idea was for a stealthy air-launched tactical missile that could jointly serve all branches of the U.S. armed forces. It should be noted that in the history of modern weapons, "joint" systems ideas have often proved to be wishful thinking; the services have such disparate requirements that a "one-size-fits-all" system winds up so heavily compromised that it ends up fitting one or *none*.

In this case, work began in 1986 on the top-secret Tri-Service Stand-Off Attack Missile (TSSAM). The air force and navy would have acquired an air-launched TSSAM as AGM-137A, while the U.S. Army might have bought a ground-launched MGM-137B. The project was canceled in 1994 without having been flown because the air force and navy had refocused their attention on the Joint Air-to-Surface Stand-Off Missile (JASSM) program.

Like the TSSAM and the ACM, the JASSM was expected to make use of low-observable (stealth)

A stylishly illuminated studio image of an AGM-158 Joint Air-to-Surface Standoff Missile (JASSM). (Lockheed Martin)

An artist's conception of an AGM-158 Joint Air-to-Surface Standoff Missile (JASSM) attacking an enemy warship. Note the missile tubes on the ship and the absence of anti-aircraft fire. (Lockheed Martin)

solid rocket booster. Guidance is by inertial navigation with GPS support and an imaging infrared target seeker. The powerplant is a Teledyne CAE J402-CA-100 turbojet like that used in the short-range AGM/RGM/UGM-84 Harpoon anti-ship missile. The range for the AGM-158A is 230 miles, but the AGM-158B JASSM-ER ("Extended Range"), first tested in 2006, has a 620-mile reach.

technology. Both Lockheed Martin and McDonnell Douglas were selected in 1996 to submit competitive design proposals under the respective designations AGM-158 and AGM-159. In 1998, the Lockheed Martin proposal was selected for production. Although the "J" in JASSM stands for "Joint," the missile was entirely an air force program for nearly two decades. The navy dropped out in favor of a variant of the Harpoon missile, the Boeing AGM-84H/K Standoff Land Attack Missile-Expanded Response (SLAM-ER). However, the navy later expressed interest in coming back aboard the JASSM program for the LRASM variant discussed below.

Like the air force AGM-86C CALCM, the AGM-158A delivers a conventional payload. It is 14 feet long with a wingspan of 7 feet 11 inches and weighs 2,250 pounds without its

Flight and operational testing of the AGM-158A, which began in 1999, was marred by a disturbing number of problems that were addressed at the customer's expense. At last, the AGM-158A entered service in 2009, followed by the AGM-158B in 2014.

Right in the window! This dramatic video frame illustrates the targeting precision of an AGM-158 Joint Air-to-Surface Standoff Missile (JASSM). (Lockheed Martin)

An AGM-158 Joint Air-to-Surface Standoff Missile (JASSM) flies in formation with an F-16. (Lockheed Martin)

The missiles are carried by tactical strike aircraft such as the F-16 and F-15E, as well as by strategic bombers. The B-52 can carry 8 in its bomb bay, plus 12 on its external pylons. The B-1 can carry 24, while the B-2 can be armed with 16. The air force has even studied the notion of retiring its conventional AGM-86C CALCM in favor of the AGM-158B. In addition to the U.S. Air Force, AGM-158 missiles are in service with the air forces of Australia, Finland, and Poland.

Stealthy Anti-Ship Cruise Missiles

As discussed in chapter 7, the U.S. Navy undertook an anti-ship missile initiative in the 1970s that included the short-range AGM/RGM/UGM-84 Harpoon and the long-range RGM/

UGM-109B Tomahawk Anti-Ship Missiles (TASM). As noted in the previous chapter, the TASM was gradually removed from the inventory at the end of the Cold War as the perceived threat from the Soviet navy faded, but the expanding Chinese Navy was then perceived as a possible future adversary on the world's oceans.

The revival of interest in twenty-first century anti-ship cruise missiles comes under the heading of the U.S. Navy's Offensive Anti-Surface Warfare (OASuW) program. Within this, the service considers various long-range cruise missiles to complement or even replace the short-range Harpoon anti-ship missile.

One OASuW option, discussed in the previous chapter, is the modification of existing Raytheon Block IV TLAMs into a Maritime Strike Tomahawk (MST) variant. Another alternative is the stealthy AGM-158C LRASM, which the navy ordered into limited production in 2014.

In addition to promoting the "nonstealthy" MST concept, Raytheon responded to Lockheed Martin LRASM by proposing a stealth cruise missile of its own for the OASuW requirement. Actually, it was not Raytheon's *own* missile, but a variant of an existing stealth anti-ship missile that it could adapt. The missile was the Nytt Sjømalsmissil (New Sea Target Missile) developed by the Norwegian firm Kongsberg Defense and Aerospace (KDA), the creators of the AGM-119 Penguin, a short-range anti-ship missile used by the U.S. Navy since 1994.

Having earned a large contract from the Royal Norwegian Navy for missiles to arm its frigates and patrol boats,

Striking in succession, two Joint Air-to-Surface Standoff Missiles (JASSM) hit their target at the White Sands Missile Range in New Mexico. (Lockheed Martin)

A prototype Long-Range Anti-Ship Missile (LRASM) launches from an air force B-1B Lancer during flight testing in August 2013. DARPA designed the free-flight transition test (FFTT) demonstration to verify the missile's flight characteristics and assess subsystem and sensor performance. This test vehicle detected, engaged, and hit an unmanned 260-foot Mobile Ship Target (MST) with an inert warhead. (DARPA)

Kongsberg rebranded the Nytt Sjømalsmissil for export as the Naval Strike Missile (NSM) and lined up orders from Poland between 2008 and 2014, where it would be used as a land-based weapon. The NSM, meanwhile, offered the flexibility of operating as a land attack missile as well as an anti-ship missile. In September 2014, the NSM was successfully test fired from aboard the littoral combat ship USS *Coronado* as part of the U.S. Navy's Over the Horizon Weapon System (OTH-WS) evaluation.

In 2014, meanwhile, Raytheon and

A Long-Range Anti-Ship Missile (LRASM) mass simulator integrated on an F/A-18E Super Hornet at NAS Patuxent River in 2015. (U.S. Navy)

This Joint Strike Missile (JSM) is pictured on the wing of an F/A-18E Super Hornet during a fit check. (Raytheon)

Kongsberg proposed a "multi-role" NSM variant called the Joint Strike Missile (JSM) for the OASuW requirement, putting it into direct competition with the JASSM. One aspect of the JSM project to which Kongsberg has devoted a great deal of attention is adapting two of the missiles to fit into the internal weapons bay of the Lockheed Martin F-35 Joint Strike Fighter.

It is not certain how the Raytheon-Kongsberg JSM, and indeed the Offensive Anti-Surface Warfare program, will be affected by the Maritime Strike Tomahawk program, though the OASuW objectives are focused on a stealthy missile, whereas the MST is not.

Going Hypersonic

Another path of development for twenty-first century cruise missile technology is the creation of very fast missiles. In the early pages of this book are the stories of many supersonic cruise missiles: the Regulus II, the Navaho, and the mysterious Boojum, but one thing they have in common is that they never became operational. The only operational supersonic American cruise missile was the Hound Dog. None of the well-known cruise missiles that have populated popular culture since the 1980s have exceeded Mach 1. As we look to the future, though, there is perhaps a role for cruise missiles flying not merely at supersonic speeds (above Mach 1) but at hypersonic speeds (above Mach 5).

"If only the Pentagon had employed hypersonic weapons instead of subsonic Tomahawk cruise missiles when it went after al-Qaeda head Osama bin Laden in August 1998," wrote James Drew in a 4 March 2016 analysis piece for *FlightGlobal*, "the terrorist leader might have died, potentially avoiding the 9/11 attacks of 2001."

He cited the Mitchell Institute report *Hypersonic Weapons and U.S. National Security* by Richard Hallion, Marc Schanz,

The Joint Strike Missile (JSM), pictured here during a fit check on a Lockheed Martin F-35B, is an air-launched version of Kongsberg's Naval Strike Missile. (Raytheon)

Artist's conception of a Lockheed Martin F-35 Lightning II launching a pair of Joint Strike Missiles (JSM). (Raytheon)

pression lift produced by its own shock waves. Powered by a Pratt & Whitney Rocketdyne SJY61 scramjet engine, the X-51 was first flown at hypersonic speed in May 2010. It flew for 210 seconds above Mach 5 in May 2013 on its longest-duration powered hypersonic flight. This compares to the X-15, which reached Mach 6.7 at 102,100 feet nearly half a century earlier in October 1967.

Also in May 2013, the air force announced that it would apply X-51 technology to its High Speed Strike Weapon (HSSW) program. Envisioned therein was a cruise missile similar in size to the 25-foot X-51 with a range of around 500 miles. It would be air-launched, as the X-15 and X-51 were both air-launched, from a B-52.

A year later, in May 2014, John Leugers, the principal aerospace engineer at the AFRL munitions directorate, confirmed to Marina Malenic of *Jane's Defence Weekly* that his laboratory was "taking lessons learned from X-51 and using

and Curtis Bedke, noting that the last winged, manned craft to achieve hypersonic speed—other than re-entering Space Shuttle orbiters—was the X-15 of the 1960s.

When it comes to winged, unmanned hypersonic vehicles, the one most often mentioned as a potential prototype for a hypersonic cruise missile is the Boeing X-51 Waverider. Developed and managed under the auspices of NASA and the Air Force Research Laboratory (AFRL), the Waverider takes its name from its utilization of the com-

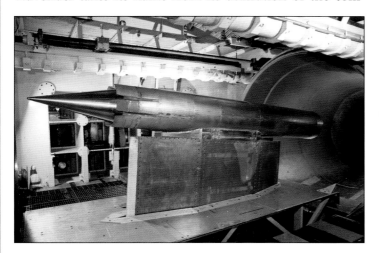

A hypersonic cruise missile engine at the NASA Langley Research Center on 30 May 2002. This engine was used in the first-ever ground test of a full-scale, fully integrated hypersonic cruise missile using conventional liquid hydrocarbon fuel. A team led by the Johns Hopkins University Applied Physics Laboratory (APL) in collaboration with the newly developed Hypersonic Flight Demonstration Program conducted jointly with the Defense Advanced Research Projects Agency (DARPA) and the Office of Naval Research (ONR) were developing experiments to produce a future high-speed strike weapon, capable of speeds of more than Mach 6 with a range of 700 miles. Hydrocarbon fuels are non-toxic and safe to carry aboard ships. (Photo courtesy DARPA/ONR/NASA)

DARPA, Pratt & Whitney Rocket-dyne, and Boeing were participants in the X-51A Waverider technology demonstrator program. (USAF)

The X-51A Waverider hypersonic flight test vehicle was uploaded to an Air Force Flight Test Center B-52 for fit testing at Edwards AFB on 17 July 2009. It finally completed its first powered hypersonic flight on 26 May 2010. (USAF)

The X-51A Waverider reached speeds of more than Mach 5 for 210 seconds on 1 May 2013 in its longest-duration powered hypersonic flight. The Air Force Research Laboratory was developing X-51 technology in part for operational deployment in vehicles such as the High-Speed Strike Weapon (HSSW). (USAF)

them in development of HSSW," but he added that ordnance and a guidance system were under development in two demonstration programs, the High-Speed Air-Breathing Weapon Concept (HAWC) and the Tactical Boost Glide (TBG) program.

Also in 2014, referring to hypersonic research in Russia and China, Acting Assistant Secretary of Defense for Research and Engineering Alan Shaffer said that the United States doesn't want to be "the second country to understand how to control hypersonics." In their 2016 report, Hallion, Shanz, and Bedke observed that "U.S. investment in hypersonics research and development is now at risk due to indecision and vacillation. Having pioneered hypersonic flight, the U.S. must redouble its efforts to retain its lead."

In 2016, Mark Lewis, the director of the IDA Science and Technology Policy Institute, told the Air Warfare Symposium in Orlando, Florida, that the X-51 had "fully lived up to all the expectations of analysis and computation [and was] a very practical configuration. It burned a practical amount of fuel, JP-7. It was a flight-scale system, so you can look at the X-51 and see how you could go from that experimental vehicle to a real operational missile. . . . Most importantly, it proved that air-breathing propulsion technology, beyond any reasonable doubt, functions correctly by delivering thrust greater than drag and accelerating the vehicle essentially uphill in the atmosphere."

As the X-51 flight test program wound down, the Air Force Research Laboratory was developing X-51 technology for operational deployment in vehicles such as those being studied by DARPA under the High-Speed Strike Weapon (HSSW) program.

The Long-Range Standoff Weapon

In August 2017, the U.S. Air Force took a step toward replacing the cruise missiles that had been acquired in the 1980s in one of the largest single weapons deals of the twenty-first century.

As the U.S. Air Force was looking at nurturing the AGM-158B as a potential replacement for its AGM-86C Conventional Air-Launched Cruise Missile (CALCM), it was looking for the successor to its AGM-86B nuclear-armed Air-Launched Cruise Missile (ALCM). Introduced to much fanfare in the 1980s, the ALCM was supposed to have been replaced by the stealthy AGM-129 Advanced Cruise Missile (ACM) before the turn of the century. Instead, it was the AGM that went away.

During the second decade of the twenty-first century, the air force defined its need for a new-generation ALCM, a missile known as the Long-Range Standoff Weapon (LRSO). On 23 August 2017, it was announced that the service had contracted with Lockheed Martin and Raytheon to develop LRSO proposals that they had previously presented.

Boeing, which built the ALCM and submitted an LRSO proposal, did not make the cut. Company spokeswoman Didi Van Nierop said that Boeing was "disappointed."

Valerie Insinna of *Defense News* reported that Lockheed Martin and Raytheon would each "rake in about $900 million for a 54-month technology maturation and risk reduction phase. . . . Because the LRSO program is highly classified—even more so than the service's program for new intercontinental ballistic missiles—it declined to release the exact value of its contracts to Lockheed and Raytheon."

She added, "The air force says its current inventory of ALCMs is still safe to use despite the fact that the [35-year-old] weapon only has a 10-year lifespan. However, it has become less effective as enemies bolster their own air defenses and is harder to maintain, as suppliers dry up and parts go obsolete."

The "54-month technology maturation" process would be evaluated by the Air Force Nuclear Weapons Center at Eglin AFB and a single contractor would be named.

"This weapon will modernize the air-based leg of the nuclear triad," Air Force Secretary Heather Wilson said in a statement. "Deterrence works if our adversaries know that we can hold at risk things they value. This weapon will enhance our ability to do so, and we must modernize it cost-effectively."

The same thing had been said about each generation of ALCMs and SLCMs since they first appeared in the 1970s with a guidance system that allowed the cruise missile concept to fulfill its potential, a potential that men like Charles Kettering and Hap Arnold had seen a century earlier.

This artist's conception shows a potential future hypersonic vehicle of the type being developed under the High-Speed Strike Weapon (HSSW) Program, which is a collaborative effort of DARPA, AFRL, Lockheed Martin, and other contractors. (DARPA)

Appendix

CRUISE MISSILE SPECIFICATIONS

Kettering Bug (Kettering Aerial Torpedo)
Manufacturer: Dayton-Wright Airplane Company
Length: 12 feet 6 inches (3.8 m)
Wingspan: 15 feet (4.5 m)
Weight: 530 pounds (240 kg)
Range: 75 miles (120 km)
Speed: 50 mph (80 km/h)
Guidance system: Sperry gyroscope and an aneroid barometer/altimeter
Propulsion system: 4-cylinder, 40-hp De Palma internal combustion engine
Warhead: 180 pounds (82 kg) high explosive
First tested: 1918
First deployed: Never

Curtiss-Sperry Flying Bomb
Manufacturer: Curtiss Aeroplane and Motor Company
Length: 15 feet (4.5 m)
Wingspan: 25 feet (7.62 m)
Weight: 500 pounds (227 kg)
Range: 50 miles (80 km)
Guidance system: Sperry gyroscope
Propulsion system: 100-hp Curtiss OX-5 V-8
Warhead: 1,000 pounds (450 kg) high explosive
First tested: 1918
First deployed: Never

TDR-1
Manufacturer: Interstate Aircraft and Engineering
Length: 37 feet 11 inches (11.6 m)
Wingspan: 48 feet (15 m)
Weight: 5,953 pounds (2,700 kg)
Range: 425 miles (684 km)
Speed: 140 mph (225 km/h)
Guidance system: SCR-549 television guidance
Propulsion system: Two 220-hp Lycoming O-435 piston engines
Warhead: 2,000 pounds of weapons, bombs, or a torpedo
First tested: 1942
First deployed: 1943

JB-2/KGW-1/LTV-N-2 Loon
(V-1 Derivative)
Manufacturer: Republic-Ford, Willys-Overland
Length: 27 feet 1 inch (8.26 m)
Wingspan: 17 feet 8 inches (5.38 m)
Diameter: 34 inches (.86 m)
Weight: 5,000 pounds (2,300 kg)
Range: 150 miles (240 km)
Speed: 425 mph (684 km/h)
Guidance system: Radio control
Propulsion system: Ford PJ31 pulsejet
Warhead: 2,000 pounds (910 kg)
First tested: 1945
First deployed: Never used in combat

SSM-A-1/B-61/TM-61/MGM-1 Matador
Manufacturer: Glenn L. Martin Company
Length: 39 feet 7 inches (12.1 m)
Wingspan: 28 feet 7 inches (8.7 m)
Diameter: 4 feet 6 inches (1.2 m)
Weight: 12,000 pounds (5,400 kg)
Range: 700 miles (1,127 km)
Speed: Mach 0.9
Ceiling: 35,000 feet (10,500 m)
Guidance system: Matador Automatic Radar Control (MARC) radio-link for A model; Short-Range Navigation Vehicle (SRNV) system ("Shanicle") for C model
Propulsion system: Allison J33-A-37 turbojet, with Aerojet solid-fuel rocket booster
Warhead: W5 nuclear
First tested: 1949
First deployed: 1954

TM-76/MGM-13/CGM-13 Mace
Manufacturer: Glenn L. Martin Company
Length: 44 feet 9 inches (13.6 m)
Diameter: 4 feet 6 inches (1.2 m)
Wingspan: 22 feet 11 inches (7 m)
Weight: 18,750 pounds (8,500 kg)
Range: 800 miles (1,300 km)
Speed: 650 mph (1,040 km/h)
Ceiling: 40,000 feet (12,200 m)
Guidance system: Automatic Terrain Recognition and Navigation (ATRAN) for A model; inertial navigation for B model
Propulsion system: Allison J33-A-41 turbojet with Thiokol solid-fuel rocket booster

Warhead: W28 thermonuclear
First tested: 1956
First deployed: 1959

SSM-N-8/RGM-6 Regulus
Manufacturer: Chance Vought
Length: 34 feet 4 inches (10.5 m)
Wingspan: 21 feet (6.4 m)
Diameter: 56 inches (1.4 m)
Wingspan: 21 feet (6.4 m)
Weight: 10,300 pounds (4,670 kg)
Weight with booster: 14,000 pounds (6,350 kg)
Range: 600 miles (960 km)
Speed: 600 mph (960 km/h)
Ceiling: 40,000 feet (12,200 m)
Guidance system: Radio ground control
Propulsion system: Allison J33-A-14 turbojet with Aerojet solid-fuel rocket boosters
Warhead: Nuclear (later thermonuclear)
First tested: 1951
First deployed: 1954

SSM-N-9/RGM-15 Regulus II
Manufacturer: Chance Vought
Length: 57 feet 6 inches (17.52 m) (without nose probe)
Diameter: 50 inches (1.27 m)
Wingspan: 20 feet 1 inch (6.12 m)
Weight: 23,000 pounds (10,400 kg)
Weight with booster: 23,000 pounds (10,400 kg)
Range: 650 miles (1,050 km) at Mach 2
Speed: Mach 2
Ceiling: 59,000 feet (18,000 m)
Guidance system: Inertial guidance
Propulsion system: General Electric J79-GE-3 turbojet with Rocketdyne solid-fuel rocket booster
Warhead: W27 thermonuclear
First tested: 1956
First deployed: Never

B-64 (later SM-64) Snark
Manufacturer: Northrop
Length: 67 feet 2 inches (20.5 m) (without sensor probe)
Height: 14 feet 10 inches (4.5 m)

Wingspan: 42 feet 3 inches (12.9 m)
Weight without booster: 49,600 pounds
  (22,500 kg)
Weight with booster: 60,965 pounds (27,650
  kg)
Range: 6,300 miles (10,180 km)
Speed: Mach .9
Ceiling: 50,250 feet (15,320 m)
Guidance system: Star-tracking celestial
  navigation
Propulsion system: Pratt & Whitney turbojet,
  with two Aerojet solid-fuel rocket boosters
Warhead: W39 nuclear
First tested: 1949
First deployed: 1960

B-63 (later GAM-63) Rascal
Manufacturer: Bell Aircraft
Length: 32 feet (9.7 m)
Diameter: 4 feet (1.2 m)
Wingspan: 16 feet 8 inches (5.1 m)
Weight: 13,500 pounds (6,120 kg)
Range: 100 miles (160 km)
Speed: Mach 1.6
Guidance system: Remote-control from
  launching aircraft
Propulsion system: Liquid-fuel rocket
Warhead: W27 thermonuclear
First tested: 1951
First deployed: Never

XB-64A (later XSM-64A) Navaho
Manufacturer: North American Aviation
Length: 87 feet 7 inches (26.7 m)
Length (booster): 92 feet 1 inch (28.1 m)
Diameter: 7 feet 10 inches (2.4 m)
Wingspan: 42 feet 8 inches (13 m)
Weight with booster: 300,500 pounds (136,000
  kg)
Range: 6,300 miles (10,000 km)
Speed: Mach 3.25
Ceiling: 80,000 feet (24,000 m)
Guidance system: N-6 celestial navigation
Propulsion system: Two Wright XRJ47 ramjets
  augmented by an XLR71 liquid-fuel rocket
  booster
Warhead: None (originally a W4 nuclear war-
  head was considered)
First tested: 1956 (XSM-64)
First deployed: Never

ADM-20 Quail
Manufacturer: McDonnell Aircraft
Length: 12 feet 11 inches (3.9 m)
Height: 3 feet 4 inches (1 m)
Wingspan: 5 feet 5 inches (1.65 m)

Weight: 1,200 pounds (540 kg)
Range: 400 miles (650 km)
Speed: Mach .95
Ceiling: 50,000 feet (15,200 m)
Guidance system: Preprogrammed autopilot
  with terrain matching capability
Propulsion system: General Electric J85
  turbojet
First tested: 1957
First deployed: 1961

AGM-28 Hound Dog
Manufacturer: North American Aviation
Length: 42 feet 6 inches (13 m)
Diameter: 28 inches (.7 m)
Wingspan: 12 feet (3.7 m)
Weight: 10,000 pounds (4,500 kg)
Range: 700 miles (1,100 km)
Speed: Mach 2.1
Ceiling: 55,000 feet (16,800 m)
Guidance system: KS-120 (later KS-140) star
  tracker plus radar altimeter
Propulsion system: Pratt & Whitney J52
  turbojet
Warhead: W28 thermonuclear
First tested: 1959
First deployed: 1959

AGM-86B Air-Launched Cruise Missile (ALCM)
Manufacturer: Boeing
Length: 20 feet 9 inches (6.32 m)
Diameter: 24.5 inches (.62 m)
Wingspan: 12 feet (3.66 m)
Weight: 3,200 pounds (1,452 kg)
Range: 1,500 miles (2,400 km)
Speed: 550 mph (885 km/h)
Guidance system: AN/DSW-15 (later AN/DSW-
  23) with TERCOM and Litton LN-35 inertial
  navigation system, later incorporating
  multi-channel onboard GPS Receiver
  Interface/Precision (GRIU/P)
Propulsion system: Williams F107-WR-101
  turbofan engine
Warhead: W80 thermonuclear
First tested: 1976
First deployed: 1981, operational by 1982

AGM-86C and AGM-86D Conventional
Air-Launched Cruise Missile (CALCM)
Manufacturer: Boeing
Length: 20 feet 9 inches (6.32 m)
Diameter: 24.5 inches (.62 m)
Wingspan: 12 feet (3.66 m)
Weight: 3,200 pounds (1,452 kg)
Range: 1,500 miles (2,400 km)
Speed: 550 mph (885 km/h)

Guidance system: AN/DSW-15 (later AN/DSW-
  23) with TERCOM and Litton LN-35 inertial
  navigation system, later incorporating
  multi-channel onboard GPS Receiver
  Interface/Precision (GRIU/P)
Propulsion system: Williams F107-WR-101
  turbofan engine
Warhead: Blast fragmentation (AGM-86C),
  AUP-3 hardened target penetrator (AGM-
  86D)
First tested: 1987 (AGM-86C); 2001 (AGM-86D)
First deployed: 1991 (AGM-86C combat
  debut); 2003 (AGM-86D combat debut)

BGM/RGM/UGM-109A Tomahawk Land
Attack Missile, Nuclear (TLAM-N)
Manufacturer: General Dynamics with
  McDonnell Douglas as a second source;
  Hughes Aircraft 1992–1997; Raytheon
  thereafter
Length: 18 feet 3 inches (5.56 m)
Length: 20 feet 6 inches (6.25 m)
Diameter: 20.9 inches (.53 m)
Weight: 2,600 pounds (1,180 kg)
Weight with booster: 3,180 pounds (1,450 kg)
Range: 1,550 miles (2,500 km)
Speed: 550 mph (880 km/h)
Guidance system: AN/DSW-15 (later AN/DSW-
  23) with TERCOM and Litton LN-35 inertial
  navigation system, later incorporating
  DSMAC and GPS
Propulsion system: Williams F107-WR-400
  turbofan (-402 in Block III)
Warhead: W80 thermonuclear
First tested: 1976
First deployed: 1984

BGM/RGM/UGM-109B Tomahawk Anti-Ship
Missile (TASM)
Manufacturer: General Dynamics with
  McDonnell Douglas as a second source
Length: 18 feet 3 inches (5.56 m)
Length: 20 feet 6 inches (6.25 m)
Diameter: 20.9 inches (.53 m)
Weight: 2,600 pounds (1,180 kg)
Weight with booster: 3,190 pounds (1,450 kg)
Range: 1,550 miles (2,500 km)
Speed: 550 mph (880 km/h)
Guidance system: Radar guidance with AN/
  DSQ-28 active radar seeker
Propulsion system: Williams F107-WR-400
  turbofan (-402 in Block III)
Warhead: WDU-25B unitary conventional
  explosive
First tested: 1976
First deployed: 1983

BGM/RGM/UGM-109C Tomahawk Land Attack Missile, Conventional (TLAM-C)
Manufacturer: General Dynamics with McDonnell Douglas as a second source; Hughes Aircraft 1992–1997; Raytheon thereafter
Length: 18 feet 3 inches (5.56 m)
Length: 20 feet 6 inches (6.25 m)
Diameter: 20.9 inches (.53 m)
Wingspan: 8 feet 7 inches (2.6 m)
Weight: 2,700 pounds (1,220 kg)
Weight with booster: 3,435 pounds (1,558 kg)
Range: 540 miles (870 km)
Speed: 550 mph (880 km/h)
Guidance system: AN/DSW-15 (later AN/DSW-23) with TERCOM and Litton LN-35 inertial navigation system, later incorporating DSMAC and GPS
Propulsion system: Williams F107-WR-400 turbofan (-402 in Block III)
Warhead (Block II): WDU-25B unitary conventional explosive
Warhead (Block III): WDU-36B with PBXN-107 conventional explosive
First tested: 1980
First deployed: 1986

BGM/RGM/UGM-109D Tomahawk Land Attack Missile, Conventional (TLAM-D)
Manufacturer: General Dynamics with McDonnell Douglas as a second source; Hughes Aircraft 1992–1997; Raytheon thereafter
Length: 18 feet 3 inches (5.56 m)
Length: 20 feet 6 inches (6.25 m)
Diameter: 20.9 inches (.53 m)
Wingspan: 8 feet 7 inches (2.6 m)
Weight: 2,700 pounds (1,220 kg)
Weight with booster: 3,300 pounds (1,490 kg)
Range: 540 miles (870 km)
Speed: 550 mph (880 km/h)
Guidance system: AN/DSW-15 (later AN/DSW-23) with TERCOM and Litton LN-35 inertial navigation system, later incorporating DSMAC and GPS
Propulsion system: Williams F107-WR-400 turbofan (-402 in Block III)
Warhead: 166 BLU-97 Combined Effects Bomblet (CEB) submunitions
First tested: 1987
First deployed: 1991

BGM-109G Gryphon Ground-Launched Cruise Missile (GLCM)
Manufacturer: General Dynamics
Length: 18 feet 3 inches (5.56 m)
Length with booster: 20 feet 6 inches (6.25 m)
Diameter: 20.4 inches (.52 m)

Wingspan: 8 feet 7 inches (2.6 m)
Weight: 2,650 pounds (1,200 kg)
Weight with booster: 3,250 pounds (1,470 kg)
Range: 1,550 miles (2,500 km)
Speed: 550 mph (880 km/h)
Guidance system: AN/DSW-15 (later AN/DSW-23) with TERCOM and Litton LN-35 inertial navigation system, later incorporating DSMAC and GPS
Propulsion system: Williams F107-WR-400 turbofan
Warhead: W84 thermonuclear
First tested: 1980
First deployed: 1983

BGM/RGM/UGM-109E Tomahawk Land Attack Missile (TLAM-E) AKA Tactical Tomahawk (TacTom)
Manufacturer: Raytheon
Length: 18 feet 3 inches (5.56 m)
Length: 20 feet 6 inches (6.25 m)
Diameter: 20.9 inches (.53 m)
Wingspan: 8 feet 9 inches (2.67 m)
Weight: 2,600 pounds (1,180 kg)
Weight with booster: 3,330 pounds (1,510 kg)
Range: 1,000 miles (1,600 km)
Speed: 550 mph (880 km/h)
Guidance system: INS, TERCOM, DSMAC, and GPS
Propulsion system: Williams F107-WR-402 turbofan
Warhead: WDU-36B with PBXN-107 conventional explosive
First tested: 2002
First deployed: 2004

AGM-129A Advanced Cruise Missile (ACM)
Manufacturer: General Dynamics with McDonnell Douglas as a second source Hughes Aircraft 1992–1997; Raytheon thereafter
Length: 20 feet 10 inches (6.35 m)
Diameter: 2 feet 5 inches (.7 m)
Wingspan: 10 feet 2 inches (3.1 m)
Weight: 3,500 pounds (1,334 kg)
Range: 2,300 miles (3,700 km)
Speed: 500 mph (800 km/h)
Guidance system: Inertial navigation supplemented with TERCOM and LIDAR
Propulsion system: Williams F112-WR-100 turbofan
Warhead: W80 thermonuclear
First tested: 1985
First deployed: 1990

AGM-158B Joint Air-to-Surface Stand-Off Missile Extended Range (JASSM-ER)
Manufacturer: Lockheed Martin
Length: 14 feet (4.3 m)
Wingspan: 7 feet 11 inches (2.4 m)
Weight: 2,250 pounds (1,021 kg)
Weight with booster: 4,400 pounds (2,000 kg)
Range: 620 miles (1,000 km)
Speed: Circa Mach .8
Guidance system: GPS-aided inertial navigation system (INS), terminal infrared homing and automatic target recognition
Propulsion system: Teledyne CAE J402-CA-100 turbojet with Mk114 jettisonable rocket booster
Warhead: 1,000-pound (450-kilogram) WDU-42B blast-fragmentation penetrator
First tested: 1999
First deployed: 2014

AGM-158C Long-range Anti-Ship Missile (LRASM)
Manufacturer: Lockheed Martin
Length: 14 feet (4.3 m)
Wingspan: 7 feet 11 inches (2.4 m)
Weight: 2,500 pounds (1,100 kg)
Weight with booster: 4,400 pounds (2,000 kg)
Range: Up to 1,000 miles (1,600 km)
Speed: Circa Mach .8
Guidance system: Jam-resistant GPS/INS, passive RF and threat warning receiver, and an imaging infrared (IIR) seeker with automatic scene/target matching recognition
Propulsion system: Teledyne CAE J402-CA-100 turbojet with Mk114 jettisonable rocket booster
Warhead: 1,000-pound (450 kg) blast-fragmentation penetrator
First tested: 2013
First deployed: 2018

X-51 Waverider
Manufacturer: Boeing
Length: 25 feet (7.62 m)
Weight: 4,000 pounds (1,814 kg)
Range: 460 miles (740 km)
Speed: 4,000 mph (6,400 km/h) (Mach 6)
Ceiling: 70,000 feet (21,300 m)
Propulsion system: Pratt & Whitney Rocketdyne SJY61 scramjet with solid\-fuel rocket booster
Warhead: None
First tested: 2010
First deployed: N/A (technology demonstrator)

Index

A Northrop SM-62 Snark cruise missile rests on the skid strip at Cape Canaveral Auxiliary AFB after a landing accident on 16 April 1957. Many of the first-generation American cruise missiles were designed to be recoverable, at least in their test phase. (USAF)

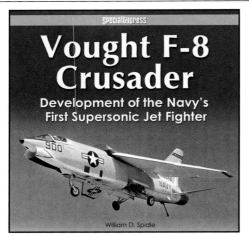

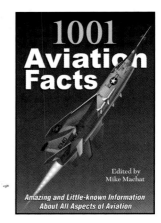
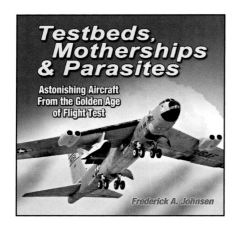
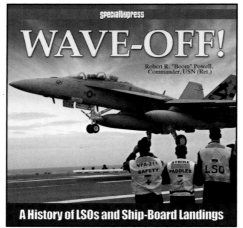
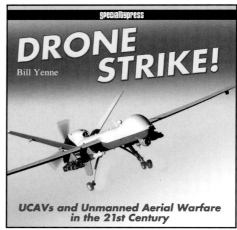